Woodbrooke College

200 38687

D1493247

Presented to

Woodbrooke Library

By *Beatrice Collier*

Date *July, 1960.*

Selly Oak

Birmingham, 29

Alinari

ST. FRANCIS (detail)

Cimabue

ELIZABETH GOUDGE

SAINT FRANCIS
OF ASSISI

GERALD DUCKWORTH & CO., LTD.
3 Henrietta Street, London, W.C.2.

First published 1959

All rights reserved

© ELIZABETH GOUDGE, 1959

270.4 FRA/GOO

PRINTED IN GREAT BRITAIN BY
WYMAN AND SONS, LTD., LONDON, FAKENHAM AND READING

For
HÉLÈNE DUTTON

CONTENTS

PART ONE

FRANCESCO BERNADONE

PART TWO

KNIGHTS OF GOD

PART THREE

THE KINGDOM

Contents

PART FOUR

THE POWER AND THE GLORY

ILLUSTRATIONS

from the Church of S. Francesco, Assisi

AUTHOR'S NOTE

SUCH a number of books have been written about Saint Francis, and so many of them works of scholarship, that a writer who is not a scholar should apologize for the presumption of attempting yet another. My only excuse is that I wanted to write it so much that I had to, my hope that it may serve to introduce Saint Francis to a few who do not know him well and perhaps make them want to know him better. At the end of this life they will find a short list of books which will give them a deeper knowledge of him than this one can do. Though some are out of print they are all to be found in the free libraries. Where I have quoted from the *Fioretti* I have used the translation of Dr. Hugh Martin. The translation of *The Canticle of the Sun* is that of Matthew Arnold. The chapter headings from the *Laude* of Jacopone da Todi are from the translation of Mrs. Theodore Beck. The quotation at the end of the book is from Saint Bonaventure's *Life of Saint Francis*; that on page 188 is included by kind permission of the publishers, Geoffrey Bles, Ltd.   E.G.

PART ONE

FRANCESCO BERNADONE

Chapter One

THE BEGINNING

O why didst Thou create me,
Great God of Heaven above?
Redeem me, and await me,
Through Jesus Christ my Love?
    Jacopone da Todi, *Lauda* xcviii

I

It is never the beginning of the story to say a child is born, nor is it the end to say a man has died, for long preparation leads up to every birth, and a death leaves behind it a power for good or evil that works on in the world for longer than the span of life from which it grew. In the case of those whom we call the saints this power is immeasurable. They are the true makers of men. Other great men may alter the material aspect of life for millions, for generations, but the saints make us for eternity. By emptying themselves, by getting rid of self altogether, they become the channels of God's creative power and by Him, through them, we are made. Not alone through them, we know, for every occasion in life makes us, and sometimes the touch of God comes directly upon us, but through them more than we realize. In this life we cannot know how much we owe to saints we have never heard of, or to saints who live with us unrecognized, but there are a few saints whose light sends such a beam through the darkness of this world that the darkness not only cannot extinguish it but is forced to recognize it and cannot forget it.

Francis of Assisi is one of these. He lived eight centuries ago and he died in early middle age, yet few of us in the Western world today, even if we know little about him, are not aware of him. Like a fresh stream springing up in the desert he is the source of so many good things. His influence upon European music, art, drama and politics, has been a study for many scholars, yet it is as a Christian that he matters to us, as a humble poor man who set himself to tread as closely as he could in the footsteps of Christ, perhaps as closely as any man has ever done, and by so doing shames us. Looking at him we see what it means to be a Christian, and what it costs. His story is not only endearing, it is terrifying. Yet without the fear and shame he would not have so much power over us, for we know in our hearts that what is worth having costs everything. And so his power lives on and we cannot measure it because it is nowhere near its end.

He was born in Assisi in 1182, but we do not know in what season of the year, though it is good to imagine that he who so loved light and fire was born in summer, in the days of the pride and beauty of the Italian sun, and that his mother, as she waited for his birth, looked out from some green bower upon her roof top over the vast landscape of plain, forest and mountain that was to be the setting for her son's life and death. The Italian ladies of the Middle Ages spent much time upon the flat roofs for their houses were dark, with small windows that in the absence of glass had to be closed with shutters against wind and weather. Their turbulent menfolk lived mostly in the streets, when they were not riding out to fight their neighbours, and upon the roofs the women had peace and quiet to do their spinning and weaving and to sing their songs. All the people of Assisi sang a great deal for this was a century of song. The country people had their laude, centuries' old litanies and hymns befitting the different seasons, and twenty years before the birth of Francis the singing bards of Provence, the troubadours, began to invade Italy, and their songs were sung everywhere in the castles of the nobles, the houses of the merchants, and up and down the streets of every city.

According to tradition the Lady Pica Bernadone was a lady of Provence, of gentle birth, the daughter of the Count of Boulement. Provence was at this time the most civilized of the provinces of Europe, and the Lady Pica was probably more cultured than the other ladies of Assisi, gentler and more fastidious and sensitive, and perhaps for this reason lonely in her fine house, in exile from her native land, and lonely too in her husband's long absences. Pietro Bernadone was a cloth merchant and much of his life was spent in commercial journeys. The richest of the merchants were those who dealt in textile stuffs. They were also the bankers of the time, and their wagons were often laden with the sums levied by the Popes in England and France. They travelled to the great fairs in Europe in stately cavalcades that were strongly guarded. At these fairs they did business with merchants from every country in the known world, even from Africa, Egypt and Greece, for the Crusades had done much to break down the barriers between one country and another and this was an age of travel. They talked to each other in the lingua-franca, the international language of Europe. They were cosmopolitan men, and at this time they were fast becoming almost the equals of the nobles in importance, merchant princes whose arrival at a castle was a major event. In Provence they were considered nobles of a second order and when Pietro Bernadone came to the castle of the Count of Boulement, and wooed and won the Lady Pica, her marriage would not have been considered a *mésalliance* for her. As our story goes on we shall think that Francis was more like his mother than his father. He was sensitive as she was, gentle and fastidious, and perhaps from her he inherited his capacity for fruitful loneliness, but it was probably from his father that he inherited his courage and determination, for success such as Pietro Bernadone enjoyed is not built up without these qualities, and certainly it was from his father that he inherited his early extravagance and love of ostentation.

The house where Pica waited for her child was built near the market place, in the centre of the hum and stir of the city's life. Assisi in those days was not the quiet city that we know today but full of turmoil and excitement, rent at intervals by savage feuds with neighbouring cities, and by the struggle against the German nobles that was convulsing nearly all Italian cities at this time. For seven hundred years Italy had endured one Teutonic invasion after another. This barbarous people passed over the country like a recurring pestilence, leaving each time not only devastation behind them but also new deposits of their hated selves. The German nobles built themselves strong castles on mountain crags, seized the lands about them, enslaved the

peasants and assaulted the cities. But they never succeeded in sub-
duing the cities in any social sense; they usually ended in being
thrown out or absorbed. At the time of Francis's birth, Assisi,
after a hard struggle, had lost her independence to Conrad of
Lutzen, now Duke of Spoleto and Count of Assisi. From his
castle on the mountain above he looked down upon her and she
lay at his feet in apparent subjection. But she was only biding
her time. In the background of her life was the great continuing
struggle between the Pope and the Emperor, between the Guelfs
and the Ghibellines of which her own small struggle was an echo.
On the whole the Ghibellines were the party of the nobles who
upheld the Emperor and were opposed to the growing power of
the Papacy. The Guelfs represented the indigenous Italians and
included the merchants and the middle classes, who looked to the
Pope for support in their fight for civic liberty. Later Francis was
to fight his own hard battle for freedom, deliverance from the
bondage of the world and of himself, but the love of freedom,
that of all things seems to raise men and nations to the noblest
endeavour of which they are capable, came to him in part from
the spirit of the time.

Assisi, built on a spur of Monte Subasio, was an old city even in
those days, though all the new building that had taken place in her
had given her a colourful appearance. The Emperor Charlemagne
had destroyed most of the Roman town with its colonnades and
temples, though the old walls had stood up against his assaults for
so long that he had had to enter the city at last by a ruse. The gate
had been opened to him by one of his own men, who had climbed
into the town through a drain during the night. Having got
inside he razed the city and put the population to the sword for
having resisted him, and one wonders that Francis had such a love
for Charlemagne. He did, however, order the rebuilding of the
city, and the new Assisi rose in beauty from the ruins of the old
buildings. The ground floors of the new houses, up to a height of
ten or twelve feet, were built of stone, the rosy stone that was
quarried from Monte Subasio, and supported the timbered walls
and balconies above, which were plastered over and painted with
bright colours. The cathedral of San Ruffino in which Francis

preached was not yet completed but the bells of the episcopal church of Santa Maria Maggiore, and of the churches of San Giorgio and San Nicholas, rang out over the city and over the city walls to the countryside beyond. In the thickness of the walls were ancient gateways, opening upon views of incomparable beauty.

From all the small windows and from the roofs of the city there were glorious views, for the name Assisi that was once Ascesi, Ascent, describes it well. The crowded houses climb up the hill one behind the other and look over each other's shoulders. The Lady Pica, in the days before her child's birth, watched anxiously from her windows or her roof, hoping that her husband, away on his travels, would come back in time so that she would not be alone in her ordeal. In the morning, as the sun rose over the crest of the mountain behind her, she saw the forested plain of Umbria bathed in golden light, the river Tescio flashing like glass, the castled villages on their fortified heights surrounded by terraced vines, olives and cypress trees and small bright fields, the whole glorious scene ringed round with cloud-like mountains. Distant cities were built on the spurs of the mountains and on a clear morning she could see the terrible Perugia rising up on her great isolated hills as though to search out her enemies. Assisi was one of them and to Assisians she was not a reassuring sight in the early morning, when the rising sun lit up her invincible Etruscan walls and her seven hundred strong towers. At evening, when the sun dropped behind the mountains at her back, she disappeared into the deepening shadows and in the starlit sapphire night she disappeared altogether. Winding across the plain through the forest were the rough roads that followed the tracks of the old Roman ways, but though Pica knew where they were and watched them she did not see her husband's train of guarded wagons lumbering home, and he was not with her when her labour came upon her.

Tradition says it was long and hard and that as the hours passed and her child was not born she asked to be taken to the stable that adjoined the house, that she might feel a little nearer to Mary the Mother of God, and that in the stable her child was born. Today the little place is a chapel, the Chapel of the Infant Francis.

The babe was christened in Santa Maria Maggiore and was
called Giovanni after John the Baptist. Pica could not have chosen
a better name for him for in the years to come he was a man who
made ready in the hearts of men a highway for his God. But
Pietro Bernadone, when he came home to delight in his firstborn
son, called him Francesco, the little Frenchman, because of his
love for France and his French-born wife. And Francis all his life
loved all things French, and in moments of deep emotion it was
always the French tongue that came to his lips. No two names
could have suited him better, symbolizing as they do the two sides
of his nature, the knightly and the ascetic.

With his father so much away the great influence upon Francis
in his childhood was that of his mother. He learned Latin and his
letters from the priests of San Giogio, who kept a school next to
the church at the eastern gate of the city, but from Pica he learned
French, and the legends of chivalry that the minstrels were singing
all round Europe at the courts and fairs, the stories of Charlemagne and Roland, of Tristram and King Arthur, stories of
heroism and knightly deeds that lit up the little boy's lively
imagination and appealed to the courage and gaiety that were a
part of him from the beginning. Like all sensitive and imaginative
children he lived in a world of vivid daydream and was himself by
turns knight, troubadour, crusader and lover of a fair lady, and he
organized all the other children in many wonderful games. For
he was always a leader and whatever he did others flocked after
him. He had that unconscious sense of drama which all great
men possess, that sixth sense which has been called the sense of
theatre. In his life of Saint Francis Sabatier draws an attractive
picture of the children playing in the streets that were their play-
ground when their fathers were out of the way at business or war.
By day they played at soldiers and processions up and down the
steep narrow ways, and at evening they went singing and dancing
to one of the open squares of the city, those terraces that occur so
often in Assisi and that are like look-out towers from which you
can gaze out at the great and frightening distances that are beyond
and below. Here perhaps Francis sometimes grew silent, his chin
propped on some parapet, looking at the distant mountains and

dreaming of the great world beyond them. Rome was there, and the fair land of France, and the Holy Land where men fought and died to win back the holy places for Christ. He would be a knight and ride to all those fabulous places, and fight great battles and win undying fame. He longed for knighthood more than he longed for anything else.

With his mother he went for walks outside the city walls, but they did not go far because it was unsafe to go beyond the circle of cultivated land that surrounded each town and village and abbey; beyond in the forests were robbers and wolves ready to pounce upon unwary children. Close to Assisi were numerous chapels and wayside shrines and it is said that Pica took him to the little church of San Damiano and that they prayed there together. Built on the mountain slope not far from the city, and facing them as they turned homeward, was the Benedictine abbey of Monte Subasio with its fields, olive groves and vineyards spread about it, a symbol of the wealth and power of the Church at this time.

Yet all was not well with this powerful Church. The wayside chapels were often ruinous and neglected and in the wealthy abbeys were many men who had gone there to escape from the danger and turmoil of the times rather than to worship God. Many of the clergy had become corrupt and ballads ridiculing them were sung all over Europe. Benefices were put up to the highest bidders and bishops extorted money from simple priests. There was much superstition and heresy and the Pope himself declared that only fire and sword could cleanse the corruption of the times. Sermons were preached in Latin which the poor folk could not always understand. They longed for God but they were confused, ignorant and suffering. They needed a poor man like themselves, humble and simple as they were, to come out from among them and preach to them repentance and the love of God. The times were ripe for that resurgence of the saints that was on its way.

II

The years passed uneventfully until Francis was sixteen years old and then they lifted him on the flood of great events. In

January 1198 the great Pope Innocent III ascended the pontifical throne, confronting a new Emperor less vigorous than his predecessors, and a fresh passion for liberty spread over the country. The Pope's policy was to increase the power of the papacy by welding the Christian states into a confederacy under his rule, and he set himself to eject the German nobles from those provinces over which the Pope had formerly claimed overlordship. He demanded that Conrad of Lutzen should deliver up his fortress, the Rocca Maggiore of Assisi, and surrender all his holdings to the Pope. The old Duke knew he could do nothing else and he set out for Narni, a city to the south of Assisi, to make his submission to the cardinals there. It was for this that the people of Assisi had been waiting for so long. As soon as he had gone they stormed out of the city up the mountain to the castle and battered it into ruins. Then they attacked the houses of the nobles within the city and set most of them on fire; built so largely of wood they burned easily, and Perugia, the city of Imperial sympathies, saw the leap of the flames with her terrible watching eyes. And she too bided her time. Vengeance accomplished, the people of Assisi set to work to rebuild the ruinous old walls of the city. The whole population laboured on these walls, Francis without doubt among them, learning the trick of carrying stones and wielding a trowel that later stood him in good stead. One can picture the scene in winter sunshine, the great panorama below the city perhaps snow-covered, the distant mountains looking as though cut out of crystal, the laughter and the singing carrying far in the clear frosty air. One can imagine the excitement, the surge of joy in freedom, and one can picture too the boy Francis, his thin brown face alight with eagerness, his dark eyes flashing, not caring if his shoulders ached with the weight of the stones he carried on them or that his hands were bruised and torn. The storming and destruction of the Rocca, the burning of the houses and the rebuilding of the walls was probably the most exciting thing that had yet happened to him. It was his initiation into manhood.

As the eldest son he was destined for his father's business and worked with his father, learning the art of money-getting. One cannot imagine that he was very proficient at this, but he loved getting rid of it for he was both generous and extravagant. Once a beggar came to the warehouse and begged alms for the love of Christ. At first Francis refused him, for his father had probably brought him up to regard poverty as disaster and beggars as contemptible, but the beggar had not been gone for very long before he suffered one of those quick revulsions of feeling that were typical of him, and reproached himself bitterly. "He asked me in the name of Christ, how could I have been so hard-hearted?" he reproached himself, and ran out of the warehouse and down the street and did not rest until he had found the beggar and made him a generous gift; and from that day he never turned away anyone who begged in the name of Christ.

As once he had been prince among the children so now he was prince of the young men and boys of Assisi. Even the sons of the nobles recognized the born leader in him and followed him delightedly. He outdid them all in extravagance, in wild fantasies, in largess and laughter. Once the dancing, singing children were in bed the streets were theirs, and when their feastings were over they would pour out into the narrow ways carrying their torches, a torrent of noise and light and colour that kept the citizens awake until the dawn came, the Assisian love of processions as strong in them as when they were children. Pietro Bernadone protested at the princely expenditure, for Francis spent an inordinate amount of money on the fantastic clothes he designed for himself, and on the wine for the feasts, but he loved the boy and was proud of this son of his, who not only took his place as easily with young men of rank as though he were himself of noble birth, but was also their accepted leader.

Yet he did not dominate them, and that he should always have been able to lead men without having in his character one trace of that love of power which mars the character of so many leaders of men, is one of the remarkable things about him. He had ambition, but it was a romantic and chivalrous ambition and had even then an other-worldliness about it. He was determined to be a great man, but a man after the pattern of Galahad and Roland rather than Alexander, a champion of great causes and a lover of

Christ. For even now he was passing beneath the dominion of Christ, even if he did not know it. When the name of Christ was mentioned he was always suddenly quiet. If he heard an obscene word he would turn his head away and he did not succumb to the grosser temptations. Perhaps it was partly in this fastidiousness that his power over his companions lay; without the slightest affectation of superiority he was yet a little different from themselves. And then they must have delighted in his abounding vitality, his brilliant fantastic imagination, "the charm of his gentleness and his courtly bearing". He had a clear and musical voice and like all young men of that time knew how to play the viol and sing to it the songs of the troubadours that he loved so well. And he was immensely generous, both as friend and host, prodigal of himself as well as of his possessions. Altogether an unusually attractive young man, even if he had no good looks to commend him except his slender grace of body and his large dark shining eyes. Pica, when her neighbours commented upon these things, and being Italian they no doubt commented with much vociferation and reiteration, replied quietly, "I will tell you how this son of mine will turn out; he will become a son of God."

Perugia did not wait for long. Some of the German nobles who had had their homes destroyed became émigrés within her walls and the remainder of the Imperial party still living in Assisi spent their time intriguing against her and finally appealed to Perugia for help. Perugia was delighted to give it and four years after the destruction of the Rocca the two cities were at war. Foligno joined Perugia, and the smaller cities, Nocera, Spello, Rosciano and Bastia, allied themselves under the red and blue flag of Assisi. All the men of Assisi, from eighteen to sixty years of age, joined the army, Francis serving in the cavalry and providing his own horse and equipment. The city hummed with the noise of preparation, the ring of hammer on anvil as armour and weapons were forged and repaired, the shouting of commands, singing and laughter, the yells of excited children, and then the neighing of the war horses being exercised outside the walls. Then they were ready and in all their glory streamed out of the city gates with trumpets sounding and banners floating in the wind.

From the city walls the old people, the women and children, watched them go. Pica would have been there, and Pietro if he was at home, full of mixed pride and dread like other parents of young sons. From Perugia the cavalry and infantry streamed out, and the two armies met each other not far from Perugia, where an old Roman bridge that had known the tramp of the Legions crossed the Tiber at Ponte San Giovanni. Uccello's picture of the rout of San Romano in the National Gallery, though it is of later date, nevertheless gives one the feeling of this little battle. There are the floating banners and the long thin trumpets, the knights in their heavy armour wielding battle-axes and pikes, the plunging horses with their bright trappings, and to one side of the picture a bare-headed boy, whose helmet must have fallen from his head, riding along as peacefully and quietly as though the battle were no more than a tourney, a boy who might be Francis himself. In the distance is the Italian landscape, a little hill, a terraced field, an apple-tree and a hedge of roses in full bloom. By the standard of the Legions, by the standard of our fearful battles of today, this battle was a very small affair, but it was a savage little fight all the same. A Perugian poet wrote of it:

"Fallen are the lords of Assisi, and their limbs are all mangled,
Torn apart and defaced, so their own cannot know them;
There is no head where the foot is, their entrails are scattered,
The eye no longer looks from the socket, its one-time window."

Perugia with her greater power won the fight with ease and Francis was among those who were taken prisoner. Perugia was never very merciful to prisoners and Francis and his companions had to march bound through the streets of the grim city, dragging their conquered banners in the dirt behind them to the Palace of the Captain, to be thrust into the dungeon there. The imprisonment lasted for nearly a year, while negotiations for peace dragged on between Assisi and Perugia, and through the whole ordeal Francis was merry amongst his depressed and irritable companions, for he had his private country of escape, his daydreams in which he was the hero of every story that his picturesque imagination could weave about himself. The men with him thought he was mad to be so merry. "Would you know why I am merry?" he retorted. "I see the day when all the world will bow in homage before me." But he was not too absorbed in his dreams to be unaware of the suffering near him. One of the prisoners had in some way injured one of the others and the rest of them would have nothing to do with him. He was left by himself, miserable and bitter. Francis was always so beloved and popular himself that he could not bear it. He sought him out, won him by gentle compassion, and finally healed the breach and brought him back into the circle of comradeship. And so the year dragged on and they were set free at last. They came out into the sunlight again, rode across the plain and saw Assisi on her hill among the tall cypress-trees, the vineyards and the olives. They rode in through the gate of the city and were at home.

Chapter Two

THE LEPER

Pardon, Lord, we sinners pray,   Thou art Love and Courtesy,
Our offences purge away,   Nought ungracious dwells in Thee;
Let us taste, if so we may,   Give, O Love, Thyself to me,
Of Thy love a little share.   Lest I perish in despair.

Jacopone da Todi, *Lauda* LXXXVI

I

IT is now that Francis begins to come closer to us. Through his
early youth he seems rather like a prince in a fairy-tale, charming
yet remote, but now there begins in him that hunger for God
that is the same in every age, so completely the same that the
psalms could be the cry of our own hearts, and though the
experience of Francis even in the earliest days of his conversion
transcends that of most men yet it is something that we recognize
as having a universal quality. This is the path that all men must
tread, either in this world or the next, if they would come to God.
His own quality of inner light illumines it for us, illumines it for
an almost incredible distance, so far did he travel while yet in this
world, but we must set out upon it for ourselves.

Conversion is rather an ugly word for the stretching out of
God's hand to take a soul to Himself, a process often so exquisite
and tender that to try and describe it can seem a desecration. Yet
there is nothing more fascinating than to watch it in a life as lovely
and luminous as that of Francis. For his was no sudden conversion
like that of Saint Paul, but one that was subtle and gentle, suited
to his gentle nature.

When he returned home he became ill with fever, so ill that
there seemed no hope for him. The suddenness and completeness
of the collapse suggests that in spite of the laughter and fun in the
Palace of the Captain his experience had thrust deep into his sensitive nature. The mutilation and death of friends in the little

battle, the humiliating entry into Perugia and the long imprisonment, shut away from the air and the light and the beauty of the
world that he adored, had been the cause of a hidden suffering that
had exhausted him. Perhaps in spite of the comfort of his private
daydreams his laughter in the prison had had more of sheer courage in it than even he had realized. His courage stood by him,
too, in this first experience of severe illness. He did not succumb
to it, and characteristically his first action, as soon as he was on his
legs again, was to stagger along to the nearest gate to feast his eyes
upon that same beauty of the habitable world. It was the spring
of 1204 and he was twenty-two years old.

He came to the Porta Nuova through which he and Pica must
have passed so often on their walks, and stood there leaning on his
stick. Before him was spread one of the loveliest views in the
world, in the glory of the spring. The sun shone warmly upon
him and the birds were singing. To his left was Monte Subasio,
to his right the Umbrian plain with its woods and fields and
castled hills. The garlands of young vine leaves were freshly
green, there were poppies growing in the corn and the tall
cypresses soared up black against the blue sky. In the far distance
were the celestial mountains. Fringing the stony paths were the
spring flowers, and lavender and rosemary bushes, and their
breath came up to him on the wind. This was what he had
longed for in prison, and through the days of fever. And it
meant nothing to him. He looked at the beauty of earth and it
gave him no joy. He had thirsted for a drink of water and was
given an empty cup. He did not know it but in the desolation,
the dryness of that moment, God touched him. There is no point
in anything without God. The beauty of the earth is so much
emptiness unless God fills it. The emptiness was the beginning of
his lifelong hunger for God.

He went home and perhaps his life at Assisi seemed to him
now a little meaningless, for he seized eagerly upon the chance
of escape from it that the next few months brought to him. A
certain knight of the city, Count Gentile, called for volunteers to
ride with him to fight for the Pope in southern Italy. They were
to join the armies of Walter de Brienne, Prince of Taranto, a

gallant and chivalrous figure who had captured the imagination of all young men everywhere. Francis answered the call at once, flinging himself into the new adventure with all his old ardour and eagerness; the Prince of Taranto was just such a hero as he had dreamed of being himself, and moreover he was a Frenchman. And this was a real war, waged for freedom and religion, and in it he might himself become a knight. This was his chance to do what he had always longed to do, to win his spurs. And perhaps he thought that on this adventure he might win the lovely lady who would be his bride.

His parents, who so tenderly loved him, entered into all his plans with sympathy and approval and gave him a splendid outfit. Not one of the young nobles would ride to war more magnificent than he. And then, just as they were on the point of departure, Francis discovered that one of the men who were to ride with him, a young man who was already a knight, was poor and ill-equipped. Francis could not bear it. That a man who had already won his spurs should have to ride to war shabbily, while he who was not yet knighted had everything he wanted, was intolerable. It was the outcast prisoner at Perugia over again. It was as it would be all through his life; if he saw other men having less than he had he could not bear it. He gave all his magnificent equipment to the other man. It must have been a blow to his father and mother but by this time they would have known that with Francis anything was to be expected.

When he went to bed that night, with his head full of the knight he had succoured, of the adventure to which he was committed and of the lovely lady, he dreamed a dream. He dreamed that he was in the palace of a fair bride, and it was full of armour hanging on the wall as though waiting for a company of knights to come and take it, and the arms were all marked with the cross of Christ. He wondered who was the owner of this palace and all the weapons and armour, and then he knew in his dream that these things belonged to him and his knights. He woke up delighted and when he was asked why he was so happy he said, "I know I shall be a great prince." The men of the Middle Ages attached great importance to their dreams, seeing in them not only pictures of events that were to come but also intimations of the will of God. And that being their faith no doubt for them it was so, for God guides us through that which we believe, in our time and in our circumstances. Francis took this dream literally, for as his biographer Saint Bonadventure expresses it, "he had not yet practised his mind in examining the divine mysteries, and knew not how to pass through the appearance of things seen unto the beholding of the truth of things unseen."

The next day the cavalcade set out. Francis was once more equipped with the best his father could give him, and bore on his arm the little buckler of a page. When he came back, he would have told his father and mother and excited young brothers, he would be carrying the knight's shield. Assisi watched them ride down to the plain and wheel away towards the south, and was immensely proud of them.

That day they rode thirty miles through the forests and came at nightfall to Spoleto, where they rested, and here again there came to Francis the touch of God, and this time he knew it for what it was. He was lying still, perhaps beside a camp fire, perhaps in some friendly room where through the small unshuttered window he could see the stars. He was not asleep, he was in that state between sleeping and waking when the veil between one world and another sometimes grows thin, and he heard the Voice. To hear the Voice is not an uncommon occurrence. Lovers of God, and Francis in his generosity was that already, have heard it in times past and do today, but they find it hard to explain it to us who do not hear. They say, "You do not hear it with your bodily ears, and yet you hear, and afterwards you know the actual words that have been spoken". Saint Bonadventure puts it very simply. He says Francis "heard the Lord speaking unto him by night, with the voice of a friend." The Voice said, "Francis, who can do better for you, the lord or the servant?" And Francis replied that the lord could do best for him. And the Voice said, "Why, then, do you leave the lord for the servant?" And Francis asked, as he was to ask at every turning point in his life, "Lord, what would'st Thou have me to do?" And the Voice said the same words that Saint Paul had heard when he asked the same question. "Return to your own country and you will be told what to do."

Francis did not sleep at all that night and very early the next morning he rode back to Assisi.

We see here the emergence of his particular brand of tough courage. He had built every high hope that he had on this adventure, and now he was asked to turn his back on it. He had ridden out from Assisi to the cheers of the people, leaving behind him a family immensely proud of him, and now he must ride back to face the ridicule of Assisi and the deep hurt and disappointment of those who loved him. He must ride home stripped of his hopes and dreams and still carrying on his arm only the buckler of a page. For a man so young and ambitious this stripping must have been bitterly hard. Yet his biographers say that he rode home gaily, in a manner that reminds us of a saying of King Alfred: "If thou hast a woe tell it not to the weakling, tell it to thy saddle-bow and ride singing forth."

There is no record of his reception at Assisi, but it is a proof of his courage that whatever it was he lived it down in such a manner that in a short while he had won back all his old ascendancy and was once again the leader of the young men in the gaieties of the city.

II

He went back to the old life, there being nothing else to do while he waited for his orders, but he did not go back to it in the same way because he was not the same man. He had never cared about his father's business and he cared about it even less now, and the feasting and the gaiety no longer gave him the old delight. It seems that just as the beauty of the world became meaningless to him as he stood at the gate of the city, so now he felt the same sort of emptiness in the life of pleasure. And he was noticing things more. As the young men paraded the streets at night in their gorgeous clothes, with their torches and their singing, Francis often leading them with the wand of the master of the revels in his hand, there were watchers in the shadows. Assisi, like all cities, had her poverty and the poverty of the Middle Ages could be horrible. In the dark alleys that were hidden away between the fine houses of the nobles and the merchants were filthy little rooms, squalor, disease and misery. There was little help or hope then for the sick, the crippled and the blind, little to relieve their pain or comfort their dying. There were religious orders in Italy who cared for the poor, such as the Crucigeri, the Cross Bearing Brothers, who looked after the lepers, but they could do no more than touch the fringe of the misery. For most of the suffering poor their chief hope was to display their wretchedness in the streets, outside the churches and the houses of the rich, in the hope of a coin being flung to them. Francis had been generous with his coins since the beggar had asked alms of him in the name of Christ, but the eyes of his mind had been turned inward to that pageant of his dreams, the knights and the tourneys and the great things that he would do. But those dreams had gone now and there too was an emptiness that was gradually filling with the men in the shadows. He noticed them now as he walked by. The torch-lit procession of the young men through the streets brought a little excitement into their lives. They crept up from their wretched hiding-places to warm themselves for a moment or two in the warmth and colour. And perhaps some of them in their bitterness cursed under their breath. In the light of the torches Francis saw the twisted limbs, the sores and dirty rags, and in spite of the perfume that scented his own fine clothes and the smell of the wine he had drunk their stench came to him and sickened him. He had always had a fastidious horror of mutilation of any sort, of dirt and smells. He especially shrank from lepers, and when he had to pass one he "turned aside his face, stopping his nostrils with his hand". But now in this flight from what he hated he was somehow coming to a dead end. Poverty was catching up with him, and soon he would have to turn and confront her.

One night after a feast they all poured out into the streets as usual but Francis, though he was master of the revels that night, gradually fell behind the others. And once more God touched him, not with the former gentleness but with some sort of piercing thrust that went so deep that it almost robbed him of consciousness. He said afterwards, "Had I been pricked with knives all over at once I could not have moved from the spot." Missing him his companions turned back and when they saw his face they were afraid and stared at him, for he seemed changed into another man. Then, recovering themselves, they began to tease him and asked him if he was in love. Only falling in love, they thought, could explain his behaviour. "Yes," said Francis, "I am in love with a bride nobler and richer and fairer than you have ever seen." They all roared with laughter and the riotous procession once more proceeded on its way.

What did Francis mean by his reply? It would seem that in that moment of piercing experience poverty changed her aspect for him. He came face to face with her and saw her for what she is, not a loathsome thing to be shunned but something stern and terrible indeed, but holy. It was she who took the infant Christ into her arms in the stable, who was His companion all His life and into whose eyes He looked upon the cross. It seemed to Francis that no man can truly love Christ without loving her too, or live a life of love without living in some degree in poverty, for one is the logical outcome of the other. Love must give or it is not love. Francis was born to be a great lover and as love is all of a piece he could have loved deeply in the human as well as the divine sense. If he had ridden on from Spoleto with the rest it would have been to become to some woman what Tristram was to Isoult or Abelard to Heloise. He had relinquished the search for his lady when he turned back but now she had sought him. The bride of whom he had dreamed was the Lady Poverty, and he began from that moment to serve her. The time of waiting was over and this was the first thing that he was told to do in his own country.

Until now he had given a coin or two to those who begged from him, but now he went out to look for the poor with food and money to relieve them. When he ran short of money he would give them even the clothes he was wearing rather than do nothing for them. One day, his father fortunately being away from home, he spread the table where he and his mother were to

dine alone together with food for a large number, and when
Pica asked him what he was doing he said it was for the poor.
"But his mother, loving him beyond her other sons, bore with
him in such things, taking note of what he did, and marvelling
greatly thereat in her heart." And as well as serving the poor of
the city Francis did what he could to help poor priests. He bought
vessels for their churches and sent them to them secretly. And he
was learning to pray. "He went oft-times, and as it were in
secret, daily unto prayer." All that he did now he did hiddenly
for he was not sure of himself. "Not yet was he wholly free from
the vanity of the world."

This experience of learning to pray brought him great suffering
and drove him out to desert places even as Christ was driven by
the Spirit into the wilderness. His life now began to be stamped
with the pattern of the life of Christ, the great pattern impressed
upon the small one. In the misery of his mind at this time he can
hardly have been aware of pattern, perhaps was never aware that
his life was like a poem, a symbolic drama of the journey through
the world of a maker and redeemer of men. His wilderness was
not far, only the country beyond Assisi where he wandered either
alone or with a friend who was good to him at this time and with
whom he found himself able to talk a little. He would explain his
wanderings by saying he was looking for hidden treasure. On the
far side of the river Tescio were the cave cellars of a large Roman
villa, Le Grotte, where it was said there was hidden treasure. One
street boy of Assisi would call out to another, "Give me a soldo!"
And the other boy would answer, "No, go to Le Grotte." Francis
would go into one of the caves to pray, leaving his friend to
wait for him outside, and sometimes the listening friend would
hear him cry out in anguish. Francis was a mystic, a man whose
mind could directly apprehend something of the glory of God,
and his longing for Him was too great to be borne. Looking up
to God he saw himself in the light of His love and holiness and
that too could not be borne. He saw the hideousness of sin and
repented of it in agony and fear, and saw too how he was bound to
the treadmill of his sinful self, revolving round and round upon
what he hated. Until he could break away from self, be done

with it, he could never be free to run after God and live for Him alone. And so Francis entered upon this battle of winning himself for God. It would be bitterly hard for him, for he had lived for a long time in a world of fantasy with himself the hero of all his dreams. It would take years of penance and struggle to push out this tawdry hero and enthrone Christ in his place. But Francis did not doubt that this heavenly treasure was worth winning; no one who has felt the touch of God even in the smallest degree ever doubts that; and he trod the path upon which he first entered in the cave to the end.

This first hard struggle with himself had another side to it, for the soul that would love God entirely must love man entirely also. He knew in his heart that he was called to serve the Lady Poverty in a far closer identification than anything he had achieved yet, for he was still only serving as a rich man serves, giving out of his abundance and going back to his own comfortable home at night. He was making no compromise in spiritual things, Christ and the tawdry hero were not to share the throne in the centre of his being, it was to be Christ's alone, however desperate the fight to make it so, but in the matter of poverty he was struggling after compromise. How could he plunge down into it all, become one with those wretches whom he saw in the streets, poor and hungry and dirty as they were? His nerves gave way and he imagined himself becoming like them, diseased and horrible, blind, or a leper. He, Francis Bernadone, delicate and fastidious, might catch leprosy and look like one of those ghastly creatures from whom he always turned his head away. Surely God couldn't be calling him to have anything to do with lepers? Surely God couldn't be asking that of him?

About this time he came to know the Bishop of Assisi, who was possibly his confessor, and it may have been Bishop Guido who made the sensible suggestion that he should go on a pilgrimage. For the men of the Middle Ages a pilgrimage was not only a religious exercise, it was change of air and scene and an excellent rest cure. And so Francis set out to visit the tombs of the Apostles, following the Tiber southwards to Rome. We do not know if he travelled with a party of pilgrims or whether he rode alone with

c

perhaps just a servant to attend him, both of them with daggers ready to defend themselves against the bands of robbers who were always on the prowl, but in either case the journey would have been an exciting joy to him. He was throughout his life an inveterate traveller and this was the first of his long journeys.

With his imagination and his sensitiveness Rome would have shaken him to his foundations, and emotion must have been at its height as he walked up the marble steps to the Basilica of Saint Peter's, and remembered that just over four hundred years ago his hero Charlemagne had mounted them too, to kneel and pray before Saint Peter's tomb as he was about to do now. He went through the silver door into the shadows within. With other pilgrims he kissed the foot of the great statue of Saint Peter and then went up the nave to the shrine. He kneeled before the altar, looking down through the grating to the tomb below, and prayed. In years to come he would learn to be so absorbed in prayer that he would be oblivious of the comings and goings about him, but at this time he was still only twenty-four years old and out of the corner of one eye he was aware of what the other pilgrims did, and was horrified at the smallness of their offerings. The Prince of the Apostles, he thought, should have more honour than this in his own great church. They were tossing down small coins with the same carelessness with which he himself had often thrown them to the poor. In a sudden fury of indignation he pulled out his own purse and flung the whole of its contents through the grating "with such a crash that all they who were standing by did marvel greatly at so splendid an oblation". It was a touch of the old Francis, madly generous and impulsive and not averse to being the central figure in a little drama, but the crash of that total giving was not without its effect upon him.

He went down the dark nave and out into the bright sunlight and was confronted with the beggars on the marble steps, parading their sores and their rags, their filth and misery, clutching at the passers-by with their hot hands and crying, "*Un soldo, signore. Per amor di Dio.*"

But now, for the first time, he could not give for the love of God, for he had just flung all his available money down the grating. Temporarily he was destitute too and had nothing to give but himself. Well, why not do it? Why not give himself to these men, be one of them for the day, to see what it felt like, put himself to the test. He would wear the livery of the Lady Poverty just for one day and see if he could endure it. He seized hold of an astonished beggar and persuaded him to lend him his clothes for the day, and in some hidden place he stripped off his fine clothes and put on the beggar's verminous rags. He went back to the steps and stood there all day, begging alms for the love of God, and he begged in French, the language that he always used when he was deeply moved. It was a great moment in his life. He had won his first victory over the pride that was a part of his fastidiousness, and taken his first step towards the final plunge that he so desperately dreaded.

Back in Assisi he continued in prayer and self-denial, seeking for the heavenly treasure and begging God to show him what he ought to do. He withdrew more and more from his old life for "it was whispered into his spirit that spiritual merchandise hath its beginning in the contempt of the world, and that the warfare of Christ is to be begun by victory over self".

And very soon the grace of God enabled him to win his greatest victory yet. He was riding home to Assisi one day across the plain, along the road that brought him fairly close to the leper hospital of San Salvatore, that was administered by the Order of the Crucigeri, when suddenly to his horror he saw a leper in his path and the old loathing, the old dread of deformity, rose up and choked him. A short while ago he would have yielded to his fear, he would have swerved aside on his horse, flinging a coin to the poor wretch and covering his face with his hand, but there was a power within him now that was stronger than his fear. He did violence to himself, fought down the sickening dread and gave himself into the hands of love to do with him what love would. He jumped off his horse, came to the leper and put the money into his hand. Then he gently took the hand and kissed it, putting his lips to the rotting flesh. It was an act of courage, for to touch a leper was considered a sure way to catch the disease, above all to touch him with the lips. It was also an act of reverence, for this kiss upon the hand was the traditional homage accorded to a priest as a representative of Christ. Francis at this supreme moment of his life saw in the suffering creature the suffering Christ. Then he put his arms about the man and the astonished, shaken leper, perhaps with enough eyesight left to see the blazing love in the young man's eyes, gave him the kiss of peace. Francis mounted his horse again and rode back to Assisi with joy in his heart.

THE CRUCIFIX

O Deepest Wisdom, counting all things dross,
Save love of us, so wretched and forlorn;
O Love Incarnate, counting gain for loss,
Sharing our life, yet of the Spirit born;
Uplifted to embrace us on the Cross,
Love spared Thee not, Thy hands with nails were torn,
Enduring Pilate's scorn,
That dreadful Day,
Our debt to pay,
Upon Thy Cross of Love.

Jacopone da Todi ?
Lauda XC "Amor de Caritate", which has been ascribed to Saint Francis.

I

FROM that day onwards he began to visit the lepers, giving them alms and kissing their hands. Years later he wrote in his will, "The Lord Himself led me amongst them, and I showed mercy to them; and when I left them what had seemed bitter to me was changed into sweetness of body and soul." His road to God was one that would pass always upwards through alternate light and shadow, and now that first period of suffering was over and his self-conquest had released him into happiness. This life of prayer and service that he was living now, irradiated through and through by love, was the life of the Kingdom of Heaven and he lived it to the full in peace and joy and an anguish of pity. He must have marvelled at the strangeness of this double life. About him was the beauty of the Italian scene that was as the landscape of paradise, and the peace of paradise was in his heart, and yet at the same time his eyes saw the agony of these men and his heart was transfixed by it. All the time, in spite of sweetness of body and soul, he must have been asking himself the question that has always tormented men. Why? Why this dreadful suffering? Francis was a simple man, not the type to be tormented by intellectual problems, and he already knew the love of God too well to doubt it, but he would hardly have been a man if he had not asked himself, "How can the God of love, who made the world so fair, permit such suffering?" He would have felt too that his present service of God in His poor was still not enough, for behind him there was still the security of his home. What did God want him to do?

One day he was passing close to the church of San Damiano. It stood on a small hill looking out over the plain, with a house for the priest beside it, and about it grew olive trees and bushes of rosemary and lavender. It was a lovely, fragrant place, but the little church was old and had fallen into ruin. Francis, that day, felt an overwhelming impulse to go in and pray there. Inside the church, with its ruined walls and broken floor with weeds thrusting up through the paving stones, was a simple stone altar with a crucifix behind it. Francis knelt down before the altar and prayed for guidance. He said, "Great and glorious God, and Thou, Lord Jesus, I pray Ye, shed abroad Thy light in the darkness of my mind . . . Be found of me, Lord, so that in all things I may act in accordance with Thy Holy Will." That was the prayer of his whole life, that he might do God's will, and he wanted to find God not only because of the joy of the finding but because the deeper his union with God the more perfectly would he be able to do His will. As he prayed he looked at the crucifix. It still exists and we can see it today at the church of Santa Chiara at Assisi. It is a Byzantine crucifix, painted upon wood, and it represents Christ with head up and eyes open looking out over the suffering world. The attitude of the figure is as though He was saying, "Come unto Me." Francis, gazing at the compassionate figure, went on praying, "Be found of me, Lord." And then once again, as at Spoleto, he heard the Lord speaking to him with the voice of a friend, and saying, "Francis, go and repair My church, which as thou seest is wholly in ruin." For a moment or two, as at Assisi when he fell behind the others, God touched him and he was terrified; in his body all his senses died and this world no longer enclosed him. He came back to consciousness again, and to the realization that his Lord had asked some service of him, and he said, "Gladly, Lord, will I repair it."

He stayed there praying, his eyes on the crucifix, and he was filled with a love for Christ greater than any he had felt before. The first time he had heard the Voice it had been, he truly believed, God's Voice speaking within him, but this Voice had seemed to come from the cross itself, it had been Christ speaking from the hidden place of the Atonement. He began to under-stand a very little what it had cost God to redeem mankind, the unbelievable humbling of the Incarnation, the poverty and labour and homelessness of Christ's life on earth, the humiliation and agony of His passion and death. He realized that though the sufferings of Christ in His human body were ended yet the At-one-ment was always going on. Christ still reigned from the cross, looking out over the suffering world, drawing all men to Himself on His cross that He might unite them to God in Him-self. When Francis had kissed the leper's hand he had seen Christ in him, but now he saw the mystery of pain the other way round; he saw all the suffering held in Christ, knew that only on the other side of the cross are the still waters and the green pastures to be found. In coming to the cross of Christ he had come to the only place where questioning could find rest. If it could not be entirely answered yet it shrank away into unimportance in the face of such unutterable love as this. From that moment Francis bore the seal of the cross upon his spirit, as at the end of his life he would bear it upon his body. Though he never ceased to love the sick and poor in Christ, and served them devotedly until the end, it was the suffering of Christ Himself that now began increasingly to possess his mind. He could never forget the passion of Christ. Once when he was seen weeping, and a friend asked him why he wept, he answered, "I weep for the passion of my Lord Jesus Christ, for whom I ought not to be ashamed to go mourning aloud throughout the whole world."

His prayer ended Francis got up and went out of the church full of joy because he had been told what he had to do. Later he would know that God's command had a deeper content than he had at first understood, but his youth and humility could not realize that now. He obeyed the command of the moment with the simple literalness that was always his. All his life his humble acts of obedience, following one upon another like the links in a chain, led him on at last to the whole content of God's will for him. Outside in the sunlight he found the old priest who looked after the church sitting under the olive trees and he gave him a large sum of money to buy oil, so that there should always be a lamp burning before the crucifix. Then he mounted his horse and rode away.

At first the rebuilding of San Damiano did not seem to him a difficult task for as a rich man's son he was still thinking in terms of money. Gold would buy the stones and mortar he needed. Gold did everything. All you had to do, when any sort of service was asked of you, was to put your hand in your pocket. At the moment his pocket was momentarily empty but to fill it was an easy matter; especially as his father was away. He took some rolls of valuable cloth from the warehouse, loaded them on his horse, signed himself, the horse and the cloth with the sign of the cross, for they were all alike now given to God, and rode away southward to Foligno. He rode through the streets into the marketplace and in front of the church of Santa Maria Infra Portas he sold both the cloth and the horse, and then walked back the ten miles through the forest to Assisi. It was possibly during this long walk that he came to an important decision. This selling of the horse was his first bit of self-stripping in the material sense. He had given away money, but it was his father's, and he had given away his clothes, but new ones could quickly be fashioned from the cloth in his father's warehouse, but his horse was his own and loving animals as he did he must have found it hard to part with that horse. But perhaps this sacrifice helped him to make up his mind to take the next step, and leave his home. How could he remain in such comfort when the Christ who had spoken to him from the cross had had nowhere to lay His head, and when beggars slept huddled in doorways and in filthy dens that were not fit to house a dog? He would ask the priest at San Damiano if he might share his little tumbledown house with him.

The old priest, when Francis had kissed his hand and told him the whole story, was willing for Francis to live with him but refused to have anything to do with the money gained at Foligno; he feared the wrath of Pietro Bernadone when he should come home and find out what his son had been doing in his absence. Francis threw the money on to a window-ledge in the little church and forgot about it, for if the priest would not let him use it for the rebuilding of San Damiano it had no further value for him.

He settled down with the kind old priest, sharing his poor dwelling and his scanty food. We can picture him serving the priest's mass and praying in the church before the crucifix, weeping for the sin of the world and its cost to the poor man crucified, vowing himself like a knight keeping his vigil to the service of Christ and the Lady Poverty. But he was still a rather unsteady knight, for he shared the old priest's nervousness as to what Pietro Bernadone might presently say and do, and noted that close to the priest's little dwelling there was an underground cave where he would be able to hide himself if the worst happened.

It happened immediately upon Pietro's return from his travels. The disappearance of the bales of cloth, of the horse, of the money that had been received for their sale, and of Francis himself, was for his father the last straw that broke him down. He had been patient with his extraordinary son and generous to Francis both in his extravagance and his lavish almsgiving. It is a measure of his love for his son that Francis seems to have had no qualms of conscience about selling the valuable cloth and appropriating the proceeds. His father had always so loved and indulged him that he took it for granted that what was his father's was his too. And no doubt Pietro's patience would have lasted longer had not Francis in his latest escapade dealt him two hard blows in his two vital spots, his business instinct and his pride. The loss of the cloth, sold by his son for far less than its great worth in the open market of Foligno, the most important commercial town of the region, was not to be borne and nor was the shame of his present way of life. That Francis should be generous to the poor from the height of his social superiority was one thing, and brought honour to the name of Bernadone, but that he should leave his home and actually share their way of life was quite another. The boy had made himself an object of ridicule to the city and in so doing had humiliated his father as well as himself. Pietro had been so proud of his eldest son, had built such high hopes upon him. They crashed now and in heartbroken misery and rage he summoned some of his friends to help him and set out for San Damiano to bring Francis back to his home and his senses. But some member of the household, and no doubt it was Pica, had warned Francis, and when his father arrived he was nowhere to be found. Pietro had to go home again frustrated, to nurse his anger and sorrow in increasing bitterness.

Francis stayed in the cave for a month, afraid to come out and face his father. This shrinking is hard to reconcile with the courage that distinguished him all his life. Perhaps it was largely made up of compunction. He was realizing now how much suffering he was causing his father and mother. "For I am come to set a man at variance against his father ... and a man's foes shall be they of his own household," is one of the harder sayings of Christ. It cuts both ways. The making of a saint, the burning out of the dross in the fire, can be a gruelling process not only for the saint but also for his unfortunate family. Francis, vowed to the service of Christ and His poverty, was ironly determined not to forsake them, but he was afraid to confront the pain and grief of Pica and Pietro. And how could he explain about this love for Christ that now possessed him so utterly? It was a thing so new and precious. To try and talk about it to the uncomprehending and the contemptuous would seem a sort of desecration. Perhaps he was also afraid that his father might curse him, and there is nothing an Italian fears more than the parental curse.

His month in the cave was a time of great suffering for him. He was kept alive by food secretly brought by a friend, but only God could comfort him as he struggled along the hard way of prayer and penitence alone in his dark hiding-place. But comfort came, moments of light that illumined his mind and spirit like sunshine, and shame came, and courage. God's gift of courage is also the command to use it and when it was given to him he knew that he must come out and face his father. This was the next step, and unless he made that simple act of obedience he was no servant of his Master.

II

So he came out of his cave into the sunshine and dragged himself up the steep stony way to the city, weak and haggard after the long period of suffering and struggle, dirty and ragged and unkempt. When he came into the streets of the city the people looked at him at first with pity, for they did not recognize him. Then the word went round, "It is Francesco Bernadone!" and their pity turned to contempt. They began to laugh and jeer at him and to pelt him with mud and stones, and then, as he bore it patiently and kept struggling along his way, up the Piazza Nuova towards his father's house near the market-place, they decided that he was mad and the cry went up, "*Pazzo! Pazzo!*" Italian children love a madman. They came tumbling up out of the dark alleys and presently a yelling crowd of them surrounded Francis, and the mud and stones came faster. Pietro heard the yells of "*Pazzo!*" in his house and came out into the street to see the fun. The dishevelled lunatic, bruised and mud-bespattered and half fainting with exhaustion, was his own son.

Pietro's always choleric temper became an uncontrollable madness. Shouting furiously at his son and the crowd alike he seized Francis, and carried him indoors. But he felt no pity for his son; he did not give himself time for pity. He gave Francis a cruel flogging and flung him into a small underground cave dungeon, still to be seen today, and here for a few days Francis stayed alone, the sounds of the house coming to him as from a great distance, in his home but shut away in pain and semi-darkness from all the laughter and love that once had centred around him. His fears in the cave at San Damiano could scarcely have conjured up anything harder to bear than this, but he bore it, and with gladness, for Christ had been jeered at on the way of sorrows and Christ had been flogged. The treatment which Pietro had hoped would break him strengthened him, for it gave him fellowship with the sufferings of Christ. When Pietro came to tell him he was leaving home on another journey he found his son still steadfast. In a last pitiful effort to break him by harshness he put manacles on Francis's hands and then went away sick at heart.

Then Pica came to Francis, took off his manacles, looked after him and comforted him. There is no record of what they said to each other on what seems to have been the last occasion when they were ever alone together. Perhaps they never spoke of it, and it remained for both a hidden treasure which they only looked upon in memory and prayer. Pica's efforts to persuade Francis to yield to his father had no success, and possibly she did not try very hard, for she had always known that this best-loved of her children belonged in a special sense to God. And so she gave him to God, and brought him to the door of the house and said good-bye, and watched him walk away from the home to which he would never return. When Pietro came back he heaped reproaches on her, and this picture of her enduring Pietro's wrath for Francis's sake is the last we have of her. It would be good to think that she lived long enough to see her son loved and revered by the whole of Italy, but it seems more likely that she died while still in middle age, for in after years Francis was to say that he knew only two women by sight, and these two would seem to be Saint Clare and the Lady Giacoma di Settesoli. There is no mention of his mother. He always paid great honour to those women who had given their sons to the Order he founded, calling them the Mothers of the Order, but again there is no mention of the Lady Pica. Though we know so little about her yet she remains one of the great figures of the Franciscan story. Through all that she taught her son, through all that she was in herself, she predisposed him to hear and obey the call of God when it came to him.

III

But Pietro and Francis had not finished with each other, and the last act in the struggle between father and son was as dramatic as anything in the vivid drama of the life of Francis. Each was as determined as the other. Pietro was not going to leave one thing undone in his effort to bring his son to his senses, and nothing that he could do would shake Francis now in his allegiance to Christ.

Francis, when he left his home, went straight back to San Damiano, and Pietro upon his return pursued him there. But this time Francis did not hide in the cave but came bravely out to meet him. His father stormed at him and struck him with his fist, but he bore the anger and blows humbly and patiently. And Pietro realized that violence was a useless weapon. He tried to quieten his anger, to speak gently and bargain with Francis. He should go his own way, he said, if he would renounce his inheritance and give back the money he had taken at Foligno. Perhaps Pietro hoped in his heart that the family, and his place in it as his father's eldest son, still meant something to Francis and that in the last resort he would not give them up, but Francis willingly agreed to renounce his inheritance. What he would not do was to give back the money. He had given it to the church and he considered that it was no longer his to give.

Pietro rode back to Assisi in angry misery but not yet hopeless. He went straight to the palace of the commune in the market-square and laid his trouble before the consuls. He had their sympathy and they sent a herald out to San Damiano to summon Francis to appear before the communal court. Perhaps Pietro hoped his sensitive gentle son would never face a family wrangle before the consuls. And Francis, confronted with the herald, did refuse to appear, but not for reasons of shame. He said that as a man dedicated to religion he was not subject to the civic authorities but only to the Bishop. Pietro went to the Bishop, and Francis was summoned to appear before the episcopal court. This time he consented, saying, "I will come before the Lord Bishop gladly for he is the father and lord of souls."

The day fixed for the trial came. It was a chilly morning in early spring but not too cold to deter the citizens of Assisi from flocking to the Bishop's palace to see what would happen between the father and son. The quarrel in the Bernadone family must have been the great topic of conversation in the city at this time, some taking one side and some the other, Pietro's contemporaries full of sympathy for him and solidly behind parental authority, the young men who had been Francis's friends quite sure he had taken leave of his senses but backing him against his father all the same. The older men and the young ones in their gay clothes and rich furred coats streamed into the hall of the palace and filled it to capacity, but when they had taken their places perhaps the poor men to whom Francis had been so generous crept about the door and stood there shivering in their rags in the cold wind, to see what would happen to the white-faced boy whom they had last seen being stoned in the street.

Bishop Guido came in in his robes and gravely took his place and Pietro and Francis came forward and faced each other, one on each side of his throne. It must have surprised many to see that Francis had put on a suit of his old bright clothes. Did he mean to give in? But there was no sign of yielding on his stern young face as he stood listening to his father stating his case and claim against him. Pietro ceased speaking and it was the turn of Francis, but he kept humbly silent. Then the Bishop gave judgement and though he loved Francis it was for the father against the son. Francis must return the money. He had no right to wealth gained by selling goods that belonged to his father, no, not though he wanted the money not for himself but for the rebuilding of a church. The Bishop summed up by saying with a certain scorn, "God does not wish His church to be succoured with goods which perhaps are gotten by injustice." But because of his love for Francis, and because he believed that God had indeed some great purpose for him, he went on to speak gently to him. "Have thou then faith in the Lord, my son, and play the man, and fear not, for Himself will be thy helper, and will give thee in abundance whatsoever is needful for the work of His church."

Francis had brought the money with him and he gave it back. He had been willing to submit to the judgement of the Bishop, and perhaps he had now seen for himself that he should not have sold that cloth. It was not as a rich man that God wanted him to rebuild San Damiano but as a poor one. The way to do it would be shown him as soon as he had put all compromise behind him and given himself utterly to the poverty of Christ. The Bishop's words put fresh heart into him for he believed they came from

God Himself. They gave him courage to do what he believed he had to do and had planned to do when he dressed himself in the old bright clothes. For a long time now he had been gradually stripping himself of one thing after the other, of his dreams, friends, comforts and pleasure, his revulsions and fears, self-love and self-will, and now he did the last thing needful, the last thing that cut him off for ever from his old life. In fervour of spirit he stripped off his gay garments and tossed them on the floor at his father's feet, saying, "My Lord Bishop, I will give back unto him with a light heart not only the money that belongeth unto him, but my clothes also." Then standing up before all the people, clothed in nothing but his hair-shirt, the garment of penitence, he cried out in his clear resonant voice, "Hear ye all, and understand: until now have I called Pietro Bernadone my father, now I give back all that I had of him, desiring to say only, 'Our Father, Which art in heaven,' with Whom I have laid up my whole treasure and on whom I have set my whole trust and hope."

It was an arresting action, and if it seems typical of that love of striking a fine figure that had distinguished the younger Francis that is not the truth about it, for that was the sort of nonsense he had now left behind him. Dramatic he had to be, for drama was part of him, as it is in greater or lesser degree of all the Italian people, who must make a picture of a thing before they thoroughly understand it, but this was a new sort of drama, a piece of symbolism glorifying not himself but God. In later years his biographer Thomas of Celano was to say of him, "He made of his whole body a tongue to preach the gospel," and he was beginning now. His half-naked figure proclaimed that we bring nothing into this world and we shall take nothing out of it excepting only the garment of penitence, that unless a man be born again in self-naughting and humility he cannot enter the kingdom of heaven, that in heaven alone is our treasure and in God alone our trust and help. By this final stripping Francis had made of himself an integrated personality; body, mind and soul he was forged together by his burning love of Christ into a sword of integrity. It was said of his sermons in later years that they pierced his hearers, and this his first sermon was no less piercing than those that were to come, and the unconscious power with which he could sway a large concourse of people was as evident now as when he was at the height of his fame. The emotions of the crowd packing the hall swung away from his father and over to him in sympathy, and many of the people wept, not only in pity for him but as we weep when some chord of music touches us unbearably, making us aware of those high and far-off things for which in our hearts we confusedly long but for which we are too cowardly to pay the price. Bishop Guido, weeping with the rest, was swept up to participate in the drama. He got up and put his own cloak around Francis, who perhaps now was shivering and exhausted, chilled by the cold wind that swept in through the unglazed windows and drained by the tremendous effort he had made. To the onlookers it seemed an act as symbolic as Francis's own. The homeless for Christ's sake are never left without the protection of His church about them.

Pietro had won back the money but it gave him no joy. There was nothing left for him to do but to take his pound of flesh and go. With grief and wrath he gathered up his son's bright clothes, leaving him with not a single garment to put on, and left the hall, hearing behind him the angry murmur of the crowd. Then he went home broken-hearted.

Some clothes were brought for Francis, a tunic belonging to one of the Bishop's farm-labourers, and a pair of rough felt boots. Francis took a piece of chalk and marked a cross on the tunic. Now he was truly a knight of Christ and the bridegroom of the Lady Poverty. He said good-bye to the Bishop and went down the hall to the door, outside which the sick and ragged beggars had gathered. He passed out into their company to be one with them for ever.

Chapter Four

THE BUILDER

Ah! when Christ is grafted on the spray,
All the withered wood is cut away;
See the freshness springing from decay!
Changing to a wondrous unity.

Lo, I live! yet not my self alone;
I am I, yet am I not mine own;
And this change, cross-wise, obscure, unknown,
—Language cannot tell its mystery.

Jacopone da Todi, Lauda LX

I

FRANCIS did not at once start the rebuilding of San Damiano. Like a lark set free from captivity he needed first to try his wings. He felt that he must go away from Assisi, away even from his beloved lepers and the old priest at San Damiano, and experience his new freedom alone with God.

He went forth singing, happy as he had been after he had kissed the leper, experiencing once again the joy of self conquest, the sense of shackles falling and wings unfolding. It was spring in the world as well as in his soul when he left Assisi and climbed up the mountain passes towards Gubbio. There was green grass under the melting snow and warmth in the sunshine. The swelling buds had misted the trees with colour and birdsong was echoing in the woods. The little streams, swollen with snow-water, were chiming over the stones, and on the wind came the scent of wet moss and ferns and the first spring flowers opening in hidden places. He was so happy that he sang the songs of the troubadours in the beloved French tongue, his wonderful voice ringing out as musically as the streams and the birdsong. He climbed up through the changing woods, through the oaks and the pines and out on to the high, bare mountain slopes above, where the wind was cold and invigorating as a draught of iced wine. Down below him he could see Assisi clinging to the slopes of Mount Subasio, and the whole vast Umbrian plain, and the mountains piled against the blue of the sky. Now he could hear the larks singing overhead, and understand as never before the passion of their joy in space and light. He was as free as they were and shared with them and with all birds and beasts and flowers this adventure of utter dependence upon God alone. It gave him a new feeling of brotherhood with them, a sense of one-ness with the whole universe, that seems to men so vast yet in God's sight is no more than a drop of dew fallen down upon the earth. Perhaps he laughed, looking at the little toy cities in the distance, and remembering how men toiled and sweated, quarrelled and fought for more and more in the way of food and drink, shelter and clothing, and called it supporting themselves, and forgot that what supported them was the finger of God alone. Were He to withdraw that gentle upholding they and the whole universe would fall into the abyss. He laughed, realizing that he was free of the whole worrying mess of earthly clutter, aware of the paradox of man's glorious peril and his perfect safety.

He went on and came to a lonely wooded place where the hills began to decline towards Gubbio, and now his story takes a humorous twist, an anti-climax after the spiritual grandeur of the scene in the Bishop's palace. He was always poised between grief and joy, never quite knowing whether man's condition calls more for weeping or laughter, and through the splendours of his life there ran always a homely thread of fairy-tale comedy. It took the form now of a band of robbers who leaped out at him from their hiding-place and demanded who he was. Even in this startling moment he remained confident and unafraid, and able to remember that his name was John. "I am a herald of the great King!" he called out joyously. At which crazy answer they pulled off his tunic and his boots and toppled him over into a snowdrift. "Lie there, thou fool herald!" they said, and made off. Francis got up laughing and "with yet louder voice began to make the woods echo with praises unto the Creator of all".

But in such chilly weather he could scarcely wander through the world with nothing on but a hair-shirt, and he made his way to a monastery, probably that of Santa Maria della Rocca near Valfabbrica, knocked at the door and suggested to the astonished monks that he should be their servant in exchange for food and clothing. They let him in, put him to work in the kitchen, gave him food but refused him garments. Francis worked for them for a few days and then, with no ill-will but anxious for something to put on, left them and set out for Gubbio, where he had a friend who might come to his rescue. Years later, when he was famous, he received profound apologies from the prior of this monastery, and we can imagine with what delighted humour he received them.

The old walled city of Gubbio, built on the lower slopes of Monte Calvo, must have been astonished to see Francis in his hair-shirt wandering up its steep streets. No doubt they laughed at him and no doubt that in his present joyous frame of mind he laughed back, for by this time he was becoming used to being a source of amusement. He never minded being laughed at, indeed he rejoiced in being God's fool, the only thing he could not bear was the fame and adulation that most men live for. But if Gubbio laughed, his friend in the city, perhaps the same friend who had stood by him through the hard days at Le Grotte, entertained him more kindly. He fed him and also found for him the garments of a pilgrim, a tunic with a leather belt, sandals, wallet and staff. For a while Francis worked in the leper hospital at Gubbio and then he tramped joyously back to Assisi. The robbers had done him no harm and he had not starved, for the God in whom he had trusted had not deserted him.

II

Once more settled at San Damiano he set himself to obey the command of Christ and rebuild the ruined church. In the lengthening days of spring, when the fruit blossom was fragrant in the orchards and the warm brilliant sunshine poured over the city, Francis the troubadour was a familiar figure as he went singing his Provençal melodies through the streets of Assisi, the

children tumbling at his heels. When he reached one of the open
squares, those high level terraces to which he had gone in procession as a child and with the young men in his boyhood, he stopped
and sang a few hymns, and when he had collected a small crowd
about him he stopped singing and spoke to them. He told them
about the church of San Damiano with its ruined walls and broken
floor with weeds pushing up through the paving-stones, and its
holes in the roof through which the rain came, spattering the
altar and the figure of Christ looking out over the suffering world.
And then he begged for stones for the rebuilding of this little
house of God. In those days when there was so much building
going on in the city, including the building of the new cathedral,
there was plenty of cut stone about and it was often used for
barter. Money was little used except by the rich. The poorer folk
supplied their necessities by exchanging one thing for another.
And so Francis sang for his stones. Some thought him mad,
others, remembering the princely young figure of the past, and
seeing him now in his pilgrim's dress, worn with prayer and
fasting and work that was too hard for him, were profoundly
moved. "Who will give stones for the rebuilding of San Damiano?" he would say. "Whoso gives one stone shall have one
reward; whoso gives two stones shall have two rewards; whoso
gives three stones shall have three rewards." And they brought
him the stones, and somehow he got them out of the city, and
down the steep pathway to San Damiano, where he girded up
his tunic and set to work with a will, putting to good use the
knowledge of building that had come to him as a boy when he
laboured at the rebuilding of the walls of Assisi. And as he worked
he sang. How his frailty accomplished all this manual labour,
or indeed any of the mighty tasks of his life, is a mystery hidden
within the mystery of sanctity itself.

He was not left to work alone, for in all that he did his infinite
attraction drew men after him as the music of the Pied Piper drew
the children. Friendly peasants came and worked with him, and
sang and laughed with him, and there was so much happiness at
San Damiano that the citizens of Assisi came down in their free
moments to watch the fun, and passing travellers stopped and

wondered what was going on, and to them Francis called out, "Come and help us, for this church will one day be a convent of ladies whose life and fame will glorify our Heavenly Father in all the world." And they would help too, sunning themselves in the loving charm of this young lunatic. For no doubt they dismissed what he said about the future of San Damiano as moonshine, and not as the intuition of a man whose growing selflessness was being illumined more and more by flashes of light from the timeless country where the fulfilment of the will of God is already perfected.

But work on San Damiano did not make Francis forget the lepers. He would take time off to be with them, either at San Salvatore or at the hospital of Santa Maria Maddalena, and his service to them had undergone a change since the days when he had given them money and kissed their hands. Saint Bonaventure in his life of Francis gives a grim picture of what service to lepers entailed for him now. "He would bathe their feet, and bind up their sores, drawing forth the corrupt matter from their wounds, and wiping away the blood." One of the lepers had gone on pilgrimage to the tombs of the Apostles in Rome to pray for healing, for the fearful disease had eaten away his mouth and jaw. But he came back with his prayer unanswered, and his despair can be imagined. Meeting Francis on the road he knelt down and would have kissed his footprints, so dearly did these lepers love him, but Francis bent down and took him in his arms and kissed his terrible face, and Saint Bonaventure tells us that in that moment the leper's prayer was answered. This is the first recorded instance of the way in which the love of God was able to heal men through the love of Francis.

When a man is determined to break himself in for God he takes every opportunity for self-conquest that offers itself. No matter how small it is, it brings its added strength. One day Francis was in need of oil for the lamp which burned always now before the crucifix at San Damiano, and he went up to Assisi to beg for it. It was evening and he saw lamps burning in a house and turned towards it, but when he came near he saw a company of his old friends having a party there, the kind of party at which in old days he had been the leader, and he turned away ashamed. It would be too embarrassing, both for them and himself, to go in then, and he felt he could not do it. Then he realized that he was being a coward and he conquered himself. He went in to the feast and stood among his old friends in their gay clothes, he in his worn pilgrim's gown, and confessed that he was a coward who had been ashamed to come among them, and asked them for some of their oil for the love of God.

There was another thing that he did that was even harder. The old priest at San Damiano, who loved him, was distressed to see him so exhausted at the day's end and knowing how delicately he had been nurtured he took great pains to cook tempting little meals for him. Francis realized suddenly that this was not true poverty. If he was not careful he would soon be enjoying the little comforts of the priest's poor home as much as he had once enjoyed the luxuries of his father's house. And so he took a bowl and went up to Assisi and begged for his food from door to door, for the love of God. The astonished housewives gave him such scraps as they had and when he had enough to make a meal he went away to a quiet place and sat down and looked at the nauseating fragments in his bowl. Fastidious as he was his gorge rose. How could he possibly swallow this disgusting mess? But this was the sort of food that poverty had to eat, and he was vowed to poverty, and he must eat it. So summoning all his courage, shuddering with revulsion at every mouthful, he set to work.

As he ate a strange thing happened to him, for the feeling of nausea passed and he began to eat with appetite, and not only that but to feel a glow of happiness all through him. For with the self-conquest there had come to him one of those moments of light that came so often when he prayed, and the light illumined many things. He realized that this poor meal was a sacrament of the providence of God. God spreads a table for His little ones, for the birds and beasts and for the poor who put their trust in Him, and is Himself their servant, as Christ was the servant of His disciples when he knelt before them to wash their feet and then gave them His body and blood to be their food. He saw also that the providence of God is a circle of loving and giving, God serving His poor through the bounty of His rich, and His poor offering up their thanks to Him. And he saw more deeply into the meaning of the Trinity, the love that gives and the love that accepts, returning love again, and the love that is the gift between them, Father, Son and Holy Spirit. And entering a little more deeply into the meaning of poverty he saw that it can be more blessed to receive than give. Until now he had only given, he had poured himself out in love and service, and perhaps his giving had not always been quite free from the taint of pride; for the power to help others, even though it may seem wholly good, is still power; but he had not set himself humbly to receive the service of God and man. With this humble receiving, he understood now, true humility must begin, and without it there is no true poverty. To Peter's cry of, "Thou shalt never wash my feet!" Christ had answered, "If I wash thee not thou hast no part in Me", and unless he could learn to say with Peter, "Lord, not my feet only, but also my hands and my head", he would have no part in the poverty of Christ. From that day onwards he had a great reverence for beggars because they were to him the symbol of this humble acceptance, and he called the eating of this food that had been begged for the love of God eating at the table of the Lord.

Day by day now he ate nothing except these scraps of food that he begged in the streets. It was not the bread of idleness, for idleness in any sort or form was always abhorrent to him, it was the bounty of God that gave his body strength for the rebuilding of God's church and the nursing of His sick.

But Pietro Bernadone could hardly be expected to see it in this way. That his eldest son should now be a common beggar was for him the final humiliation and whenever he met Francis in the street he cursed him. He could have done nothing more cruel, for he knew very well the numinous dread and fear awakened by the parental curse, and he knew his son's sensitiveness, but by now his love had so wholly passed into bitterness that he did not care how much he hurt Francis if only he could hurt him enough. At first he was successful and had his son quivering and wretched under the flaying of his tongue, but not for long, for Francis had that most enviable of gifts, the ability to confront every challenge, small or great, with the perfect response. Sometimes this response came in swift symbolic action, sometimes in a few words so perfectly phrased that they have never been forgotten. Sometimes it was the leaping out of his own ready wit, but often something much deeper than that, the answer of divine inspiration. Whichever it was it gave a vivid freshness to his life. On this occasion he bribed an old beggar, the bribe being half shares in the miserable scraps he collected, to accompany him round the streets and be a more loving father to him than his own. Whenever they encountered Pietro, and Francis was cursed, he would turn to the old beggar who would bless him and make over him the sign of the cross. The blessing of this adopted father took away Francis's fear and must have annoyed Pietro extremely.

To the mockery of his brother Angelo Francis's answer came from the depths of him. One day, when he was perhaps toiling along with a load of stone, he met Angelo strolling through the street with a companion, and Angelo said loudly to his friend, "Go and ask Francis to sell us a drop of his sweat." Francis laughed and called back in the joyous French tongue, "Nay, I sell it more dearly to my Lord!"

III

The months passed and San Damiano was finished at last, with sound roof and walls and floor to house the treasure of the crucifix, and Francis turned to another ruined shrine outside the city, San Pietro, and then he laboured at the restoration of Santa Maria Maggiore beside the Bishop's palace. When these were finished it was the turn of the little church which with San Damiano is now one of the holy places of the world.

Two miles from Assisi, and less than a mile from the leper hospital of San Salvatore where he worked, was a shrine that Francis must always have loved because it had been for long a holy place and legends had twined themselves about it, and old and far-off stories had always fascinated him. Also it was hidden in the woods, ruined and deserted, and he loved the quiet places.

The church itself was a small stone building with gables at each end. Over the altar, painted on the wall, was a fresco of the Assumption of our Lady with angels surrounding her. Not far from it were a well and the fallen walls of a ruined building. The woods had taken the ruins to themselves and made them beautiful. Brambles and creepers had climbed over them and flowers grew in the crannies of the stones. Where once bells had rung out there was now the chiming of birdsong, and birds made of the church a nesting-place. "The sparrow hath found her an house, and the swallow a nest where she may lay her young; even thine altars, O Lord of Hosts, my King and my God." Francis must have sung the eighty-fourth Psalm many times in these ruins for at this time he left San Damiano and came to live here in the woods, and the birds, accustomed to his comings and goings, would have been undisturbed when he joined his singing to theirs.

The little church was so old that it had perhaps once been a pagan temple or tomb. According to the legend that Francis loved, four pilgrims, coming back from the Holy Land in the fourth century, had found this place. They were happy pilgrims, for their eyes had seen the holy places and their feet had trodden the very paths where once their Lord had walked, but they were footsore and tired and they thought that they would stay here. They had with them a precious relic that they had brought from our Lady's sepulchre in the Holy Land, and with this relic they sanctified the pagan shrine and they called it Saint Mary of Jehosaphat, and they sang to God and praised Him within its walls. After a while they went away but the shrine was not deserted because the angels had taken a fancy to it and they came and sang there. Visiting hermits also came sometimes, and they heard the angels singing, and so did peasants passing through the woods, and children who came gathering flowers, and so it came to be called Santa Maria degli Angeli, Saint Mary of the Angels, and the fame of its holiness spread abroad like the fragrance of a flower. It was as a flower that Saint Benedict found it, growing here in the woods in quietness and peace, and he loved it so much that he took possession of it for his Order. He bought a small plot of land around the shrine and called it the Little Portion, Portiuncula, and he built for his monks the monastery whose ruins were still there when Francis came. They lived there for six hundred years and then, the times being so dangerous, they went away to the safety of the Benedictine fortress on the slopes of Monte Subasio. When Francis came to rebuild the church it had been left for nearly a hundred years to the angels and the birds.

Francis, who called the life of prayer the life of heaven, was no doubt very much aware of the angels as he worked and sang in the echoing woods, but beneath his happiness he was in great perplexity. What did God want him to do next? Christ had said to him "Rebuild My church", but he did not know of any more rebuilding that he could do. When Christ had said, "My church", had He meant San Damiano, or had He meant something greater, something of which that little shrine was the symbol? Francis knew how the symbol can be a shadow of truth, and yet when you pass beyond it to what it foreshadowed that too is only a shadow of something greater still, and so you pass on and on as you are able, from one handhold to another, and yet each shadow in its own place is the truth. He knew now that he must mount a little further but he did not know how, and he prayed as he had prayed at Spoleto, "Lord, what wouldst Thou have me to do?"

Chapter Five

MY GOD AND MY ALL

I beseech Thee, O Lord, that the fiery and sweet strength
of Thy love may absorb my soul from all things that are under
heaven, that I may die for love of Thy love as Thou didst deign
to die for love of my love.

Writings of Saint Francis

I

EARLY one morning, on February the 24th, 1209, when Francis
was twenty-seven years old, he came from the little shelter he had
made for himself in the woods and walked towards Santa Maria
degli Angeli. It was completed now and to please him the old
priest from San Damiano came sometimes to say mass there and
today Francis was going to serve the mass. It was Saint Matthias's
day. Very reverently he made the church ready, sweeping the
floor with a broom, made of sprigs of heather fastened together,
dusting the plain stone altar and the window-ledges, seeing that
everything was in order in this tiny place. If he had known that
this was to be not only a great day in his own life but also in the
history of the world he could have been no more awed and ex-
pectant than he was already. Nothing could be greater than the
coming of Christ the King in the sacrament of the altar. Soon the
little church would be as holy as the courts of heaven, and angels
and archangels would be thronging there. "My soul hath a
desire and longing to enter into the courts of the Lord: my heart
and my flesh rejoice in the living God." He put away his broom
and knelt down upon the altar steps to pray. The silvery light of a
morning in early spring grew stronger and through the unglazed
windows and the open door came the woodland sounds, sweet
sharp flutings as the birds made trial of the spring day and the
stirring of the trees as the morning wind blew down the world.
And then at last the footfall of the priest was heard coming

through the wood. Presently Francis heard his greeting, "*Dom-inus det tibi pacem*," the Lord give thee peace.

The priest stood before the altar and his server knelt upon the steps. The words of the divine office rose and fell, the birds sang in the wood and the bolder among them hopped in and out of the open door. The moment came to read the portion of scripture which was at that time the gospel for the day, and as the priest turned towards Francis and began to speak there seemed a great silence in the world.

"And as ye go, preach, saying, The kingdom of heaven is at hand. Heal the sick, cleanse the lepers, raise the dead, cast out devils: freely ye have received, freely give. Provide neither gold, nor silver, nor brass in your purses, nor scrip for your journey, neither two coats, neither shoes, nor yet staves: for the workman is worthy of his meat. And into whatsoever city or town you shall enter, inquire who in it is worthy; and there abide till ye go thence. And when ye come into an house, salute it. And if the house be worthy, let your peace come upon it; but if it be not worthy, let your peace return to you. . . . Behold, I send you forth as sheep in the midst of wolves."

No interior voice this time, no dream, no sudden visitation of God such as had struck him almost unconscious in the streets of Assisi, only the quiet deep conviction that this was for him. This was what he had to do. These were Christ's words to His apostles. Christ was calling him to be an apostle as he had called those other poor men long ago. He was saying, "Follow Me."

The priest turned back to the altar and the prayers and praises continued peacefully, Francis's voice steady and quiet as he made the responses. Mass was celebrated and God visited His people. When it was over the priest and server continued to kneel for a while in silent prayer. The birdsong was louder now and the sunshine stronger. Then they rose and Francis asked the priest if he would read the gospel to him again and explain it. Together with his impetuosity there was always in him this humble reliance upon the help of others, even when he believed that he had had direct revelation from God. It was said of him "He believed his

companion's advice to be safer, and others' views seemed to him
better than his own. He used to say that anyone who kept back
the treasure-chests of his own opinion had not left all for the sake
of God." But what the priest said only strengthened his own
certainty. He got up full of joy, pulled off his sandals and wallet
and flung them aside. And then he carefully learned by heart the
command that he had heard. "This," he said, "is that which I
am fain with all my might to fulfil."

He spent that day making himself ready, praying and thinking,
and as always the practical thing that he did was the outward
expression of his thought and enables us to follow it a little way.
For this new adventure he made himself a new garment, a
habit shaped like a cross, with a hood, and instead of his belt he
girded himself with a rope. Upon the tunic the Bishop had given
him he had chalked a cross; he had been a servant wearing his
Master's badge on his livery. But now he clothed himself in the
cross itself. "Put ye on the Lord Jesus Christ." He had set himself, as far as a man may, to imitate Christ in all things, with arms
stretched out both ways in love to God and man. He would have
had no illusions as to what was before him. To love God meant
perfect obedience to the will of God and he knew from the
example of his Master what suffering that might bring. To love
men meant living a sanctified life, or God's grace would not reach
them through the channel of his spirit, and sanctification calls for
hard and ceaseless discipline. In deep humility, in fear and
trembling as well as joy, he put on his habit. How could he, a
weak and sinful man, carry this cross? Only by living so close to
Christ that they would carry it together. Perhaps he thought of
the rope that he wore as a symbol of the love and obedience that
bound him to Christ. Or perhaps he thought of it as one of the
symbols of the suffering of Christ, remembering the rope with
which they had bound his Master's wrists in the Garden of Gethsemane. And so he made ready, and prayed in the little church,
and the next morning he went barefoot up the stony way to
Assisi to preach, saying, "The kingdom of heaven is at hand."

Except for that first silent sermon in the Bishop's palace he had
not preached before, but his Lord was with him and his preaching

took hold of the people almost at once. They did not mock him now. Two years had passed since the children had cried out "*Pazzo! Pazzo!*" in the streets and through those two years he had shown a courage and perseverance of which no madman is capable. The austerity of his life, the rebuilding of the churches and the nursing of the lepers had made the people respect him. Earlier they might not have listened to what he had to say but now they were very ready to listen. His preaching was something new and fresh to them. The lay preachers to whom they occasionally listened in the streets were usually heretics or men with a grievance. Francis was no heretic and he had no grievance. Like Saint John before him he preached simply as the herald of the great King, proclaiming the kingdom of heaven. His preaching, like himself, was utterly simple. He would go quietly through the streets and when he saw a few citizens together he would greet them saying, "The Lord give thee peace," and then standing at a street corner, or on a flight of steps leading up to an arched doorway, he would talk to them of repentance and of the life of love that is the life of the kingdom, and then one after another men, women and children would gather around him until the street or square where he was standing was full of people. Though his preaching must have increased in power as his life went on, Francis from the very beginning seems to have been a compelling preacher. He had a strong and beautiful voice, grace and charm, and the actor's ability to use voice and gesture harmoniously together. And to these natural gifts he added sincerity and authority. For he knew what he was talking about. He had himself repented in agony and tears and after much suffering he had found the peace of God. He knew what it meant to love God and to be loved by Him, and he had yielded himself to love for ever. His words were not empty "but full of the might of the Holy Spirit, piercing unto the marrow of the heart, insomuch as that his hearers were rapt in amazement as they listened".

The quality of his preaching is seen in the type of men who were the first to give up all for Christ as he had done. They were not very young men, and not beggars or outcasts who had lost their all already, and neither was there anything of hot-headed

enthusiasm or fanaticism about them. They were a wealthy
business man, a lawyer, a farmer's son and a priest, and they did
not come to Francis without thinking first what they were doing.
His appeal was not to facile emotion but to the deep hunger for
God within men, a hunger of which they may be only vaguely
aware until something pierces them "unto the marrow of the
heart", some grief or beauty or holiness which awakens them to
know the purpose for which they were made.

The two who came first were Bernard da Quintavalle and Peter
Cathanii, the business man and the lawyer. Peter was a doctor of
laws and a lay canon of the cathedral and he had the distinction of
having studied in the famous law schools at Bologna. Francis
must have been deeply moved and astonished when he came to
him and asked that he might be his pupil in the school of love.
The humility of this scholar, who had discovered that learning
and intellect left him hungry still, and turned for help to a young
man who could equal him in neither, was well matched by the
humility of Francis, who had set himself to learn patience of the
homeless poor. Francis felt great reverence for the learning of
Peter, and Peter for the selflessness of Francis, and they talked
together often of the God whom both men served and of
Peter's desire to do what Francis had done and strip himself of all
that he had for Christ's sake.

Bernard da Quintavalle also had this strong passion for the
costing simplicity of singlemindedness; as had all men who
followed the light of Francis who was its most perfect embodi-
ment. His house was close to that of Pietro Bernadone so that he
and Francis must have always known each other, though perhaps
not well, for Francis was the younger and the extravagance of his
youth would not have commended him to the cautious, sober-
minded Bernard. But the extraordinary change in Francis
impressed him, his steady patient labour and now the sincerity of
his preaching. He paid a secret visit to Francis, as once Nicodemus
visited Christ by night, and after that he frequently asked Francis
to spend the night with him and they talked together. This
friendship must have given great joy to Francis and comforted
him a little for the loss of his father, for Bernard was one of the

merchant princes of Assisi, holding much the same sort of position as Pietro, and yet he could understand Francis as Pietro had not been able to do. When Francis came to visit him Bernard had a bed prepared for his guest in his own bedchamber, and must have been happy to think that for once in a way Francis could stretch out at ease on a soft mattress and have a little warmth and comfort. But Francis never stayed for long in his comfortable bed. As soon as he thought Bernard was asleep he would slip noiselessly out of it and kneel to pray. One night Bernard, who had only seemed to be asleep and was in reality awake, hard-pressed and struggling for decision, watched Francis and marvelled at this silent prayer of adoring love. But now and then as the hours passed a few words would break from Francis, and always the same words, "My God and my All," and Bernard realized that this was what he wanted, that God should be his All, this God of mercy who gave Himself so entirely to those who gave themselves entirely to Him. For this God he had longed all his life but he had been held back from Him by divided allegiance, pulled one way by love of God and the other way by his great possessions. Watching Francis he made up his mind. He would follow Christ in the way that he had done.

When Bernard told Francis of his decision Francis was as careful for him and for Peter as he had been for himself in Santa Maria degli Angeli. Before they decided that what they wanted was the will of God they must seek this will through humble prayer. So in the early morning, when the sun was rising over Assisi and the shadows were long and blue in the streets, the three went to the Piazza San Giorgio, entered the Church of San Nicholas and knelt down to pray in the cool stillness and quiet within. The altar, and the book of the Gospels that lay near it, were touched with the light of the rising sun, and they heard the birds singing, for it was April and the world was turning towards a new beginning. After a few moments Francis, acting for the first time as a leader of other men, left Bernard and Peter and knelt before the altar and prayed for the three of them the prayer that he always prayed, that was the prayer of his life, that was his life, for he lived now only to do the will of God. We do not know what words he used, though thinking of this scene we remember the words he used on another occasion. "God Almighty, eternal, righteous and merciful, give to us poor wretches to do for Thy sake all that we know of Thy will, and will always what pleases Thee; so that inwardly purified, enlightened, and kindled by the fire of the Holy Spirit, we may follow in the footprints of Thy well-beloved Son, Our Lord Jesus Christ. Amen." Then he got up and going to the book of the Gospels he opened it three times in the name of the Holy Trinity, and read out to Bernard and Peter the words to which the will of God directed his eyes when he opened the book. The first time he read from St. Matthew's Gospel words which seem to us now especially applicable to Bernard the rich man. "If thou wouldest be perfect, go, sell all that thou hast and give to the poor, and thou shalt have treasure in heaven; and come follow Me."

The second reading from St. Luke seems for Peter, whose intimate treasures of knowledge and intellect must have seemed to him as precious and indispensable as scrip and staff to a pilgrim, and far harder to part with than Bernard's gold. "Take nothing for your journey, neither staff nor scrip nor bread nor money, neither have two coats."

The third reading from St. Matthew belongs to Francis, who had already clothed himself in the cross. "If any man will come after Me, let him deny himself and take up his cross and follow Me."

Francis turned round to his companions. "Brothers, this is our life and rule for ourselves and for all who will join our company." He came back to them and knelt beside them again, and the three prayed together, lifting up to Christ their gold and frankincense and myrrh, all they had and were, their prayer, their suffering and death. Outside the thick walls of the old church the city was stirring to life but within them there was stillness, peace and silence, and in this silence the great Franciscan Order was born.

II

A few days later, on April the 16th, Assisi was humming with excitement. The people had heard already that the rich man

Bernard da Quintavalle had sold his house and all his possessions, but when word went round as to what he was doing with the proceeds they could not contain themselves. They ran out of their houses, calling to their neighbours to come with them, and surged up the narrow streets to the Piazza San Giorgio to see a sight they had never seen before, a rich man giving away all his wealth to the poor. Beggars in rags and barefoot children, the old, the sick, the blind and the cripples were jostling together in the sunlit piazza, and the rich men were watching in amazement, shamed or contemptuous according to their nature. But being Italians their amazement would not have been silent. The uproar must have been magnificent. At the heart of it all were Francis and Bernard distributing Bernard's wealth to the crowd as calmly as though they were giving crumbs to hungry birds. Peter Cathanii was perhaps with them, but he had had few possessions and his giving would have been less spectacular; though perhaps when he gave to some beggar the price of his precious books the few coins weighed more in God's sight than the whole of Bernard's wealth put together. Francis, as he handled the gold and silver, sang loudly above the noise of the crowd. It was the last time in his life that he ever touched money, that he increasingly hated as the symbol of avarice, but this his last encounter with it was sheer joy; it flowed through his fingers like gold and silver rain upon the parched earth of the suffering of the poor.

Among the more outraged of the onlookers was an old priest named Sylvester. In the days when Francis had gone singing through the streets of the city, begging for stones for the rebuilding of San Damiano, Sylvester had been so touched by his valour and his music that he had momentarily failed to keep a firm hold upon his common sense, and had given him good dressed stones for which he might have received a very fair price elsewhere. But now the singing of Francis merely annoyed him. Here was all this good money being flung away to undeserving vagabonds, who had done nothing whatsoever to earn it, while he for his stones had had no more payment than a smile and a song. He made his way to Francis and said, "Brother, you did not pay me enough for those stones; give me now a share of this money."

Francis listened courteously. "Thou shalt have thy due, sir priest," he said, and going to Bernard's cloak, where the money was piled, he took out two handfuls, and then two more, and gave them to Sylvester with that same charming gentle smile that had been Sylvester's undoing before. "Hast thou now thy payment in full, sir priest?" he asked sweetly, and Sylvester said, "I have it in full, brother," and took it home rejoicing.

But during the next few days he thought constantly of Francis, and that something about the young man which at their first meeting had pierced right through his native prudence and carefulness, and made him behave in so unaccountable a manner, got through to him again. It uncovered that hidden longing within him, that hunger, and he felt most uncomfortable. It was because years ago, in his own youth, the hunger had made him uncomfortable that he had so carefully wrapt it up in prudent care for worldly things. Now Francis had released it and he compared his own greedy old age, with its confused and tortuous desires, with the straight clean channel of the young man's love for God, and he said to himself, "I am a wretched man." Sorrowing for the wretchedness he went to bed and to sleep and dreamed a curious and arresting dream. He dreamed that he saw a mighty cross. The top touched heaven and the arms stretched from one side of the world to the other, and the foot was set in the mouth of Francis, the young man who preached Christ crucified and Him alone. Sylvester awoke convinced that Francis was a true servant of Christ and the founder of an Order that would spread throughout the world. During the days that followed the old man remained alone in his house, and he wept and did penance for his sins.

Meanwhile Francis, Bernard and Peter had gone back to the Portiuncula and made a shelter for themselves in the woods, and Bernard and Peter put on the cross-shaped habit of the Order, and girded themselves with rope as Francis had done, and through the warm spring days they prayed together and waited upon the will of God.

On April the 23rd, Saint George's day, mass was said very early in the church of San Giorgio near the east gate, where Francis had once learned his letters. Among the worshippers was a young countryman, a farmer's son, kneeling alone, his sunburnt face covered with his hands that were broad and strong and hard from driving the plough. He knew about Francis, probably he had heard him preach in the streets of Assisi, and he knew Bernard had given all his money to the poor, though it is not very likely that he had been in the piazza that day because the spring work on the farm would have kept him busy. The story of these two men, Francis and Bernard, had taken him captive. They had been rich men and yet they had chosen to become poor for the love of Christ. For days he had thought about them as he went about his work in field and byre. He had been told, perhaps, that Francis frequented this church, that from his boyhood's days must have been dear to him, and had come here hoping to see him, for surely he would be here upon Saint George's day. But when he lifted his face from his hands and looked about him, feeling shy because the rest of the congregation were well-dressed city folk and he wore only his countryman's tunic and rough boots, he did not see him. Abashed, he hid his face again and prayed, and gave himself humbly into the hands of God.

He came out of the church after mass and stood in the bright sunlight wondering what to do. Other members of the congregation stared at him curiously, and did not know that when they themselves were long forgotten the name of Brother Giles would be revered all over the world. He had been told that Francis was living now in the woods, near Santa Maria degli Angeli, but he did not know where that was. However he went out of the city gate and walked down towards the great wooded plain. When he reached the crossroads near the leper hospital of San Salvatore he stopped and prayed that God would bring him to the place where Francis was, and when he opened his eyes again he saw Francis coming out of the wood. He ran forward and knelt down and said, "Brother Francis, I want to be with you for the love of God." Francis bent over him, put his arms around him and lifted him up with great joy, and took him down through the woods to Bernard and Peter, and said to them, "See what a good brother the Lord has sent us." And then the four of them ate their first meal together and were very merry.

A short while after this they looked up and saw an old man coming towards them through the aisles of the trees, approaching them humbly and with diffidence, and to their astonishment they saw that he was Sylvester.

III

But these five men had not come together in the woods to enjoy each other's company, not even only to worship and love God; though hereafter the love and worship of God was to be the atmosphere of their life, in which they lived and which they carried with them wherever they went; they had come together to do the will of God, and that was to "preach, saying, the kingdom of heaven is at hand". They set out at once, Francis and Giles going north-west through the mountains towards the March of Ancona, Bernard and Peter going to another province. Sylvester does not seem to have gone on this first journey. Perhaps he had to see to the disposal of his possessions in Assisi, and when that was done he would have come back to the Portiuncula and prayed for the others at Santa Maria degli Angeli. He was the priest of the brotherhood, and prayer, and the offering up of the love and worship of the Order in oblation before the altar, would have been especially his work.

Francis went up through the mountain passes singing, as he had sung when he went through the mountains to Gubbio, but this time he was not alone, and he was so naturally friendly and loving that he must have rejoiced in the simple, sturdy Giles with his gift of dry humour, and found him a delightful companion in misfortune. For this first missionary journey could hardly be called successful. The people in the walled villages and cities of the March, and the travellers whom they met on the way, did not know what to make of this strange couple in their cross-shaped garments, walking so painfully on bare, bruised feet, with no staff to help them, no cloak as protection against bad weather, nothing at all except their gift of peace. "The Lord give Thee peace,"

Francis would cry in the streets and on the stony mountain ways, and then when he had gathered a crowd of curious sightseers about him he would speak to them of penitence and the love and fear of God, and Giles would exhort the people to listen to Francis because no man could give them better counsel.

But these people were unaware of their need for counsel "for at that time the love and fear of God were everywhere extinct and the way of penitence was utterly unknown". Such knowledge of God as they had was largely a mixture of religious superstition and old pagan beliefs, and they were hardened in the sort of thoughtless carelessness that is more impervious to the simple truths of love and penitence than mortal sin itself. Francis was a stranger to them, not as at Assisi a man who had grown up in their midst and whose changing life they had witnessed, and he made little or no impression on them. They thought he and Giles were drunk, and laughed at them accordingly, or else they ran away, thinking they were wizards who would cast evil spells upon them. Sometimes they played cruel tricks upon the brothers. They would place dice in their hands and try and make them play with them, and they would take hold of their hoods from behind and carry them on their backs as though hanged by a halter. One man, however, had a penetrating thing to say about them. He said, "Either these men are saints or they are stark mad." Something in Francis must, in this man, have pierced "unto the marrow of the heart", or he would not have realized that this was an open question.

And so Francis and Giles returned to the Portiuncula hungry and weary failures, but undismayed, and presently Bernard and Peter joined them in the same state of mind; for none of them had thought that the doing of the will of God is an easy thing, or that the hard hearts of men are anything but a stubborn field to plough. Their sore feet had been treading in the footsteps of Christ and that in itself was joy enough for them.

Back in the woods again three more men came to join them, Sabbatino and John of the Hat, so called because he would insist on wearing a hat in violation of the rule of the Order, and Morico who was one of the brothers of the Crucigeri, the brotherhood who nursed the lepers at San Salvatore. He had been dangerously ill at the hospital and had sent a message to ask Francis for his prayers. Francis had prayed for him, and sent him a piece of bread which had been dipped in the oil of the lamp which burned before the altar in Santa Maria degli Angeli, and when he had eaten it he had recovered. Ever afterwards Morico followed Francis. There was no need of a change of heart for him for when he put on the cross-shaped habit of the Order it was the symbol of something he had always borne.

The Franciscan family now numbered eight men and their life began to take on the shape of custom. They had no proper dwelling-place, for Christ had not had where to lay His head and they wanted to be like Him, but they made themselves thatched huts, such as Italian shepherds build today, where they could take refuge in bad weather and where they could sleep for a few hours before they rose to begin their day with prayer. It was still dark when they began their prayer, and sometimes cold and wet, so that they shivered in their little huts, and often they were sick and weary, but nothing was allowed to interfere with their prayer for it was their life's blood and all that they did and were was rooted in it. Those who were beginners in prayer had to learn it the hard way, through all the alternations of dryness, self-disgust and shame, boredom and hopelessness, shot through with those moments of light that made it all worth while. They had Francis to help them, for he had come this way before them, in the cave at Le Grotte and in the cave at San Damiano, and they had the love of each other, that love of a small closely knit community suffering the same things together which is about the toughest love on earth. "They cherished one another with a right inward love, and served each other, and nourished him, even as a mother doth her only and well-beloved son." And they had the worship of God, the slowly growing heaven of contemplation, filling up the empty spaces left by the things of the world of which they had stripped themselves. What pleasure and comforts were to other men worship was to them; this looking up into the face of Christ and telling Him how much He meant to them.

Their days were days of labour. They nursed the lepers, for of

all the works of mercy this was always the one that was nearest the
heart of Francis, they preached the Gospel in Assisi and the
countryside about them and they toiled for their bread by helping
the labourers in the fields, though whatever they were doing they
broke off at the set hours of prayer to spend a few minutes in
adoration. Through the summer months in which these eight
worked together they must have found great joy in this toil,
mowing or turning the grass, and at evening sharing the labourers'
meal in the fields, their bread and cheese and dried beans, with
perhaps a salad of herbs and thin brown wine. When the toil was
done the bagpipers entered the fields and led the laden carts back
to the village with music. For this was Umbria and so there was
always music. Over the corn the labourers chanted ancient
incantations, rhythmic prayer for blessings on the harvest, and
Francis and his brothers sang the praises of God. They called
themselves *joculatores Domini*, God's jongleurs, and whatever
suffering they endured they never failed to show to the world
this face of joy.

But they could not always find work and sometimes they had
to turn to the table of the Lord. Begging was not easy now for
they were no longer welcome at Assisi. The fickle city had
suffered a violent reaction of feeling and the brothers had to face
what Francis had endured when the people had stoned him and
mocked him on the way to his father's house. Even Francis
himself, when he went up to the city to beg, was received with
insults. When he and the brothers asked for scraps of food the
doors were shut in their faces and at times they came near to
starvation. They had to bear not only cruelty and hardship but
the searching discipline of apparent failure, for they and their
preaching were no longer wanted. But Francis would have kept
them merry through it all, for the Gospel to which he had
listened at Santa Maria degli Angeli had said, "Behold, I send you
forth as sheep in the midst of wolves," and if what their Lord had
foretold for them was happening to them then that was a sure
sign that they were doing His will.

Assisi's persecution, like most cruelties, was rooted in fear.
Francis alone in his poverty and repentance had touched the

citizens' hearts, but a steadily increasing company of men living this life was something that was likely to touch their pockets. Were they to take the food out of their own mouths to support these madmen? And Bernard and the others had disposed of their wealth not by handing it back to their families but by pouring it out on the undeserving poor. This was a form of robbery which if allowed to go on might end in ruining some of the wealthiest families of Assisi. And how were they to defend their city against their enemies if their young men all went trailing off to the woods after a lunatic preacher and refused to fight? Without wealth and without men that terrible Perugia would devour them.

Bishop Guido saw their point of view and shared it. At the beginning he had blessed Francis and encouraged him, but he had supposed that the young man would eventually join some religious order, not that he would himself found a brotherhood of vagrants composed of some of the most useful men of Assisi. And he was distressed for the brothers themselves. They were not fitted for this life. It was an impossible life for men who had come from comfortable homes. Winter was coming on and how would they survive, homeless, barefoot and half-starved? He sent for Francis, receiving him graciously and kindly, and reasoned with him. Things could not go on as they were. Hardness and discipline were right and proper for men whose lives were given to God, but it must be within reason, as that of the monks was within reason. They must have a proper roof over their heads and enough property to ensure a minimum of food and comfort.

Francis stood before the man who from the beginning had shown him such kindness and understanding, and it must have been hard to withstand and grieve him, but he did not waver. He knew that this life of entire poverty and absolute dependence upon God was the life to which he had been called. Poverty was the foundation stone of the brotherhood, and also its quality; if salt loses its savour it is good for nothing. But he was never blindly fanatical. He always knew why he was doing what he did and could support his actions with cogent reasons. Courteously, with all his gentle winning sweetness, he explained to Bishop

Guido why they could have no possessions. "My Lord," he said, "if we should have possessions, we should need arms to protect ourselves. For thence arise disputes and lawsuits, and for this cause the love of God and of our neighbour is wont oft-times to be hindered, wherefore we be minded to possess naught of worldly goods in this world."

The Bishop sat silent. It was perfectly true. Possessions led to greed, fear, vanity, envy and wrangling, that were as boulders blocking the passage of love that could only flow full and free when these were away. Poverty was the logical outcome of love of such a temper as this. He could say nothing. Humbled and saddened, aware of all the ambitions and disagreements that clouded his own life and the life of the Church he loved and served, he once more blessed Francis and sent him away from his presence free to do what he would. The purpose of God was at work in this apparently crazy undertaking and he must await its unfolding patiently.

IV

Francis went out from Bishop Guido freshly inspired. "The love of God and of our neighbour" knew no bounds, and Christ had not commanded His disciples to preach the Gospel in their own neighbourhood only. He had said "Go ye therefore, and teach all nations . . . and, lo, I am with you alway, even unto the end of the world." They must leave Assisi and go out on another missionary journey. They could not go very far as yet but they must go as far as they could. As autumn turned to winter, and the leaves drifted down upon them in the thin sunshine, he gathered the brothers about him in the woods and told them of the new adventure that lay before them.

Winter scarcely seems to have been a very promising time for such an undertaking, but their spirits leaped up to face the challenge of it. When the day came to set out they met together, in the little church of Santa Maria degli Angeli that was so dear to them, and Francis preached to them. He said, "Dearest brethren, let us consider our vocation, unto which God in His

mercy hath called us, not so much for our own salvation, as
for that of the many, wherefore let us go through the world,
admonishing all peoples both by example and by word to do
penance and to be mindful of the commands of God. Fear ye not,
for that ye seem weak and despised and foolish, but with easy
minds preach repentance in simple wise, trusting in the Lord,
Who hath overcome the world, for that by His Spirit He speaketh
through you, and in you, to admonish all men that they do turn
unto Him, and keep His commandments. Ye will find some men
that be faithful, gentle, and gracious, who will receive you and
your words with joy, and others, the more part, that be faithless,
proud, and blasphemous, who with reviling will oppose you, and
against these shall ye speak. Be it set therefore in your hearts to
bear all things patiently and humbly." Then one by one the
brothers knelt before Francis and he blessed them, and to each
man separately he said, "Cast thy burden upon the Lord and
He will sustain thee." Then they were ready to go. They had no
preparations to make for they had nothing to leave and nothing
to take. They had only themselves; and not even themselves
for to a man they were God's. Then two by two they set out
north, south, east and west, towards the four quarters of the
earth.

Francis and his companion went south towards the beautiful
valley of Rieti that he was to come to love only a little less than his
own valley of Spoleto. Bernard and Giles went north towards
Florence, for they hoped to get as far as Spain and visit the shrine
of Saint James at Compostella, and the other four brothers
went east and west to unknown destinations. Francis had given
them careful instructions. When they came to a church or
wayside crucifix they were to stop and pray, and say devoutly,
"We adore Thee, O Christ, and bless Thee, in all Thy churches
that be in the whole world, for by Thy holy cross Thou hast
redeemed the world." Wherever they went, in city or castle or
house they were to give the Franciscan greeting, "The Lord give
thee peace," and they were to comfort the sorrowful, and bid
them fear and love God and keep His commandments.

The treatment they received on this journey was not much

better than that of the previous one. People thought them wild men from the hills, or thieves, and would not give them shelter in their houses or barns, so that they had to spend the winter nights in the porches of churches and houses. It was hard for them to give a satisfactory account of themselves. When they were asked to what order they belonged they could only reply that they were penitents, natives of Assisi, an answer which did not give satisfaction. They were mocked and ill-treated, were cold and footsore and hungry. But there were some who heard them gladly and were touched by their simplicity and patience. The hard earth was yielding a very little under the plough.

The Legend of Saint Francis, by the Three Companions, gives an account of the adventures of Bernard and Giles at Florence which we can take as typical of the experience of all the brothers in the early days, before fame came to them and the Franciscan habit was honoured wherever they went.

In the great city, where Giles had never been, and which was perhaps strange to Bernard also, they tried to find shelter for the night. They went from house to house but each time the door was shut in their faces. It was getting late, dark and cold, and they were worn out after a day of travelling, so that when they found a house porch with an oven in it they said to each other that they would shelter there. But first they knocked at the door, prayed that the peace of God might rest upon the house, and asked the mistress of it if she would receive them within. She refused but she said they might sleep in the porch near the oven. Her husband protested at even this much kindness but she said there was nothing they could steal but the wood. So all that night these two great Franciscans, perhaps the greatest of all the early followers of Francis, supperless and with no cloak to cover them, lay huddled together in the porch. They slept very little and when morning came they got up and went to find a church, and when they had found one they went in and knelt down to pray. Presently the bell rang out for matins and a few worshippers came to the church, together with the ubiquitous beggars who always haunted the doors of churches. Among the worshippers was the woman who had not given Bernard and Giles either a scrap of bread or an old blanket to keep out the cold when they took shelter in her porch, and she was astonished to see them kneeling there in reverent prayer. She watched them and thought about them all through matins. When the service was over another member of the congregation, a man called Guido, began to give alms to the waiting beggars, and he tried to give money to Bernard and Giles. They refused it, and when he asked why they would not accept alms like the rest Bernard said, "True is it that we be poor, but poverty is not a hard thing unto us, as unto the other poor, for by the grace of God, whose counsel we have fulfilled, of our own accord have we made ourselves poor." The astonished Guido asked if they had had possessions, and Bernard told him they had given all they had to the poor for the love of God. The woman was listening and she was ashamed, and begged them to come back to her house and be her guests, and they thanked her humbly, saying, "The Lord repay thee." But something about them had made Guido feel ashamed too and he insisted that his house must be their lodging for as long as they liked. He took them there and looked after them, and they stayed with him for some days, and their example so touched him that after they had left him he gave much of his own wealth to the poor.

Francis, in the valley of Rieti, where the snow lay white upon the enclosing mountains, was also winning the heart of a rich man. In the town of Rieti lived a young knight, Angelo Tancredi, gallant, courteous and most charming. One night he dreamed of Francis, and Thomas of Celano, who enlivens the wordiness of his biography of Francis with occasional flashes of humour, says that after the dream "he began to purpose better things—at least, in the distant future". The story goes that later Francis met Angelo in a street of Rieti, where he and the brother who was with him were preaching, and said to him, "It is a long time now that you have carried the belt and sword and spurs of the world. Come with me and I will dub you a knight of the army of Christ." It seems a story likely to be true for Francis had this gift of knowing at first sight one whose life was to be intimately bound up with his own, and Angelo was to be to him one of the nearest and dearest of his sons. His words seem to imply that he knew it already. Angelo must have known it also, for when Francis returned to the Portiuncula he followed him.

Francis and the brother left Rieti and went north to Poggio-Bustone, a little city that clings to the fringe of the mountains looking out across the plain, and after he had preached to the people there came upon Francis the longing to be alone with God. Like his Master he had to have these times of solitude that God might re-create him and give him the strength to go on, and like Christ he liked to climb up into the loneliness of the hills. Here, with the clamour of earth fallen away below him, there was nothing to distract his prayer. There was nothing but the great silence, for him not empty but filled with the quiet upholding of God.

He left the city and followed a steep path into the mountains behind, climbing up through the woods until he reached a place where the trees thinned out and there were only the bare crags, with the snow above them, and here he found a cave where he could hide himself. For he was in misery, crushed by the thought of the wasted years of his early life and of his sins. He thought he had sinned so greatly that God could not forgive him. His was a nature of contrasts, and alternations of joy and grief were habitual with him, but this overwhelming wretchedness was partly the misery of exhaustion. It is always a temptation to an exhausted Christian to hark back to the past and wonder if the sins of which he has repented, which he has confessed and which have been forgiven, are not really after all past forgiveness. Attacking a man at his weakest it is a most subtle temptation of the devil to make him doubt the love of God without realizing what it is that he doubts.

It is difficult, reading or thinking about Saint Francis, to remember how young he was. The old chroniclers speak of him always as the blessed father or the holy man, and that gives a misleading impression of age, but at this time he was only twenty-eight. Only five years had passed since the Voice had spoken to him at Spoleto and in that short time he had passed through experiences, both physical and spiritual, that must have severely overstrained a man as sensitive and highly strung as Francis. And lately he had

had other men dependent on him, some of them older than himself, men who had flung aside their security because of what he had said to them. They were a heavy burden on his youth. How could such a sinner as he was guide other men? How could eight poor sinful men, who so far had met with little but failure and contempt in all that they had tried to do for God, convert the world? Crouched in the cave he was bowed down by the burden of his sin, weariness and hopelessness, and wept out his misery within the upholding quietness until, like a child, he had spent himself.

Gradually he became aware of what it was that held him. The passion of Christ was never far from his mind for the image of the poor man crucified had been stamped on his soul in the church of San Damiano. Perhaps now his awareness of the load of his sin passed into remembrance of another burden and he saw a man staggering uphill, crushed almost to the ground with the weight of the burden on His back. "Behold the Lamb of God, which taketh away the sin of the world." Slowly, like the dawning of light, he was flooded with the knowledge of the love of God and knew himself forgiven. And then the mercy of God lifted for a moment the curtain of the future and showed him that "he that goeth forth and weepeth, bearing precious seed, shall doubtless come again with rejoicing, bearing his sheaves with him". Thomas of Celano says, "he was . . . wholly absorbed into a certain light; the capacity of his mind was enlarged, and he beheld clearly what was to come to pass." As far as words can tell such things he tried to describe his vision to the brothers when he returned to the Portiuncula. "I have seen," he said, "a great multitude of men coming to us, desiring to put on the habit of our holy vocation and to live under the rule of our blessed religion, and their sound is in my ears as they come and go under the orders of holy obedience. I have seen the roads from all the nations full of men coming into these parts: the French are coming, the Spaniards are hastening, the Germans and English run, and great is the crowd of them who hurry along speaking other tongues."

But there were no words to describe that sense of flooding love and power that was filling him and bearing him up. As strong now as he had before been weak he praised and adored God, and then prayed that He would turn the brothers back from their journeys and bring them all home to the Portiuncula so that he could share his joy with them. He knew how often they too were exhausted and discouraged and he wanted to tell them what he knew. His prayer was answered. To all the brothers on that day there came the conviction that they must turn back. When they had all met together at the Portiuncula and saw Francis again he was so confident and so happy that "he seemed changed into another man".

Chapter Six

THE RULE

And when the Lord gave me some brothers, no one showed
me what I ought to do, but the Most High Himself revealed to
me that I should live according to the form of the holy Gospel.
And I caused it to be written in a few words and simply, and
the Lord Pope confirmed it for me.

Writings of Saint Francis

I

THIS vision of an increasing brotherhood confronted Francis with
a problem. The independent life that he and the brothers had
been living had been possible for a few men but it was hardly
possible for a larger number to live in this way without becoming
an embarrassment to the clergy, as they had already been to
Bishop Guido. Francis was a devoted and loyal son of the Church
and he wanted her blessing upon the life and work of the brotherhood. No doubt by this time he understood that the rebuilding of
San Damiano had been a picture of what Christ really wanted him
to do. He had been like a child playing with toy bricks while his
Lord, his Father God, looked on in tenderness, leading him gently
on to see that the living church is built up of souls and that the
stones that he really had to handle were the souls of men that
needed to be reborn in love. But love cannot work from outside.
To attack and criticize from outside is not love's way, and it was
never Francis's way. He saw that he and his brothers must be
living their life of gospel poverty deeply within the Church if
they were to touch her heart that had become so corrupt and
hardened by the power and ambition of the world. They must go
to the Pope and ask for his permission to be an Order recognized
by the Church, living under his protection and with his blessing.
That the little barefoot family should go straight to the great Pope
Innocent the Third, a man before whom kings trembled, was an

F

idea so daring that the brothers must have had their breath taken away when Francis put it to them. All Francis's ideas had this daring simplicity, but none of them was ever allowed to run away with him; he and the brothers prayed earnestly that they might know if this was the will of God.

God's answer came in the arrival of four new brothers, Angelo of Tancredi, the young knight who had followed Francis from Rieti, John of San Constanzo, Barbaro and Bernard de Vigilanzio. Now they numbered twelve, the number of Christ's apostles, and this seemed to Francis a sign that the time had come to take His twelve apostles to Christ in the person of the Pope, His vicar upon earth. It remained only to find a name for themselves, and to write out a rule for their little Order which could be submitted to the Pope for his approval.

They called themselves the Fratres Minores, the Brothers Minor. In Assisi the important men of the city were called majores, while those who served them were the minores, and they remembered Christ's words, "I am among you as he that serveth." And they remembered too how Christ had called His disciples His little ones. Francis wrote out a rule suited to the humblest and the poorest of the humble and the poor. It was expressed largely in Christ's own words, an expansion of the verses from the Gospels that Francis, Bernard and Peter had taken as their rule in the church of San Nicholas. It was the charter of men who had pledged themselves to obey to the letter all the hard commandments of Christ that most Christians busy themselves in explaining away, the blueprint of one of the greatest adventures that men have ever undertaken. First, Francis promised obedience and reverence to both Innocent and his successors after him. All the brothers were to take the three evangelical vows of poverty, chastity and obedience, and they were to live without any property whatever. Any brother joining the Order was to sell all his goods and give everything to the poor. They were to wear shabby clothes patched with rags or sackcloth, eat anything that was set before them and when going barefoot about the world they were to carry nothing with them. None of them was ever to have any power of any sort. No one was to be called

Prior, but all alike Brothers Minor, and in token of humility they
were to wash one another's feet. The brothers were to follow
whatever trade they knew, and be paid for their work with the
necessities of food and shelter, but not with money, and when
working as servants they were to bear no rule in the households of
those they served. They were not a mendicant order but when
necessary they were to beg for alms and not be ashamed. They
were to love one another and never wrangle or speak evil of each
other, and they were to remember that they had given themselves
and surrendered their bodies to Jesus Christ, for love of Whom
they ought to expose themselves to their enemies both visible and
invisible. They were to follow the humility and poverty of
Christ and to rejoice to be with despised persons, with the poor
and weak, the sick, the beggars and the lepers. The brothers
were to be Catholics and if any brother was to err from the
Catholic faith, and refuse to mend his ways, he should be expelled.
They were to respect all priests and religious as their superiors and
respect their Order, office and work. Wherever they went they
were to praise God and exhort men to reverence. Incorporated
in this Rule there was a great burst of praise, pouring out in a
cataract of words, breathless, exhilarating and infinitely happy.
"Let us therefore desire nothing else, wish for nothing else, and let
nothing please and delight us except our Creator and Redeemer,
and Saviour, the only true God, Who is full of good, all good,
entire good, the true and supreme good, Who alone is good,
merciful and kind, gentle and sweet, Who alone is holy, just, true,
and upright, Who alone is benign, pure, and clean, from Whom,
and through Whom, and in Whom is all mercy, all grace, all
glory of all penitents and of the just, and of all the blessed rejoicing
in heaven. Let nothing therefore hinder us, let nothing separate
us, let nothing come between us. Let us all, everywhere, in
every place, at every hour, and at all times, daily and continually
believe, truly and humbly, and let us hold in our hearts, and love,
honour, adore, serve, praise and bless, glorify and exalt, magnify
and give thanks to the Most High and Supreme, Eternal God, in
Trinity and Unity, to the Father, and Son, and Holy Ghost, to
the Creator of all, to the Saviour of all who believe and hope in

Him, and love Him, Who, without beginning or end, is immutable, invisible, unerring, ineffable, incomprehensible, unfathomable, blessed, praiseworthy, glorious, exalted, sublime, most high, sweet, amiable, lovable, and always wholly desirable above all for ever and ever."

Carrying with them this rule, and nothing else, the barefoot brothers set out on their pilgrimage to Rome. It was the spring of 1210.

II

Innocent III was a great man and a great Pope. He was now forty-nine years old and had been Pope for twelve years, and the achievements of those years were impressive. In his struggle with the German barons he had been on the whole successful. The papal armies were exterminating heresy with fire and sword and every king in Europe was afraid of him, for he had made the Papacy immensely powerful. He was a great statesman, a clever politician and a fine theologian who had studied at Bologna and Paris. He had a handsome presence and elegant though imperious manners. But he was not guilty of seeking dominance for its own sake. It was his honest belief that the Papacy needed increasing worldly power if it was to redeem the world. He seems to have felt about power as Francis had once felt about money; that you could save men with it. But he was ascetic and deeply religious and knew with bitterness and sadness that the Church was corrupted by the luxury and greed that had eaten into her clergy and laity alike. He knew that the purification of the world must begin with the Church herself but he did not know by what means she could be saved.

Arrived in Rome there can be little doubt that the weary footsore brothers went straight to Saint Peter's tomb. Francis led his little company up the marble steps, through the silver door into the cool shadows within. Their bare feet trod the marble floor silently, between the long columns of the pillars that were like their forest trees, and then they knelt together to pray at the tomb of the great apostle who had left all to follow Christ, who had lived for Him and been martyred for Him. The twelve later apostles, the little ones who had also left everything for Christ, gave themselves afresh to live and die for Him. It was only four years since Francis had knelt here alone, and now he had his brothers around him. God had been good to him and he poured himself out in love and gratitude for the guidance and safe keeping that had brought him to this great hour of his life.

They left Saint Peter's and Francis led the brothers through the busy streets of Rome towards the Lateran Palace. Was he afraid? Did he think of the man he was going to see as the Lord Pope Innocent III, the most alarming man in Christendom, or simply as Christ's representative on earth and therefore a man who would surely be loving, gentle and approachable as Christ Himself? The simplicity and fearlessness of his approach suggests that he thought of him in the latter way and was not afraid.

Knowing nothing of the difficult and complicated process of seeking an audience Francis simply left the brothers to wait for him in some quiet corner, walked into the Lateran Palace apparently unchallenged, and by extraordinary good luck managed to make his way straight to the corridor where the Pope was pacing up and down in thought. Turning in his walk his Holiness, outraged and astonished, found himself confronted by a slight young man with a sensitive, eager face, dressed in some dilapidated grubby sort of tunic, barefoot, travel-stained and very tired. He was clutching a bit of parchment in his thin nervous brown hands and sinking to his knees he began to tell the Pope, gently and humbly, about his bit of parchment. His voice was low, resonant and musical, his eyes, as he looked up in the Pope's face, were dark and very bright. Few men could withstand Francis but this was an occasion when his charm for once failed to make any impression. As soon as he could sufficiently command his anger and astonishment the Pope told Francis to take himself off and curtly turned his back upon him.

Francis crept away down a corridor which must have seemed quite endless, his whole sensitive being lacerated by the contemptuous words and the abrupt dismissal. He went back to the brothers and told them what had happened and they went out into the crowded streets again, to be jostled and stared at by the passers-by, with nothing to eat and nowhere to go. They had come all this way and the Lord Pope did not want to hear about their rule.

In the street they met Bishop Guido of Assisi, to Francis's astonishment and his, for neither had known the other was in Rome. Francis would have been less astonished than the Bishop, for he would have expected that God would send them help. Bishop Guido took them into his care, and it was probably he who brought them to Saint Anthony's hospital near the Lateran, where they found lodging. The modern biographers of Francis differ as to what sort of man was this Bishop Guido but one thing about him is quite clear; he loved Francis and could be wise for him. Among the great men about the Pope was one whom he guessed would love Francis as much as he did, and want to help him, the Cardinal John of Saint Paul, Bishop of Sabina, and he brought Francis to him.

The Cardinal, had God called him to the life of a monk or hermit, would have stripped himself as gladly as Francis had done. That would have been the easier way for him, but God had called him to the infinitely harder task of living the dedicated life within the world. Pressed upon by the luxury of the Papal court, by the ambitions, subtleties and cruelties of the men around him, he had to hold himself detached from it all, adoring Christ in poverty of spirit within the cell of his own soul. He had won his victory, and when he and Francis met each other there was between them that instant recognition of those who can truly say to Christ, "My God and my All." They understood each other.

But at first the Cardinal could see no necessity for a new Order and he would have liked to see Francis and his sons bring their fiery love into one of the older Orders for its purification. He begged them, as Bishop Guido had already done, to enter a monastery. But Francis knew he could not do that and after a few days the Cardinal realized that he was right and he went to the Pope to plead for the brothers. Describing Francis to Innocent he said, "I have found a very perfect man who wishes to live after the precepts of the Holy Gospel, and in all things to adhere to the evangelical perfection. And I believe the Lord intends by him to renew the faith all over the world." Then the Pope consented to see Francis and his brothers.

If it were possible to go back in time and to be present as a spectator at a given number of historical events it is fascinating to wonder which one would choose. The day when Francis and the brothers appeared before Pope Innocent III in consistory would certainly be one of them. Innocent sat in his great chair, his Cardinals grouped around him in their gorgeous robes, the splendour of the room where they sat gleaming about them, and before them knelt the twelve poor men who had come to beg for leave to follow Christ in the full rigour of His hard commandments. There could have been no greater contrast than that between Innocent and Francis, and Cardinal John of Saint Paul, who understood both men, must have been intensely moved as he watched them. For he knew the likeness that hiddenly united them; each man loved God, and was trying each in his own way to fulfil the will of God for His Church. Perhaps as he looked at the humble kneeling figure of Francis of Assisi the Cardinal, with the intuition of the saint, found himself possessed of a strange piece of knowledge; in centuries to come the great man seated on his throne-like chair would be chiefly remembered because of his association with the shabby insignificant young man kneeling before him.

Francis read the rule, his voice dwelling in loving reverence on the words of Christ in which it was chiefly expressed, and the Pope and his Cardinals listened, and as they listened they looked at the faces of the twelve brothers; at the sensitive face of Francis himself, and from him to the gentle knight Angelo of Tancredi, to Bernard and Peter Cathanii, and the aged Sylvester. These were not men born to hardship, they were for the most part men of gentle birth, culture and intelligence. Could they endure to the end such a life as they were proposing to lead? With nothing behind them, no certainty from one day to another of even the bare necessities of food and shelter, and their chosen companions the poor, the outcast and the lepers, surely the inevitable end would be weariness, sickness and death. This sort of thing had been tried before and had always ended in disaster. These men would come to grief too and there would be yet another failure of a religious undertaking to bring ridicule upon the Church. When Francis ceased speaking there was a murmur of vigorous dissent. The Pope gathered it up into a kind but firm refusal to ratify the rule, and advised Francis and his brothers, as the Cardinal and Bishop Guido had done before him, to enter one of the already recognized religious orders.

Cardinal John of Saint Paul got up to speak for Francis. He pointed out that these men were asking permission to follow the way of life commanded in the Gospel. To say it was impossible to do so was blaspheming against Christ, who had Himself given these commandments to His disciples. The Pope was shaken by the Cardinal's speech. What he said was true. Francis and his brothers were asking only that they might be allowed to take Christ at His word. How could that be forbidden? He decided to test this thing with time and he said to Francis, "My son, go and pray to Jesus Christ that He may show us His will; and when we know His will more certainly, we shall the more safely sanction your pious purpose."

Francis and the brothers left the presence of the Pope and the old chronicler says that Francis "ran trustfully to Christ and began to pray, bidding his brethren do the same". One would like to know where Francis prayed, in what church or garden in Rome in the springtime. Perhaps it was in the chapel of Saint Anthony's hospital, which still exists today. In whatever quiet place he knelt, waiting upon the will of God in childlike trust and patience, the answer came as to a beloved child. He who so loved symbol and parable was told a story. There was once a poor woman who lived in a desert. Here she was found, loved and wedded by a king, who begot of her handsome sons. These sons grew up nurtured by her in all gentleness, and when they were grown their mother said to them, "My dear sons, be not ashamed because you are poor, for you are all the sons of a great king. Gladly therefore go to his court and ask him for whatever is necessary to you." The sons marvelled and were glad, and knowing themselves the king's sons they esteemed their very need as riches. They went boldly to the king, and they were not afraid before him whose likeness they bore. The king, recognizing in them this likeness to himself, inquired whose sons they might be and they told him that they were the sons of the poor woman who lived in the desert. At this the king embraced them and said, "My sons and heirs you are: fear not. If strangers are fed at my table, by a greater right must I nourish them for whom all my possessions are lawfully kept." And afterwards the king ordered that the poor woman should send to his court all the sons that should be born of her, that they might be nurtured there. Francis realized that when he saw the Pope again he must tell him the story.

Innocent too had turned to God in prayer and like Pharaoh of old he had dreamed a dream. He thought that he stood in the Lateran Palace, in the place called the speculum, because of its fine view, and looked out at the church of John the Baptist and John the Evangelist, the mother church of Christendom, and as he looked at this great and beloved church he saw that the walls were cracking and that very soon it would fall into ruin. The awful paralysis of nightmare came upon him. He could not move or cry out, he could not even raise his hands to clasp them in prayer, he could do nothing except stand there in agony, as though turned to stone. And then he saw a small lithe figure crossing the piazza dressed in a shabby habit with a rope around his waist. The little man crossed quickly to the tottering building and set his shoulders against the cracking walls of Constantine's basilica. The Pope thought he would be crushed to death, but instead of that the whole church straightened and stood once more in its accustomed place, and the man who supported it turned his face towards the Pope and Innocent saw that he was the extraordinary little man from Assisi, Brother Francis, and he remembered the words of Cardinal Saint Paul, "I believe the Lord intends by him to renew the faith all over the world."

The next day Francis and the brothers were once more summoned to an audience and Francis said, "Lord Pope, I will tell you a story," and he told the story of the poor woman and her sons.

"Holy Father," he said, "I am that poor woman whom God so loved and of His mercy hath so honoured."

So to both men, in answer to their prayer, God had spoken by a parable, as He had loved to do so long ago in Galilee.

The Pope was won over now. He believed that this adventure was indeed inspired by the Spirit of God, and he must do nothing to prevent it. He told Francis he would sanction the rule and he and the brothers might preach penance and exhort men to love God and forsake evil. It was a limited commission, for the brothers were not authorized to expound the dogmas of the Church. Innocent was putting them on trial. "Go forth with the Lord, brothers," he said, "and as the Lord shall deign to inspire you, do ye preach repentance unto all men. But when God Almighty shall have multiplied you in numbers and grace, come again to me rejoicing and I will grant more unto you than this and with a greater assurance commit to you greater powers."

The brothers knelt before the Pope and Francis promised obedience to him, and the brothers in their turn promised obedience to Francis, and the Pope blessed them and sent them away rejoicing; back again to the tomb of Saint Peter to kneel there and pour their hearts out in thanksgiving. The Cardinal John of Saint Paul was equally thankful. They had all of them won his reverence as well as his love and he had taken them to his heart as his sons. Before they left he gave them the small tonsure, marking them as religious but distinguishing them from the monastic orders who wore the large tonsure, and it may have been now that Francis received the diaconate. He was never a priest but remained a deacon only to the end of his life, and though in later years he might have worn the larger tonsure he did not do so, but was content to be always the "lesser brother". And so Francis and his brothers left Rome to travel back to Assisi, no longer a company of crazy vagrants whom everybody laughed at but the Order of the Friars Minor who were destined to turn to the love of Christ such an innumerable host of sinners, from that day until this, that heaven alone can reckon up the number.

III

When the brothers returned to Assisi they did not go back to
the Portiuncula but went to live in a ruined hovel in a part of the
woods called Rivo-Torto, the crooked stream. Perhaps they did
this because they were afraid of getting too attached to the
beloved Portiuncula, of laying claim to it, they who had vowed to
lay claim to nothing but the poverty of Christ. But the Portiuncula was only a short walk away through the woods and they
could easily reach it to hear mass at Santa Maria degli Angeli.
They were close too to the leper settlement of Santa Maria Maddalena and only half an hour's walk from Assisi. They stayed at
Rivo-Torto all through that summer and well into the next
winter. It was a time of quietness in their lives, a pause and breath-
ing space before the great days that were soon to come, the days of
the expansion of the Order, the gathering crowds, the missionary
journeys, the miracles and the fame. Now that they had been
recognized and blessed by the Pope they met with no further
persecution in Assisi, and they undertook no long journeys or
great enterprises at this time. They laboured in the fields, nursed
the lepers, fasted and prayed. Francis knew it was God's will
that his sons should have this time of stillness and quiet growth,
for these first brothers were the foundation stones of the Order
and they must be humble, disciplined, strong in faith and love
and prayer before they could support, teach and train other men
and bear their witness to the world.

Rivo-Torto was a good choice as a training-ground for behind
the hovel where the brothers ate and slept a deep wooded ravine
gashed the side of the mountain, the bed of the crooked stream that
rushed down it as a torrent in wet weather, and high up in the
ravine were caves in the rock that Francis called the carceri, the
prisons, and here the brothers could fast and pray, contemplate
and adore the beauty of God in loneliness and peace. These caves
were to them what the wilderness was to John the Baptist. Here
they broke themselves in for God. Even after they left Rivo-
Torto Francis and the brothers loved and used these caves. Stark
in themselves, like the discipline practised within them, they were

surrounded by great beauty. The ravine was thickly wooded, cool and fresh at the rocky summit where there was a small oratory dedicated to the Virgin. This oratory was very old and perhaps like Santa Maria degli Angeli had taken the place of an earlier shrine. Under the oratory was a little cave where Francis would sometimes sleep between his hours of prayer and below it were those used by the two contemplatives, Bernard and Sylvester. It was the sort of place that birds love, with trees and water, and the woods echoed with their music. It was here that Francis held a contest in singing with a nightingale, which was won by the nightingale, and blessed a flock of birds which had perched upon an ilex tree. The flowers were as happy here as the birds. In the spring the cyclamen were like a host of butterflies upon the ground, and later dog-roses festooned the banks of the ravine. Fine weather must have given to the brothers days that were idyllic in their beauty and their peace.

But winter came with driving rain, snow and sleet, and winds that were like a knife, and then the big wooden cross that the brothers had put up outside the ruined hovel, and before which they prayed as a family together, was a fitting symbol of the hardship of their life. The hovel, by no means waterproof, in which they slept on straw covered with rags and laid on the damp miry earth floor, was so small that Francis had to mark each man's place with chalk on the beam above his head, so as to ensure as much order and quietness as possible for their hours of prayer. Often they had nothing to eat but mangels and were very hungry. There was only one brother who could not stick it out and who left them, John of the Hat. The Hat was no doubt a symbol of the creature comforts that he could not bring himself to abandon. One night a young brother who had added too much fasting to the normal condition of semi-starvation woke up in such pain that he thought he was dying, and cried out in fear. Francis got up at once and when he had discovered the cause of the trouble he put together such scraps of food as they had and made a little meal for the young brother, and shared it with him lest he should feel ashamed to eat alone. Then he gathered all the brothers around him and talked to them about moderation in fasting, which was designed to make of the body a tempered instrument of the spirit, not to break it. "My best beloved," he said, "I tell you that each one of you ought to pay heed to his nature; for some of you may be strong enough to be sustained on less food than others; yet it is my will that he who needs more food shall not be bound to imitate those who need less, but let each give to his body what it requires in order to be strong enough to serve the spirit. For whilst we must beware of that superfluity of food which is a hindrance both to body and soul; in like manner, nay even more, must we beware of too great abstinence, seeing that the Lord wills to have mercy and not sacrifice."

For his sons Francis always showed wisdom when faced with the difficult business of mortification. When later he discovered that many of them were wearing iron chains upon their bodies, and lashing themselves to extremity in impetuous efforts to break their self-will, he made them bring him all their instruments of torture and forbade them to use them again. But for himself he was not so wise. In this one thing only he did not practise what he preached and he shortened his life by his austerity. The normal disciplines that for his sons in the beginning of the way sufficed for mortification, the disappointments, hardships and humiliations of their life, soon became for him things that he hardly noticed. He had to go further. He could never forget the sufferings of Christ, and his longing to share them consumed him.

This time at Rivo-Torto was for the brothers a time of unusual physical danger. They were always in danger from hungry wolves, and the bandits and desperate men who roamed about in the forest, but now the war between Guelph and Ghibelline claimants to the Imperial throne brought added danger. The Emperor Otto IV, who had been crowned by Innocent only a year ago and had sworn fidelity to him, had broken his oath and once more the Germans were on the march in Umbria. Perugia was on the warpath and Assisi had shut herself within her gates. But the brothers did not take refuge in their city. They remained where they were in the forest and Francis did not allow the proximity of the barbarians to make them afraid. On the contrary, when he heard that the Emperor himself was making an armed progress through the valley on his way to Rieti he sent one of the brothers to intercept him and tell him something that Francis already knew; that Otto IV would fall from power and die ingloriously. Six years later Francis's prediction was fulfilled for Otto died defeated and discredited. As he lay dying priests surrounded his bed scourging him as he sobbed out the words of the Miserere, and he cried to them to lay on the lash more heavily as death came nearer. It is amazing that the courageous brother who came to tell him of his miserable end was not hanged off-hand on the nearest tree, but he was not. The courage and defencelessness of these poor men seemed in their own country always to protect them.

The war gave Francis a great chance in Assisi and he took it eagerly and gratefully. His greeting of, "The Lord give thee peace," was no formal one. He cared passionately for peace, worked and prayed for it, primarily for the peace of God in the soul but also for peace between nations and cities, and between one man and another. The Italian communes at that time seem to have thoroughly enjoyed quarrelling. Within Assisi there had been endless bitterness and hatred both between merchants and nobles, and between both and the poor whom they oppressed. But now their common danger, and fear of once more losing their independence, disposed them to listen to Francis when he implored them to make their peace with each other and their God. The 9th of November 1210 was a great day both for Assisi and in the life of Francis. Upon that day the citizens signed a Treaty of Concord amongst themselves. The nobles and merchants on one side, and the poor men on the other, the majores and the minores, bound themselves to work together for the common good of Assisi, and to enter into no alliance with Pope or Emperor or any other city without the consent of the whole commune. Exiles were to return, taxes were to be fixed justly and civic peace was to reign.

The Treaty of Concord was a great testimony to the extraordinary ascendancy which Francis, still so young, had won over his own people. The Pope's blessing and sanction of his little Order had silenced their fears and won their respect and his city would never again laugh at him or persecute him. But that was not all.

He himself, by the power of his preaching, had won them. If the months at Rivo-Torto were months of quiet waiting for the brothers they were not entirely so for Francis, for they witnessed his emergence as a preacher. He had been listened to when he preached at the street corners, but now that as the head of a recognized Order he could preach in the churches and in the cathedral his opportunities were immensely increased. His first sermon was preached at San Giorgio, the church that was so bound up with the life of the Order. Soon after that the canons of the cathedral asked him to preach every Sunday at the cathedral itself. To give him a little space of quiet they lent him a room in a house in their garden. He would come there on Saturday night and after a short rest would spend hours in prayer in preparation for the morning's mass, and for his sermon.

The people of Assisi had built their own cathedral, and it had been finished only a few years before Francis preached his first sermon there. Built of the stone of Monte Subasio it was at this time white and sparkling, with a rosy tinge in the stone. There were no benches and no pulpit in the modern sense; the congregation listened standing or kneeling and the preacher stood on a platform. The people applauded the preacher, or audibly disagreed with him as the case might be, and he in his turn had room on his platform for much movement and gesticulation. A thirteenth-century sermon in an Italian cathedral must have been at times a lively affair, and Francis's youth and eagerness, and the fact that he preached in the homely language of the people and not in Latin, must have made it even livelier than was usual. One can picture the eager crowd waiting for him each Sunday morning, packing the space before the pulpit. Already they must have been aware that Assisi was to possess that most treasured of all possessions, its own private and particular saint, and they whispered to each other about him as they waited; and then fell silent, for he had come and was making his way to the pulpit, a small spare figure in a patched and shabby habit, barefoot, his young face too thin and worn for his years, but with dark eyes blazing with unquenchable vitality. He mounted the pulpit and stood before them, capturing them even before he began to speak.

So many tried to put on record what they felt about his preaching that it is not difficult to realize what a great experience it must have been to hear him. He did not write down his sermons, his preparation beforehand was that night-long vigil of prayer and communion with God, and he used no rhetoric, he spoke straight from his heart as the Holy Spirit inspired him, in direct and simple language. He was naturally a fine actor but he never thought about his gift, or indeed about himself at all, he thought of nothing but Christ, the Saviour of the world, and the hunger for Him and need of Him of the people before him, and so he spoke easily and naturally, with all the force of his sincerity and burning love for God and men. Thomas of Celano said of his preaching, "He would hint in a few words at what was unspeakable and mingling ardent gestures and movements with his words transported his hearers wholly to heavenly things." Sometimes the joy of these heavenly things would so overwhelm him that words would break down altogether and he would sing and dance God's praises. His actual words, divorced from the irresistible charm of the man himself, would sometimes be difficult for his hearers to recapture afterwards. One of them said, "I never remember what words he uses, and if I do they do not seem to me to be the same."

But at other times what he said would be easy to remember because like his Master before him he often talked in parables. One grim little story that he told of the deathbed of a wily and wicked old usurer shows that he knew how to put the fear of God into his hearers. And he was not afraid of plain speaking. Bonaventure says, "Forasmuch as he did himself first practise that which he afterwards preached unto others, he feared none that might blame him, and did most faithfully preach the truth. It was not his way to smooth over the faults of any, but to smite them, not to flatter the life of sinners, but rather to aim at it with stern reproofs." These reproofs had their effect. Men who had gained their wealth unworthily gave it back to the poor and merchants who found the business world incompatible with strict integrity forsook it and became farmers instead. In his great love of souls it mattered nothing to him whether his congregation was large or small. Celano says, "He saw the greatest concourse of people as

Alinari

THE MIRACLE OF THE SOURCE

Giotto

one man; and to one man he preached most carefully, as to a multitude."

But if Francis had sometimes to be away from his sons he never for one moment forgot them. One Saturday night, when he was praying in the house in the canons' garden, and the brothers at Rivo-Torto were some of them praying and some of them keeping vigil, light suddenly filled the dark little hovel where they were. They all saw the same thing, a fiery chariot moving to and fro with over it a ball of fire of amazing brightness. At the same time spiritual light flooded their souls and they were made known to each other. They looked into each other's consciences and knew the real man as they would know him in heaven. Then the light, and the supernatural knowledge, both left them, and utterly awed they crept close to each other and asked what this mystery could mean. They all had the same explanation; Francis, though absent in the body, was with them in spirit and in prayer. When he came home the next day they found that they were right.

IV

The life at Rivo-Torto was abruptly terminated by the arrival of a donkey. Francis and the brothers were praying in their hovel when the head and shoulders of a donkey appeared in the narrow door, and the rough voice of an unmannerly peasant was heard admonishing the donkey outside, in words that he intended the brothers to hear. "Get in with you, get well within, for we shall do well in this place." Goaded from behind brother ass came trampling in, the unmannerly peasant after him. There was not room in the hovel for the Brothers Minor, the peasant and the donkey; somebody had to go and Francis decided it should be the brothers. Always so courteous himself, discourtesy was one of the few things which still had the power to upset him and against which his sense of humour seems not to have been proof. He was troubled by the man's rudeness. "Brothers, God hath not called us to provide stabling for an ass, nor an inn-parlour for men," he said, and he and the brothers went away and left the donkey and the peasant in possession.

G

Now they were shelterless again and had no place of prayer except the caves, high up in the ravine, which could not always be reached in bad weather. Though they were bound to the Lady Poverty and could have no home, as men normally understand the word, they had to have somewhere to pray and some centre from which they could go out to preach the gospel, and to which they could return. Leaving the brothers in the woods Francis went to his good friend Bishop Guido to ask if he knew of any chapel which they might use for their prayer, but for once Bishop Guido was not able to help him. He went to the canons of the cathedral and they could not help him either. Then he climbed up the mountain to the Benedictine abbey, that looks out over the great plain like a lighthouse over the sea, and laid his difficulties before the abbot. This abbot must have been an understanding and generous man for after discussing it with his monks he offered to give the Benedictine property of the beloved Portiuncula to the Brothers Minor for their own. He made only one stipulation, that if the Order should grow larger the Portiuncula should always be looked upon as the centre of the whole Order. Francis's joy was tempered by his terror of possessing anything, but that difficulty too was happily settled. The Brothers Minor were not to possess the Portiuncula but only pay rent for it; the yearly payment of a basket of fish caught in the river. The brothers always faithfully paid this rent, and the abbot never neglected to send a receipt in the shape of a vessel of oil.

Francis, when he left the abbot, must have gone with all possible speed down the mountain to the woods below to find the brothers and tell them his glorious news. God had given them the Portiuncula. When they had returned from Rome they had not gone back to the holy place that they loved above all others, for they feared to lay claim to it. But now it had come to them as a gift of God. They were homeless men, as Christ had been homeless, but they were to have their luogo, their place. Christ had had Bethany and they were to have the Portiuncula.

PART TWO

KNIGHTS OF GOD

Chapter One

THE FIRST ORDER

Where there is charity and wisdom there is neither fear nor
ignorance. Where there is patience and humility there is neither
anger nor worry. Where there is poverty and joy there is neither
cupidity nor avarice. Where there is quiet and meditation there is
neither solicitude nor dissipation. Where there is the fear of the
Lord to guard the house the enemy cannot find a way to enter.

Writings of Saint Francis

I

THE next ten years were the great years of the Order and the
Portiuncula saw the glory of them. From it Francis and his sons
went out on their missionary journeys and to it they returned. As
the Order grew in numbers and stretched out beyond the bounds
of Italy brothers from all over Europe would flock there for the
chapters, would live there for a while and go away again re-
freshed. Pilgrims came there, rich men and poor men, and whoever they were and whatever their troubles the Portiuncula
comforted them. Soon after it had been given to the Order a
man who afterwards became one of their number had a dream.
He saw a multitude of men kneeling around Santa Maria degli
Angeli and they were blind. With their clasped hands and
their blind faces upturned to Him they were imploring God
to give them sight, and while they were praying a light broke
out in the sky and fell upon their faces and they could see. The
Portiuncula was always a place of light and like a lighthouse
sent its beams flashing out into a dark and troubled world. It had
a spirit all its own, even apart from Francis and the brothers.
It had been a place of prayer for so long that like all such
places it seemed to have its own atmosphere of prayer and
peace.

The plan of the Portiuncula was that of all subsequent

Franciscan "places". The brothers did not build in stone in the early days of the Order for stone would have given an air of permanence to their dwellings, they built themselves huts of wattle and daub, with thatched roofs. Enclosing the church and the little buildings was a quick-set hedge. Within this hedge was the brothers' private enclosure, where laymen did not come and where they themselves spoke only of the things of God. They had a garden where they grew vegetables and herbs, and they had the one and only Franciscan luxury, a few flowers "that they might cause those that should look upon them to remember the eternal sweetness". Their beds were of straw and they had no chairs or tables but ate sitting on the floor, and they had only the poorest of platters and cooking utensils, for Francis wished "that all things should end in poverty, should sing out to them of their pilgrimage and exile". Enclosing the whole of the little domain was the beautiful oak wood.

After reading the old chronicles three phrases are left chiming in one's mind like music. "The castled villages . . . Into the wood . . . We that were with him." They call up three vivid pictures of the life of the Order during these early years.

The first shows us the grey-clad brothers travelling along some rough road at evening, and seeing up above them at the end of the way one of those enchanted villages perched on a rocky hilltop that one sees so often in the background of Italian pictures. The crenellated towers of the castle are black against the sunset sky and below are the crowded little houses, their walls pierced with small squares of light where lamps have been lit and set in tiny windows. The brothers, tired and footsore, quicken their pace. In the castled village they will find food and shelter for the night, and in the morning they will preach the gospel of Christ, comfort the sorrowful and minister to the sick.

The phrase "into the wood" comes again and again. It was their cathedral and they went there to pray. In the aisles of the wood each man could find his own solitude and be undisturbed in his prayer. There was no sound there except the rustling of the leaves and the singing of the birds. If God in His mercy should draw them into adoring awareness of Himself they could stay there resting in His presence and no one would interrupt them and take them away.

"We that were with him." It is spoken with infinite pride and love by those brothers whose memories of Francis we have now in "The Legend of the Three Companions" and "The Mirror of Perfection", but it could have been said with the same pride and love by all the men who gathered around him in the first great days of life at the Portiuncula. Though their numbers were being added to all the time they were still small enough as a community for Francis to know them all intimately, and to infuse every one of them with his own joy and selflessness, and complete devotion to Christ their Master. Their love for each other had its being in their love for Christ, was born of Christ and returned to Him again. They were the knights of God, not of Francis. Not for one moment would Francis have allowed their pride in him and deep love for him to have put him on any sort of pedestal. They were all humble men but he was the humblest of all and the servant of all, and so afraid was he of the authority that the Pope had given him that some other brother was always appointed to be the "mother" of the community, to whose judgement he submitted himself with the rest. The dream he had had before the journey to Spoleto, of the palace of the Lady Poverty where he was to dwell with his followers, had come true now, but the armour of the knights was emblazoned not with any device that belonged to Francis but with the cross of Christ. What was said of one brother could have been said of them all: "His heart was set on imitating Christ through the bodily and spiritual strength of the cross."

Saint Catherine of Siena said, "All the way to heaven is heaven because He said, 'I am the Way'," and because they had chosen to follow that way, upheld and carried by His cross of sacrifice, the breath of heaven was about them and they knew, even in their mortal days, even in defeat and pain and fear, the meaning of joy. It was a gift to them, the resurrection gift of Christ who said, "Your heart shall rejoice, and your joy no man taketh from you," but in the thought of Francis to be joyful was also a command, as much so as the command to be poor and humble and to walk in love. It was their business to see that their joy was not taken from them. It was a flame to be tended and, if it went out, to be immediately lit again. He knew there was no better armour against sin than joy and would say to the brothers, "If the servants of God would study to preserve within and without the spiritual joy which comes of cleanness of heart, and is acquired by devoutness of prayer, the demons would not be able to harm him, for they would say: 'since this servant of God has joy in tribulation as in prosperity, we can find no way of entering to him nor of hurting him.'" He would allow no gloomy faces. To a grieving brother he said, "Why dost thou make an outward show of sorrow and sadness for thy offences? Keep thou this sadness between thee and thy God, but before me and others, study always to have joy, for it befits not a servant of God to show before his brother or another sadness or a troubled face."

Francis himself could be so happy, so attuned to the music of heaven, "the veins of murmuring which he heard secretly", that he could not contain his joy but would break out into singing. Sometimes in the woods he would pick up a branch from the ground, "and laying it on his left arm, he drew in his right hand another stick like a bow over it, as if on a viol or other instrument, and making fitting gestures, sang with it in French unto the Lord Jesus Christ." And then suddenly in the midst of his joy he would remember the horror of sin, and the agony of Christ Who bore our sins in His own body on the tree, and he would break down and weep.

The pattern of life that the first eight brothers had followed in the earliest days at the Portiuncula was the same now, the fourfold pattern of prayer, work, healing and teaching that was Christ's own pattern.

Prayer came first, the worship and adoration of God for which man was created, the prayer of penitence for the sin of the world, of intercession for all for whom they laboured. Francis taught them that without prayer "no good could be wrought in the service of God", and that prayer was not only for their hours of contemplation in their cells or in the wood, or for the hours when they met together to say their offices, but for always. They must pray unceasingly "whether walking or sitting, within doors or without, in toil or in leisure." To those setting out on a journey he said, "Meditate as much while on this journey as if you were shut up in a hermitage or in your cell, for wherever we are, wherever we go, we carry our cell with us; brother body is our cell, and the soul is the hermit who dwells in it, there to pray to the Lord and to meditate." He warned them against all ostentation in prayer. He himself would hide his head in his cloak when he prayed, or he would pray in deserted churches, and rise up very quietly at night, no one seeing him, and go into the wood to pray. He never let them think that prayer was easy, and taught them that they must train themselves for prayer with heroism and perseverance. The wandering thoughts that most of us take so calmly in our prayer were sin to them. Once when Francis was praying his eyes wandered to a little pot he had been making and for a moment or two he thought about it, but when he had finished his prayer he threw it in the fire, saying, "Let us be ashamed of trivial fancies when we are speaking to the great King." When consolation came to them in their travail of prayer they were to say, "This consolation, O Lord, Thou hast sent from heaven to me, a most unworthy sinner, and I commit it to Thy care, for I know that I should be but a thief of Thy treasure."

In the early days the brothers had no office books. They did have a copy of the Gospels but when one day a poor woman came begging and they themselves were in such straits that they had nothing to give her, Francis gave her their one precious book. But their poverty is this respect did not disturb them. They were themselves living the gospel and for office book they had the Lord's Prayer, which they recited at the canonical hours with a few other simple prayers and praises that Francis taught them. These hours were never forgotten. However ill and tired Francis was he would repeat them erect and bareheaded, or on his knees, "he would never lean on the wall or doorpost". There is a picture of him at the end of his life, when his journeys had to be undertaken on horseback or riding a donkey because he was too weak to walk, saying his office in the pouring rain. He stopped the horse and dismounted, put back his hood, and prayed "with as great a fervour of devotion and reverence thus, standing on the road with the rain falling on him continually, as if he had been in a church or a cell". And in this great faithfulness in prayer the brothers followed him.

All men of prayer, especially those who are called to be contemplatives, have found that the best companion of their prayer is hard physical labour. The Cistercian Order, an order of contemplatives, have from the earliest days worked in the fields, and for the Brothers Minor, too, hard work was valuable not only as a means of support for their bodies but for their souls also. Though primarily their work was rooted in their prayer it is also true to say that faithful and disciplined work prepared them for contemplation. Giles the farmer's son, who became one of the greatest contemplatives of that or any age, held strong views about the value of hard work. "Since no one," he said, "can enter upon the contemplative life unless he has first faithfully and devoutedly practised in the active, it behoveth that active to be pursued with toil and solicitude." And he said that if he had achieved anything in prayer it was because he was a strong fellow who could tackle heavy labour. All the brothers worked hard at their different crafts, whether as servants, farm labourers, shepherds, cobblers or basket-makers, and when the day's work was over they returned to the Portiuncula with the food that had been given them as wages, and this they shared together. It shows their independence of spirit that when work failed and they were forced to beg they found this the very hardest part of their vocation. Francis, though that day when he had eaten his first beggar's meal and found it the table of the Lord had turned the mortification of begging into joy, remembered his own early reluctance and was gentle with them. One young brother, who had so conquered his shame and pride that he not only begged a wallet full of scraps but carried it back to the Portiuncula singing, saw as he neared home that Francis was coming to meet him. Francis took the wallet, kissed the shoulder over which it had lain, and said, "Blessed be my brother, who goes forth promptly, quests humbly, and comes back merrily."

As prayer and work went hand in hand so did prayer and the

healing and comforting of the sick and sorrowful. For the brothers, as for their Lord, the Mount of Transfiguration and the epileptic child were not divisible. They turned from prayer that they might bring the love of God down to the pain of the world, and returned to prayer again that they might lift the pain of the world up to the love of God. All the sick and sorrowful were as their children to them but the lepers were their special charge, for they followed Francis in seeing in them, above all other men, the suffering Christ. Taught by Francis they did not call their patients lepers, a word with terrible connotations, but they referred to them always as their brother Christians. There are two stories in the old chronicles which illustrate well the patience and tenderness of Francis and his sons in dealing with these poor men.

In one of the hospitals where the brothers worked there was a very recalcitrant leper. His fearful disease had embittered him in mind and spirit and reduced him to the depths of misery. He was so impatient, so insolent and blasphemous, that the brothers were the only people who would have anything to do with him, and they had hard work to struggle on. At last even they came to the end of their tether. His violence and rudeness to themselves they could put up with but his blasphemies became more than they could endure and they went to Francis and told him they could not go on. Then Francis himself went to the hospital, found the leper and said to him with gentle courtesy, "May God give thee peace, my beloved brother."

"Peace!" retorted the leper. "What peace can I look for from God, who has taken from me peace and every other blessing, and made me a putrid and disgusting object?"

Francis tried to comfort him, telling him how strength of soul comes from patient endurance, but the sick man only broke out into bitter complaints of the long-suffering brothers who had been nursing him. "They do not serve me as they ought," he said.

Francis knew the answer to this, for during the stream of complaints he had been quietly praying for help. "My son," he said, "I myself will serve thee, seeing thou art not satisfied with the others."

"What canst thou do more than they have done?" demanded the leper.

"Whatsoever thou wishest I will do for thee," said Francis.

"Wash me all over," said the leper, "for I am so disgusting that I cannot bear myself."

So Francis heated water, putting into it sweet-smelling herbs, and then as gently as a mother with her child he undressed the man and washed him all over, and through the touch and the prayer of Francis help came to both body and soul. The sores that covered the leper's body were healed, the pain ebbed, and the darkness passed from his mind. He was at peace, and wept.

Another leper, also very ill and suffering, was in the special care of Brother James the Simple, a childlike person who had not grasped the fact that men as ill as his patient were not permitted to leave the hospital. He thought it would be a nice change for his leper if he took him for a walk to the Portiuncula, and so the two of them set out together along the road and through the oak wood to the peaceful enclosure within the quick-set hedge. Here they encountered the horrified Francis and so startled him that before he could stop himself he said to Brother James, "You must not lead these brother Christians abroad in this fashion; it is not decent, neither for you nor for them." But as soon as the words were out he was filled with remorse, realizing how much they must have hurt the leper. He went at once to Peter Cathanii, who was at that time the "mother" of the community, knelt before him and asked what he could do to show his penitence and sorrow.

"Whatever it will please thee to do, that do," said Peter compassionately.

Francis said, "I will eat out of the same dish as my brother Christian." And at the meal which followed he did so, and what that meant for a sensitive man like Francis, and what it meant in terms of the risk he ran of catching the loathsome disease, are best expressed in the explicit words of "The Mirror of Perfection": "One dish was placed between blessed Francis and the leper. But he was all ulcerated and loathsome, and especially he had his fingers shrivelled and bleeding with which he took up lumps from the dish, so that when he put them in the dish the blood and matter of the fingers flowed into it. And seeing this Brother Peter and the other friars were much saddened, but did not dare to say anything on account of the fear and reverence of the holy father." That this grim little scene was of great importance, epitomizing the spirit of the Order in which every man held himself ready to throw away his life for love's sake, after the pattern of Christ, the writer realized, for he ends his account of it with almost the same words that were used by John the Evangelist after he had witnessed the sacrifice of Calvary. "He who saw this wrote it down, and bears testimony of these things."

The "place" of the Portiuncula has such charm that it is a temptation to think of Francis and the brothers chiefly in its setting. Actually they were never there for long. They were ever on the road, travelling to distances that seem incredible when we remember that they went there barefoot, confronting dangers and difficulties that were sometimes even greater than those which met Saint Paul on his missionary journeys; for Saint Paul, travelling in the Roman Empire and speaking the Greek that was the official language in every portion of it, had a measure of protection from his Roman citizenship and could make himself understood by those to whom he spoke, but once they passed out of Italy there was no protection for the brothers, and the lingua franca was not spoken by the uneducated among them and not understood by all to whom they preached. Though in their own country the missionary journeys of the brothers were increasingly successful. beyond it they frequently ended in what the world calls failure. It could hardly have been otherwise. That they should have attempted them at all is a measure of their courage. Christ had said, "Go ye into all the world," and so they went, whether they knew the language or whether they did not, in childlike faith and obedience.

In Germany a company of brothers were stripped, beaten and driven out of the country. In Hungary they were taken for mummers and mocked and insulted. In Morocco five brothers who had entered the mosque and denounced Mohammed there were scourged and imprisoned. Let out of prison and told to leave

the country they refused to do so, and continued to preach
Christ crucified in the streets. Once again they were imprisoned
and this time they were put to the torture. Upon the rack they
were offered life if they would deny Christ, but they answered by
uttering His praises in their agony. Then they were taken from
the rack and beheaded.

It has been said that the blood of the martyrs is the seed of the
Church, and from the seed of this particular martyrdom, as from
all martyrdoms, there sprang new life, unnoticed at the time, but
one of the first sheaves of that great harvest that was reaped in
years to come when the Franciscan missionaries had travelled to
every corner of the known world. The first Christian martyrs,
dying in the Roman arena, trusted in Christ that he would give to
each one of them, as the fruit of his dying, one soul among the
spectators called to Himself by what they did. The Moroccan
martyrs had their soul, not one saved from heathendom, for he
was a Christian already, but brought into the ranks of the Order
and destined to be one of the greatest men in it. The Portuguese
Infante Don Pedro had had the bodies of the five martyrs brought
to Portugal and buried at the church at Coimbra. Many came to
the tomb to pray and among them was a young man called
Anthony. As he knelt there what these men had done took
hold of him and there flamed up in him the longing to follow
their example. A few days later he joined the Order of the Friars
Minor. He was Saint Anthony of Padua.

Francis also had his fruit of souls as the result of one of the
early missionary disasters. Not long after the brothers went to the
Portiuncula he and another brother set sail from Ancona for
Syria, with the simple but staggering purpose of converting the
infidels. But a storm arose and the ship was wrecked upon the
coast of Dalmatia. There was no way of going on, and for a while
it seemed as though there was no way of going back, for Francis
and his companion were penniless and could not pay for their
passage. And here once again the strand of comedy comes into
the Franciscan story, for Francis, humorous and undaunted, decided that the only way to get home was to go as stowaways. So
as stowaways they went, smuggled on board by one of the

sailors who had been won over as a friend by the charm of Francis, and provisioned by another friend, who had the forethought to realize that if the stowaways were to survive they must have food, a detail which one can imagine would be likely to have escaped the attention of Francis himself. But again the weather was stormy and the little boat was so long upon her way that the food ran out. This was Francis's chance. He gave the sailors his own food, sharing it out among them all. Then, in high favour with them, he preached to them and won their hearts for Christ.

For the English no Franciscan missionary journey is so important as that which brought the brothers to England in September 1224, to a land that must have seemed to them grey and cold and inhospitable after their sunny and friendly Italy. The chronicle of Lanercost tells a story of them that is typical of the courage and gaiety of all these men. Upon landing they had pushed on gallantly to London, Canterbury and Oxford, and Christmas Day found two of them in a wood near Oxford. It was bitterly cold, that penetrating cold of Oxfordshire that enters the very bones. The mud and snow of the rough path they followed was frozen hard and blood stained the track of their naked feet. They were far from home and the cold and desolation struck at their hearts as well as their bodies. It was difficult not to think with longing of the beloved Portiuncula and the brothers in Santa Maria degli Angeli joyously singing the praises of the Babe of Bethlehem. Suddenly "the younger friar said to the elder, 'Father, shall I sing and lighten our journey?' and on receiving permission he thundered forth a Salve Regina Misericordiae . . . Now, when the hymn was concluded, he who had been the consoler said, with a kind of self-congratulation to his companion: 'Brother, was not that antiphonal well sung?'"

II

Of most of these knights we know little or nothing but those who were nearest to Francis share with him his power of coming near to us. Because they were simple and humble, their way of life the Gospel way that is timeless, their close companions the

birds and beasts, the hills and trees and waters that are our friends
too, their politics, philosophy and art all summed up in the one
word love that never changes, they do not seem to belong to one
age more than another. In that as in other ways they were like
their master Christ.

To think of a few of them is to get a good picture of the
chivalry whose vanguard they were. Bernard must always come
first because he was the eldest son of Francis, called by him the
Founder, dearly loved and truly representative of all the brothers
who, "being called by God to carry the cross in their hearts, to
practise it in their lives, and to preach it by their words, were truly
crucified men in their actions and in their works." Bernard was a
quiet, steady man, loyal and reliable, a lover of the open spaces and
solitude. A story told of him in *The Little Flowers of Saint Francis*
is typical of the humility and patience of this man who in the
world had known such wealth and comfort. In the early days of
the Order Francis sent him to preach at Bologna, the city of the
famous schools where the study of law and the liberal arts was
held in higher estimation than the study of scripture, that he
might bear witness to the simplicity of the Gospel. But when he
arrived in Bologna the children in the streets, who had not seen a
Franciscan friar before, thought the barefoot dusty figure that of a
madman and followed him to the market-place laughing and
jeering and calling out *"Pazzo! Pazzo!"* When he reached the
market-place Bernard tried to sing the song of praise, hymn and
sermon in one, which Francis had taught the brothers, and which
they sang always in the market-square of every village and town
to which they came.

"Fear and honour, praise and bless, give thanks and adore the
Lord God Omnipotent in Trinity and Unity, Father and Son
and Holy Ghost, Creator of all things. Do penance, make
fruits worthy of penance, for know that you soon will die.
Give, and it will be given unto you. Forgive, and it will be
forgiven unto you. And if you will not forgive men their sins,
the Lord will not forgive you your sins. Confess all your sins.
Blessed are those who die in penance for they will be in the

kingdom of heaven. Woe to those who do not die in penance for they will be the sons of the devil, whose works they do, and will go into eternal fire. Beware and abstain from all evil and persevere up to the end in good."

But the people laughed and would not listen, so he continued his preaching in a manner all his own, he sat down and endured in silence while men as well as children threw stones and dust at him, mocked him and pulled him about by his hood. Day after day he returned to the market-place to receive the same treatment, and to preach again his silent sermon on humility and patience. A certain lawyer of Bologna, observing this unique preacher, realized that he was no lunatic and going up to him he asked him where he had come from. Bernard, still silent, put his hand in his bosom and taking out the Rule of the Order gave it to him to read. The man was moved and impressed, and turning to the people around him told them that the preacher should not be insulted but honoured as a friend of God. Then he took Bernard home with him, and later he prepared for him a "place". These gifts of "places" on the fringe of big cities were a frequent occurrence in the life of the Order, and the gift was accepted provided it was poor enough. It was generally a hut beside the city gate, with a tiny oratory attached, and as the Franciscan missionaries went farther afield they were found all over Europe. Bernard, living his life of prayer and penitence at the "place", setting out from it to preach, to nurse the sick and comfort the sorrowful, gradually became so loved by the people and so honoured by them that he got into a state of panic. His humility, that most precious treasure of the saints, was in danger, and with it his immortal soul. He fled back to Francis and said, "Father, the convent is founded at Bologna, send other brothers there to keep it up and reside there, as I can no longer be of any use; indeed, I fear that the too great honours I receive might make me lose more than I could gain." And Francis quite agreed with him and sent other brothers to take his place.

For ten years after the death of Francis, Bernard was the guardian of the Portiuncula and as a father to all the brothers who came there, and then he retired to a life of solitary prayer and contemplation. So winged was his prayer that Giles said of him that "he fed flying, like the swallows". As he had been one of the first to join the Order so he was one of the first to die. He was happy in his dying, for the brothers stood around his bed, among them Brother Giles who had come from his hermitage to cheer him with his joyous exclamation of, "*Sursum corda!* Brother Bernard, *sursum corda!*" When he felt his life going from him he asked the brothers to lift him up in bed and he said to them, "Beloved, not for one thousand worlds as beautiful as this would I have served any other master than my Lord Jesus Christ." And so he died.

Giles the farmer's son, sometimes called Egidio, is perhaps the most beloved figure of them all, of whom his brothers did not hesitate to say that he was "one of the most glorious religious whom the world has ever seen in the contemplative life." He was a great traveller who loved going on pilgrimages and would support himself on his solitary journeys by manifold labours; carrying water, making baskets, gathering faggots, beating walnut trees and cleaning out dirty kitchens. He was a mystic, who like Saint Paul was once caught up to the third heaven, a man of heroic prayer who in his old age said he knew now that martyrdom was an easy matter and that the inner life of prayer was a harder proof of man's constancy. Delightful stories are told about him in his old age when he lived in a mountain hermitage but was always ready to give shrewd and witty advice to those who visited him in his retreat, and even occasionally to issue out and comment caustically upon the changing scene. Upon one of these occasions, after the death of Francis, he journeyed to Assisi to take a look at the fine buildings that were being erected in honour of the poor and humble saint; a magnificent church to keep his bones, a papal palace and a large comfortable convent to house the Brothers Minor who once had lived in wattle and daub huts in deepest poverty. The old Giles gazed at the splendour in a silence pregnant with what he did not say, a silence lasting so long that the brothers who were proudly showing him round became uncomfortable.

"Ah," said Giles at last, "now you only want wives."

The brothers exclaimed in horror, "What is this that you have dared to say, Brother Giles?"

"I wish to say," said Giles, "that since you have abandoned holy poverty it only remains for you to abandon chastity, to which you were also vowed."

Two cardinals once visited him in his hermitage and asked him to pray for them. He said, "What need, my lords, that I should pray for you, who have more faith and hope than I?"

"How so?" they asked.

"Because," said the old man, "whatever of riches, honour and success this world can offer, you possess, and hope to win salvation; whereas I, in spite of hardship and adversity, fear to be lost hereafter."

Giles, one of whose sayings was, "Humble yourself daily in everything you do, and in everything you see," had no use for self-satisfaction. When a brother told him he had visited hell in a dream and seen no Brothers Minor there Giles said, "You did not go down deep enough." To some lazy brothers he said, "Do you think that in doing nothing you are being spiritual?"

Not all his sayings were caustic. *The Little Flowers of Saint Francis* contains a collection of them, wise and loving, for he was a great lover of God and men. "Blessed is he who truly loves," he said, "and desireth not to be loved again . . . Blessed is he who loves God with all his heart and with all his mind, who labours and suffers with mind and body for the love of God, and yet seeks no reward under heaven, but accounts himself only to be His debtor." Giles would have echoed the prayer of a Mohammedan mystic: "O my Lord! If I worship Thee from fear of hell, burn me in hell; and if I worship Thee from hope of paradise, exclude me from thence; but if I worship Thee for Thine own sake, then withhold not from me Thine eternal beauty."

The last years of Giles's long life were spent in contemplation in a small cell close to a church at the summit of a hill near Perugia, where he could look out over the whole valley of Spoleto and see Assisi and the Portiuncula. He had a little garden here and would wander up and down among his flowers, talking to the doves, and sometimes after the example of Francis he would hold two sticks as though they were a viol and bow and sing aloud the praises of God. He died in 1262, on Saint George's Day, the anniversary of his reception into the Order. His life as a son of Francis began in prayer, when he knelt in the church of San Giorgio, continued in prayer and ended in it. "Prayer," he said, "is the beginning, the middle and the end of all good."

Of all his sons Leo was closest to Francis. He joined the Order in 1210 when the brothers were still at Rivo-Torto. Francis called him "*pecorello di Dio*", the little sheep of God, perhaps in amusement that he who was named "the Lion" should be so gentle. Almost alone among those who were closest to Francis he was a literary person, a priest and Francis's confessor and his secretary. He was an exquisite penman, as can be seen from the breviary he made for Saint Clare, and it was his pen that wrote down the memories of "we that were with him". His precious "rolls and notes" formed the basis of the earliest writings about Francis, "The Legend of the Three Companions" and "The Mirror of Perfection", and the biographies of Thomas of Celano and of Saint Bonaventure. It is hardly too much to say that without Leo we today should hardly have known Francis. The gentlest and most retiring of the brothers is thus for us the most valued of them all. Particular stories in the chronicles seem especially connected with the various brothers, and Leo's is the story of perfect joy from *The Little Flowers of Saint Francis*. Though it is so famous it is not possible to write of Leo without quoting it in full.

"One day in winter, as Saint Francis was going with Brother Leo from Perugia to Saint Mary of the Angels, and was suffering greatly from the cold, he called to brother Leo, who was walking on before him, and said to him: 'Brother Leo, if it were to please God that the Friars Minor should give, in all lands, a great example of holiness and edification, write down, and note carefully, that this would not be perfect joy.' A little farther on, Saint Francis called to him a second time: 'O Brother Leo, if the Friars Minor were to make the lame to walk, if they should make straight the crooked, chase away demons, give sight to the blind, hearing to the deaf, speech to the dumb, and, what is even a far greater work, if they should raise the dead after four days, write that this would not be perfect joy.' Shortly after, he cried out again: 'O Brother Leo, if the Friars Minor knew all languages; if they were versed in all science; if they could explain all scripture; if they had the gift of prophecy, and could reveal, not only all future things, but likewise the secrets of all consciences and all souls, write that this would not be perfect joy.' After proceeding a few steps further, he cried out again in a loud voice: 'O Brother Leo, thou little lamb of God! if the Friars Minor could speak with the tongues of angels; if they could explain the course of the stars: if they knew the virtues of all plants; if all the treasures of the earth were revealed to them; if they were acquainted with the various qualities of all birds, of all fish, of all animals, of men, of trees, of stones, of roots, and of waters —write that this would not be perfect joy.' Shortly after, he cried out again: 'O Brother Leo, if the Friars Minor had the gift of preaching so as to convert all infidels to the faith of Christ, write that this would not be perfect joy.' Now when this manner of discourse had lasted for the space of two miles, Brother Leo wondered much within himself; and, questioning the saint, he said: 'Father, I pray thee teach me wherein is perfect joy.' Saint Francis answered: 'If, when we shall arrive at Saint Mary of the Angels, all drenched with rain and trembling with cold, all covered with mud and exhausted from hunger; if, when we knock at the convent gate, the porter should come angrily and ask us who we are; if, after we have told him, "We are two of the brethren," he should answer angrily, "What ye say is not the truth; ye are but two imposters going about to deceive the world, and take away the alms of the poor; begone, I say"; if then he refuse to open to us, and leave us outside, exposed to the snow and rain, suffering from cold and hunger, till nightfall—then, if we accept such injustice, such cruelty, and such contempt with patience, without being ruffled and without murmuring, believing with humility and charity that the porter really knows us, and that it is God who maketh him to speak thus against us, write down, O Brother Leo, that this is perfect joy. And if we knock again, and the porter come out in anger to drive us away with oaths and blows, as if we were vile impostors, saying, "Begone, miserable robbers! Go to the hospital, for here ye shall neither eat nor sleep!"—and if we accept all this with patience, with joy, and with charity, O Brother Leo, write that this indeed is perfect joy. And if, urged by cold and hunger, we knock again, calling to the porter and entreating him with many tears to open to us and give us shelter, for the love of God, and if he come out more angry than before, exclaiming, "These are but importunate rascals, I will deal with them as they deserve"; and taking a knotted stick, he seizes us by the hood, throwing us on the ground, rolling us in the snow, and shall beat and wound us with the knots in the stick—if we bear all these injuries with patience and joy, thinking of the sufferings of our Blessed Lord, which we would share out of love for Him, write, O Brother Leo, that here, finally, is perfect joy. And now, brother, listen to the conclusion. Above all the graces and the gifts of the Holy Spirit which Christ grants to His friends, is the grace of overcoming oneself, and accepting willingly, out of love for Christ, all suffering, injury, discomfort and contempt; for in all other gifts of God we cannot glory, seeing they proceed not from ourselves but from God, according to the words of the Apostle, "What hast thou that thou hast not received from God? And if thou hast received it, why dost thou glory as if though hadst not received it?" But in the cross of tribulation and affliction we may glory, because, as the Apostle says again, "I will not glory save in the cross of our Lord Jesus Christ."'"

Leo, like Giles, lived to be a very old man and died at the Sacro Convento at Assisi.

Ruffino was an aristocrat of Assisi, a member of the noble family of the Scefi. He is a heroic character, not heroic in the manner of the dauntless Giles, but heroic because of the lifelong battle he had to fight within himself. He was a lonely and melancholy man, beset by fears and anxieties, shy and reserved, the type that today would be called neurotic. But he was not conquered by his disabilities, he conquered them, and a quiet persevering strength in him made him at last a great man of prayer, a man whom Francis called in his absence Saint Ruffino. One of his inhibitions was an inability to speak in public. Whenever he tried to speak to people he became incapable of saying a word, whether from a stammer or from sheer nerves we are not told. But this speechlessness could not be allowed in one of the Brothers Minor, who had pledged themselves to obey the command of Christ to preach the gospel, and Francis to put an end to it commanded him to go and preach at Assisi. Ruffino in an agony implored Francis to spare him. He said that he could not do it, and held out so obstinately that Francis suddenly lost his temper and told Ruffino to go and preach at Assisi at once, and for a penance to go there without his tunic and wearing only his breeches.

There was in Francis a queer streak of harshness, amounting at times almost to cruelty. Normally he was fierce with himself only but on rare occasions the stinging lash caught the brothers too. It is hard to reconcile this harsh streak with his love and gentleness, and those who suffered from it must have been even more taken aback than we are, but it is noteworthy that only one thing called it out and that was the failure of perfect obedience. No injury done to himself had any power to ruffle the sweetness of Francis's temper, but to a religious disobedience to the rule of his Order, or to the command of his superior in the Order, is disobedience to Christ Himself, and Francis could not endure to see his Master so dishonoured. And these occasional outbreaks tell us something else about Francis, for they show the extreme tension under which he lived. He, like Ruffino, knew the torture of oversensitive nerves and though his joyousness and selflessness gave him an ease that Ruffino lacked, his control could at times snap.

With desperate courage Ruffino did as he was told. Naked except for his breeches he went up the stony way to Assisi and into the city. It is thought that the place appointed for his sermon was the out-of-doors pulpit of the cathedral, and if this is so he had quite a long way to go through the streets to reach it, with urchins running at his heels and jeering at him and the windows and doors of the city full of staring eyes. For any sensitive man it would have been a nightmare but for a son of the house of Scefi, who had walked these streets as a prince, it must have been a via dolorosa harder to endure even than that of Francis when he came from San Damiano to his father's home. But no one had the kindness to take hold of Ruffino and pull him indoors as a madman, and when he reached the pulpit he had to clamber up into it and try and preach. He had it in mind to talk to the people about honesty, but though he managed to get his mouth open words came out of it only with agonizing difficulty, and the astonished inquisitive crowd that quickly gathered found in his remarks food rather for mirth than for edification. But Ruffino did not give up. He was doing this under holy obedience, for the love of Christ, and laugh as they would he went on.

But soon after Ruffino had left the Portiuncula Francis was seized with sudden frantic remorse. He understood Ruffino, he knew the suffering his temperament caused him, and he had always been gentle with this difficult brother, but if he had brought him any healing he had undone it all now with his harshness. All his fierceness now was turned upon himself. "Son of Pietro Bernadone, thou vile mannikin," he stormed at himself, "wherefore didst thou command Brother Ruffino, one of the noblest citizens of Assisi, thus to go preaching naked? Please God, thou shalt have experience of what thou hast made another to endure." Then he too cast away his habit and wearing only his breeches set out for Assisi.

Brother Leo, that quietly efficient young man, picked up the two habits, placed them over his arm and followed gently along behind.

Francis, when he reached the crowd about the pulpit, waited unnoticed until Ruffino's poor sermon had stumbled to its end, and then he mounted the pulpit steps and stood beside him. The crowd had found one half-naked friar funny enough, two of them must have seemed more comic still. But their laughter soon ceased, for Francis was preaching to them of the poverty and nakedness of Christ. There was scarcely a moment when he was not thinking of the suffering of Christ and when he spoke of it neither he nor his hearers could remember anything else. When his sermon ended the congregation were weeping.

Leo judged this a good moment to step forward and reclothe the two saints in their habits. When he had done this the people pressed forward and lifting the hems of the worn habits they kissed them, and they showed as much deference towards Ruffino as towards Francis. From that day onward he lived the full life of the Franciscan friar, accepting the chalice of his temperament with fortitude. His long endurance brought him at last to peace, for when as an old man he lay dying Francis appeared to him and lovingly greeted him, and he died in joy.

Among the brothers there can hardly have been a greater contrast to Ruffino than Masseo, a big burly handsome man, possessed of charm, common sense and "a fair and devout eloquence". Preaching held no terrors for Masseo, he enjoyed it, and Francis liked to take him as his companion on a journey because when he wanted to go away quietly and pray Masseo would keep the people from following him by preaching to them and holding them enthralled by his eloquence. But Masseo had his difficulties too and the stories of him suggest that they came not so much from his disabilities, as did Ruffino's, as from his gifts. His charm and popularity made the battle for humility harder for him than for another, and moreover he was a hungry man and was not always able to share Francis's love of poverty quite to the full.

One day he and Francis were journeying towards Rome where they were to visit the tombs of the apostles. Francis was contemplating a missionary journey to France and he liked to begin all important undertakings by a pilgrimage to Rome. They were hungry and weary and stopped at a little town to beg for food. Francis went one way and Masseo another, and Masseo's good looks, and perhaps also the pitiful sight of a large man sagging for want of food, so touched the hearts of the housewives that they gave liberally of their scraps; but Francis, little and insignificant in appearance, was given hardly anything. When they had finished their begging the two brothers went to a place outside the town where there was a fair fountain, and a large flat stone where they could arrange the food they had begged.

When Francis saw that Masseo had been far more successful than himself he was delighted, and then, as he looked about him and saw the sky like a king's canopy over their heads, and the cool sweet water and the grass, and the stone shaped like a table lifting up the food that had been given them for the love of God, his delight deepened to an ecstasy of joy. This was the bounty of God. This was the table of the Lord, the green pastures and the waters of comfort. "Thou shalt prepare a table before me . . . Thy loving-kindness and mercy shall follow me all the days of my life."

"O Brother Masseo," said Francis, "we are not worthy of so great a treasure," and he said it over and over again in the joy of his heart, so many times that Masseo, still hungry and not able to attack the food until they had said grace, lost patience.

"Father," he protested, "how can this be called treasure, when we are in such poverty and lack the things of which we have need, we who have neither cloth nor knives nor plates nor porringer nor house nor table nor manservant nor maidservant?"

But Francis said, "This is indeed the reason why I have counted it great treasure, because man has had no hand in it, but all has been given to us by divine providence, as we clearly see in this bread of charity, in this beautiful table of stone, and in this so clear fountain. Wherefore let us beg of God to make us love with all our hearts the treasure of holy poverty."

And then at last they "made their prayer" and Masseo was able to stay the pangs that assailed him. When the meal was finished they went into a church to pray and after they had prayed for a while Francis preached to Masseo upon poverty, and when he preached to one man it was "most carefully, as to a multitude". It is a moving and wonderful discourse.

"Dearest Companion, let us go to Saint Peter and Saint Paul, and pray them to teach and help us to possess the immeasurable treasure of most holy poverty; for she is a treasure so all-worthy and so divine, that we are not worthy to possess in our most lowly vessels; inasmuch as she is that heavenly virtue through which all things earthly and transitory are trampled under foot, and every obstacle is removed from before the soul in order that it may freely unite itself with God Eternal. This is that virtue which makes the soul, while still placed on earth, to converse in heaven with the angels. This is she who accompanied Christ upon the cross; with Christ she was buried, with Christ she rose again, with Christ, she mounted into heaven; and it is she who, even in this life, gives to the souls who are enamoured of her the means of flying to heaven; inasmuch as she guards the weapons of true humility and charity. And therefore, let us pray the most holy apostles of Christ, that by His most holy mercy, He may grant to us to merit to be true lovers and observers and humble disciples of the most precious and most beloved evangelical poverty."

Masseo numbered among his many gifts musical composition and a sense of humour. He once composed a chant and being pleased with it sang it constantly. When his restive brethren asked him why he could not sing something else he replied, "When a man has found a good thing he ought not to change it." Francis had to help him to learn humility, as he had helped Ruffino to learn obedience, and he used both severity and laughter to help him along the hard way. At one time he set him to do menial tasks for the community, and kept him at it so long that the other brothers pleaded that he might be relieved. But Masseo, who wanted above all things to be humble, refused to be relieved and said to Francis, "Father, whatever thou dost lay on me, whether wholly or in part, I deem it altogether God's deed."

But he did not find it so easy to be laughed at. One day when he and Francis were journeying together Francis dropped behind to pray and Masseo, striding ahead, came first to a cross-road. "Father, by which way are we to go?" he called back.

"By that which God shall will," replied Francis.

"But how can we know the will of God?" asked Masseo.

Francis said, "By the sign I will show thee. Wherefore by the merit of holy obedience, I command thee that in the crossroad where thou art now standing thou turn round and round as children do and cease not turning till I tell thee."

So the large, hot and flustered Masseo had to spin round and round until he was giddy, and wondered why Francis made him play the child before the amused passers-by. When Francis called a halt he was facing towards Siena, and so to Siena they went, that evidently being God's will for them.

Masseo felt that no price was too great to pay for the precious gift of humility. He wore himself down with fasts, vigils and prayer, beseeching God to give it to him. But still he knew he was not a truly humble man and one day he went "into the wood" and as he walked through the aisles of that lovely place he broke down and wept because he had not attained the grace of humility. And then in the midst of his bitter weeping he heard his name whispered by that still small Voice that Francis knew so well. "Brother Masseo!" said the Voice and he answered, "My Lord! My Lord!" And the Voice said, "What wilt thou give to have this grace from Me?" Brother Masseo said, "O my Lord, I would even give the eyes from out my head!" But bargaining has no part in the generosity of God's giving and the Voice said gently, "I will thou hast the grace and thine eyes also."

The Presence withdrew, leaving Masseo so humbled by the humility and gentleness of Christ, and so filled with His light, that from that hour he was ever jubilant. He lived to be a very old man and was called Masseo of Humility.

These three brothers, Leo, Ruffino and Masseo, with Angelo the courteous knight of Tancredi, made a bodyguard for Francis during the last years of his life. They went with him to Monte Alvernia, they nursed him through his last illness, and they are buried close to him in the great church of San Francesco, watching over him still. Leo, Ruffino and Angelo are the Three Companions whose memories were written down in Leo's "rolls and notes".

Pacifico also had been a great man in the world before God called him to the poverty and littleness of the Brothers Minor. He had been William of Lisciano, the king of verses, and he had been a troubadour. As a boy he had been brought by the Emperor to the gay court of Palermo, had contested with Norman and Provençal troubadours and been crowned as poet laureate by the Emperor himself. With his honours fresh upon him, and accompanied by the usual crowd of admiring young men who troop after the hero of the moment, he went one day to a convent at San Severino in the Marches of Ancona, where he heard Francis preach and was so "pierced" by him that afterwards he went to Francis and asked if he might talk to him. And so in some quiet place they sat and talked together, the friar in his worn grey habit and the courtier in his finery, and Francis spoke gently of the royal court where he himself was a servant, the court of the King of heaven. He was still speaking when William of Lisciano suddenly cried out, "What need of further argument? Let us come to deeds. Take me away from men and give me back to the Most High Emperor." They went back to the courtiers who had come with their poet laureate and kneeling down in front of Francis before them all William of Lisciano gave himself to God, and became Brother Pacifico, so called by Francis because he had left the gay traffic of the world for the peace of Christ. If this prompt acceptance into the Order of a young man he had never seen before seems startling we must remember that Francis had a sure instinct for vocation. When another young man knelt weeping before him, begging to be taken into the Order, Francis said curtly, "Miserable and carnal boy, why do you think you can lie to the Holy Spirit and to me? Your weeping is carnal and your heart is not with God. Go, for you savour of nothing spiritual." It must have given Francis great joy to have a troubadour for his son, and when years later the Brothers Minor went as missionaries to the beloved land of France, the land of the troubadours, they were led by Pacifico.

It was once granted to Pacifico to see a vision of heaven. He and Francis were walking together one day in the valley of Spoleto, when they came to an abandoned church, one of those lonely places in which Francis liked to pray, and he said to Pacifico, "Return to the leper hospital, for I wish to remain here alone tonight, and tomorrow very early return to me."

Pacifico did as he was told and Francis went into the church to say compline and to pray, and then after a while he was tired and lay down to sleep. But he could not sleep for he felt evil all about him and he was terribly afraid. He was always acutely aware of the strength and horror of evil, not only the evil of wicked men but that diabolical unseen evil which in the spiritual world is arrayed with such power against the powers of light. He felt often in his own body and mind and soul the tides of the eternal conflict, and sometimes he would feel himself almost swept away by evil. Like all men of his time he personified in an almost human way the powers that are above and below us, their conflict interpenetrating ours. The angels and the demons were very real to him. In some dark and lonely place he would think he heard a footfall behind him, or the beat of dark wings, and he would be terrified. Yet he never ran away from the terror but stayed and faced it out, for he knew that the power of God is always mightier than any evil that can assail us, and he believed also that God can use even the demons for a good purpose. He called them "the sergeants of the Lord", and pictured them in this world bringing the afflictions that curb sin, and in the after life executing the Divine justice.

Lying in the dark church he felt the evil both within and without. Diabolical suggestions attacked his mind and about him was the dark pressing-in of fear. He got up and went out of the church, taking with him out of the holy place the evil that had fastened upon him, and under the stars he crossed himself and invoked the name of God, and the evil let go of him and he went back to the church and slept in peace.

Very early the next morning Pacifico came quietly into the church and saw Francis praying before the altar. He did not want to disturb him and so he waited outside the choir; there was a crucifix there and he knelt down to pray before it. The picture that comes into the mind is one of awe and beauty; the abandoned lonely church full of shadows and the two men kneeling in prayer, the one before the altar and the other before the crucifix, and outside the growing light of dawn and the first twittering of the birds. As his prayer deepened it seemed to Pacifico that he was caught up into heaven, and like Saint Paul he said afterwards, "Whether in the body or out of the body God knoweth." He saw in heaven many seats and one lovelier than the others for it was shining with precious stones. But it was empty. And then he heard a Voice saying to him, "This was the seat of Lucifer, and in his stead shall the humble Francis sit."

When he came to himself again Pacifico saw Francis coming

down to him from the altar and he went to him and kneeled at his feet with his arms held out crosswise, and he whispered, "Father, do me this grace, and ask the Lord that He may have mercy on me and forgive me my sins."

Francis, seeing the transfigured face of his friend, knew that he had had a vision, and he lifted him gently to his feet and they went out of the church together.

Afterwards Pacifico wondered, like so many who have lived with great and holy people, what sort of opinion Francis had of himself and he asked, "What thinkest thou of thyself, brother?"

And Francis answered, "It seems to me that I am a greater sinner than anyone in the whole world."

Then Pacifico knew that his vision had been true for in the kingdom of heaven it is only the humble who are exalted.

There were two brothers who were neither noblemen nor poets but two poor men whose intelligence was not their strongest point. They were "simple" and for that very reason Francis loved them greatly. There was no need to teach humility and obedience to Brother John and Brother Juniper. The limitations and disasters of Brother Juniper made him humble as the humblest child and the blindness of Brother John's obedience was something of an embarrassment to the Order.

One day when Francis was at Nottiano, a village to the east of Assisi, he found the church not as clean as it ought to be and set to work to clean it. Nothing distressed him more than to find churches neglected and he used to carry a broom with him on his journeys so that he could sweep them. Often, after he had finished preaching in some small town or village, he would gather the priests of the district together in some quiet place, where lay people should not hear what he said, and talk to them of the salvation of souls and plead with them that they should look after their churches and altars with careful reverence. On this particular day, while Francis was hard at work cleaning the poor little church and grieving in his heart because men loved God so little that they could let His house be dirty and neglected, he heard footsteps padding on the stone flags and looking around saw a "a rustic of strange simplicity", and the rustic said, "Brother, give me the broom for I wish to help thee." Francis gave him the broom at once and he finished the sweeping, and then the two of them sat down together, perhaps in the church porch, where they could look out over the fields that were being ploughed ready for the spring sowing and see the garlands of the vines and the silver olive trees. In one of the fields a couple of oxen stood idle, for John the rustic had been ploughing when word went round the village that Brother Francis of Assisi was in the church, and he had promptly left the plough and the oxen and run to Brother Francis. As they sat and talked together he told Francis that he had been wanting to come to him for a long time, but he had not known how to come, and he said, "It is now a long time that I have had the will to serve God. Now therefore, since it hath pleased the Lord that I should see thee, I have the will to do whatever shall be pleasing to thee."

Francis saw that this simple ploughman had it in him to be a holy servant of God, and he explained the rules of the Order to him. The thought of parting with his possessions did not daunt John. He ran off and came back with one of the oxen, his portion of the family inheritance, and told Francis that he would give it to the poor.

But when John's parents and younger brothers heard what he was proposing to do there was a fearful outcry, for they did not want to lose John and still less did they want to lose the ox. But Francis knew how to comfort them. He shared a meal with them, and talked to them and made them happy by his love and kindness. He told the parents what a great honour it would be for them to give their son to God, "to serve whom is to reign", and he went on to say that since they themselves were so poor their son should give his ox to them. At that the poor little family rejoiced greatly at the idea of giving John to God, but "chiefly they rejoiced on account of the ox", and John went with Francis to the Portiuncula with the parental blessing.

Francis so loved John's simplicity that he had him with him as his constant companion, though the companionship had its difficulties, for everything Francis did John had to do too; when Francis knelt he knelt, when Francis sighed he sighed, when

Francis looked up to heaven he looked up to heaven. When reproved he said, "Brother, I promised to do all things which thou didst, and therefore I must conform to thee in all things." John had his own wisdom. He was well aware how closely Francis followed in the steps of Christ and like the page of good king Wenceslas he thought he could not go far wrong if he came after, putting his feet in the prints that Francis left behind him. So he came after, and though he did not live much longer, being one of the few brothers who died young, "he being made perfect in a short time, fulfilled a long time. For his soul pleased the Lord, therefore hasted He to take him away from among the wicked". After his death Francis always spoke of him as Holy John.

Brother Juniper, the beloved jester of the Order, has been a delight from that day to this, and so many stories are told about him that he has become an almost legendary figure. He was a cobbler, child-like, warm-hearted, impulsive, simple, humble, selfless and very patient, and Francis loved him so much that he said he wished he had a forest of such Junipers. The other brothers loved him too but were glad there was only one Juniper, especially when it was his turn to do the cooking, for he thought it saved trouble to cook rabbits in their fur, and was surprised when the brothers were not appreciative of all he tried to do for them. Juniper was not afraid of preaching, for he liked to talk, but he preferred children to sermons and once kept a distinguished congregation waiting for him while he played see-saw by the city gate with two ragged boys.

After the death of Francis life was hard for Juniper, for a change came over the life of the Brothers Minor and he could not understand it. With the Order numbering thousands of friars the absolute poverty of the early days was no longer possible. Convents were built and equipped with books and furnishings and all these things Juniper gave blithely away to every beggar who asked for alms; for Father Francis had taught him to give to all who were in need and not to forget the command of Christ, that to him who asks for our coat we must give our cloak also. Juniper did not forget and gave away his clothes so often that at last his Superior lost all patience with him and forbade him

I

ever again to give away his habit. So Juniper let it be stolen from him instead.

Upon this occasion or another his Superior rated him so thoroughly that he gave himself a sore throat. Juniper in his selfless humility was not aware of any injustice done to himself, even though he had only been obeying Christ and Father Francis, or of any unkindness in what must have been a savage scolding, he thought only of the rasped throat. He went into the city, begged butter and flour and made a pottage, and late that night the Superior heard a knock at his door and opening it saw Juniper standing there with a lighted candle in one hand and the hot pottage in the other. Juniper smiled his child-like loving smile and said, "My Father, when thou didst reprove me for my faults I saw that thy voice grew hoarse and I weened it was through overmuch fatigue. Therefore I thought of a remedy and made this mess of pottage for thee."

For the Superior this interruption of his sleep was the last straw; and perhaps remembering the rabbits cooked in their fur he mistrusted Juniper's pottage. He lost his temper again and told Juniper to take himself off, but still Juniper stood there, full of pity and love, pleading and holding out the pottage. But the patience of the angry man before him had been tried too far and it was not accepted. The heart of a lesser man than Juniper would have broken then; he would have turned away weeping and taken the pottage to the pigs. But Juniper was made of stouter stuff and if his intellect was not strong he was richly endowed with common sense. It was good pottage and he was not minded to have it wasted. He said, "If you will not eat, my Father, I pray thee do this for me: hold the candle and I myself will eat it."

How Francis would have laughed! Perhaps that hard tired man, his successor as the Father of the Little Ones, whose chief virtue it was that he had truly loved Francis, fancied that he heard an echo of laughter in the shadows. Be that as it may, it was his heart that broke, not Juniper's. He took Juniper into his cell and they sat down and ate the pottage together.

There is one brother who has come down to posterity only by reason of the briefness of his sojourn in the Order and the suddenness of his exit from it. He seems to have thought that the life of a religious was a species of rest cure, for he "did hardly pray at all and never did work, neither would he go forth for alms; but he did eat bravely." Francis dealt with him summarily. "Go your way, Brother Fly," he said, "since you are willing to eat the sweat of the other brethren but yourself are idle in the work of the Lord. Like a barren drone you gain nothing and do no work, but you devour the labour and gains of the good bees."

Thinking over these good bees Francis described the good Brother Minor as a man having the faith of Brother Bernard, the simplicity and poverty of Brother Leo, the courtesy of Brother Angelo, the gracious and natural sense and devout eloquence of Brother Masseo, the mind raised in contemplation of Brother Giles, the continual labour of holy Ruffino, "who without intermission prayed always, for even when sleeping or doing anything his mind was always with the Lord", and the patience of Brother Juniper, "who arrived at the perfect state of patience because of the perfect truth of his own vileness which he had before his eyes".

Francis had it all. The virtues of all these men were his virtues, and he seems in a sense to have been them all, to have held them within himself that he might lift them up to God.

Chapter Two

THE SECOND ORDER

They are clean of heart who despise earthly things and always
seek those of heaven, and who never cease to adore and contemplate the Lord God Living and True, with a pure heart and mind.

Writings of Saint Francis

I

A YEAR after the brothers settled at the Portiuncula another
stronghold of prayer was established at San Damiano. Francis had
known in the days when he was rebuilding San Damiano that
nuns would live there, and so when he was confronted by a tall
fair-haired girl, aged eighteen, telling him she wanted to be one
of the Brothers Minor, his first shock would quickly have passed
into reverent acceptance of a new but expected unfolding of the
will of God. That was always the only supremely important thing
to Francis and Clare, the will of God. The difficulties in which his
acceptance of her as a member of the Order would involve them
both must have been foreseen by Francis from the first, but what
appeared to others a difficult problem was for him extremely simple;
God wanted Clare. He knew it and she knew it and so their duty
was inescapable. As unhesitatingly as he had answered Pacifico's
appeal to him to take him away from the world and give him back
to God he answered Clare's, and as unhesitatingly as Pacifico and
the other brothers Clare did what she had to do and never looked
back. Her courage all through her life had a tough masculine
quality. She was as doughty a fighter as any of them, and far more
obstinate. At the end of her life she postponed death to get her
own way in a matter near her heart and having got it died in peace.

The Lady Clare was probably born in the summer of 1193, when
Francis as a boy of eleven was the prince among the children,
leading them singing and dancing up through the streets to the
high terraces of the city. She was a daughter of the house of Scefi,

a cousin of Ruffino and possibly of Sylvester also, so that she was the third member of that noble family to enter the Order. Her father was Favorino Scefi, Lord of Sasso Rosso, a castle on the slope of Monte Subasio, though he owned also a palazzo within the city of Assisi, and she was the third of the five children of Favorino and his wife Ortolana. From the beginning the Lady Ortolana, like the Lady Pica, must have known that her child was in some special way chosen of God, for shortly before the baby's birth, when she was praying for a safe delivery, she heard the interior Voice say, "Fear not, woman, for you shall bring forth a light whose rays shall enlighten the earth," and when the child was born she called her Clare, "the shining one." And so even Clare's name marked her for that Order whose light had been seen in the dream of the Portiuncula falling upon the blind faces of the praying men.

Ortolana was a devout woman, fond of escaping from the world for a while and going on pilgrimage, and Clare was a devout little girl, who liked to escape to hidden corners to say her prayers in secret. She grew up in her two homes, the castle and the palazzo, hearing the topics of the day discussed around her, hearing the minstrels play and delighting in their music, learning to read and write and do exquisite needlework, a well-educated, cultured and beautiful girl destined by her father for distinguished and suitable marriage. But as she grew older her inclinations began to take what her father must have thought an unsuitable turn and she became absorbed not in the thought of marriage but in the sufferings of the poor. She would have been about twelve years old when the young Francesco Bernadone began to serve the poor of Assisi. Perhaps one day, passing up the street with her mother or her nurse, she saw him bending over some poor wretch who was pouring out a tale of woe to him, and the sight of the compassionate figure remained a vivid memory with her. Perhaps even then he became her hero. Everyone in Assisi knew about his father's treatment of him, his quarrel with his father and the scene in the Bishop's palace, and so she would have known too and perhaps she wept for him. She was about fifteen when he began his costly service to the lepers, and when she too began to serve the poor she saw to it that her service also was costly. She did not condescend to them as a great lady, she denied herself her food to help them. Her family let her have her way in this service; possibly they could do nothing else for her will was so strong that even the men stood in some awe of her. But to the poor she was all gentleness and her marvellous sympathy and understanding won her so much love that all men spoke of her, and of the light of heaven that seemed to shine about her in the dark and sorrowful places where she went. To many a poor sick creature, bedridden in some hovel, it must have seemed like the sunrise when the door opened and the Lady Clare came in, fresh and young and smiling, her fair hair gathered in its crespin of golden mesh, a long cloak worn over her plain belted gown. Under her cloak she carried a woven basket on her arm with bread and fruit in it, bandages and salves and bunches of sweet herbs. It was so that Francis heard of her, all love and light and courage, and he longed to see and speak with her.

She longed to speak with him. She saw him frequently for she made one of the large congregation that heard him preach in the cathedral, and as she listened to his sermons she knew that here was the man who would help her. For her life just now had reached an impasse. She had been allowed to remain unmarried for longer than most girls of her rank but now, a suitable husband having been found for her, marriage was being pressed upon her by her parents. But she knew she was not made for the conventional life of a married woman. What she wanted was nothing less than God Himself. "Like as the hart desireth the water brooks so longeth my soul after Thee, O God." But neither did she want the conventional life of a nun in one of the convents for women that were little more than appendages of the noble houses, where unmarriageable daughters could lead lives of gentle prayer interspersed with fine needlework and a little gossip. Her heroic temper was made for something more than this and what she wanted was total giving. Francis had given himself utterly and only he could understand and help her.

Her need seems to have communicated itself to him for it was he, not Clare, who brought about their first meeting. Speechlessly she had cried out to him, as Pacifico had done, "Take me away," and her chronicler says, "He was wishful to snatch this noble prey out of the reach of a wicked world." He must have been extremely certain of God's will for Clare, for to take the initiative in this way was unlike him. As a rule his dealings with women had a shattering simplicity. He avoided them whenever possible but if they insisted on talking to him about their souls he kept his eyes on the ground, or the sky, while the interview lasted. He was a naturally ardent and loving man who had cut women out of his life for God's sake and he was taking no risks. One would like to know where his first meeting with Clare took place; perhaps outside the cathedral after the Sunday sermon, with Clare in all her patrician finery curtseying to the shabby young friar who had been her hero for so long. After it Clare and her aunt the Lady Bianca Guelfucci, who understood Clare and knew all that was in her heart, often went down the hill to talk to Francis at the Portiuncula. Many other citizens of Assisi must have done the same, for his own sufferings had given him a rare understanding of troubled souls, and his natural gentleness and courtesy had been fashioned by prayer into a channel of the comfort of Christ. His visitors could not go inside the quick-set hedge, where the conventual silence held, but Francis could come out to them and talk to them in the cathedral of the wood. And so it was "into the wood" that Clare went to speak with Francis of the love of Christ. It was here that she told him that she must do what he had done and he agreed with her. It was God's will that the Order should give to Him the service of daughters as well as sons and in the wood he strengthened her for what she had to do. It was early spring and the buds were thickening on the trees.

On Palm Sunday, April the 18th, 1212, the Lady Clare left the world. In the morning she went with her family to the cathedral for high mass and the blessing and distribution of the palms. Her chronicler says that she was dressed in the festival garments of a nobleman's daughter, her scarlet robe girdled with a jewelled belt, a high stiff head-dress on her head and embroidered shoes on her feet. The cathedral was crowded, for the people of Assisi loved this Palm Sunday service, but among all the beautiful women gathered there Clare of the oval face, fair hair and delicate features was one of the loveliest. Her emotions must have almost torn her in pieces. She was here for the last time with her father and mother, brother and sisters. She must give up home and security, the fulfilment of marriage and children, of worldly dignity and gracious living, for a life of hardship for which nothing in her life so far had prepared her. And being what she was there would be no turning back, for she was not of the type that turns back. Her world would be outraged and her family heartbroken. And all this she was doing at nineteen years of age for love of a God Whom her eyes could not see and her human arms could not hold, and Whom she would not truly find until after long struggle all the self-love in her had been destroyed. She was doing what she wanted to do but it is a paradox of human life that what we want to do with the noblest part of us is not accomplished without blood and tears. When the time came for them all to go up to receive their palms Clare could not go with the others but had to stay kneeling and trembling in her place.

And then there occurred an incident that suggests that in what they were doing Clare and Francis had the approval and support not only of Bianca Guelfucci but of Bishop Guido too. When he saw that Clare had not come up with the others he left the altar, came to where she was kneeling, and put the blessed palm between her hands.

That night Clare left her home, and the little pointed doorway through which she went is still to be seen. Umbrian houses had a special door which was used only for the carrying forth of the dead and between each death was blocked up with stones. Afraid to leave the palazzo by the main door, in case she attracted notice, Clare somehow managed to move these heavy stones and passed out through the door of death. Perhaps it flashed through her mind, as she stepped out into the cool spring night, that the Lady Clare was dead and that she who now stood under the stars was Sister Clare.

Bianca was waiting for her in the street and together they went down the dark hill from the city and made their way through the forest. As they came near the Portiuncula they heard singing and saw lights shining through the trees. All the brothers, having recited matins in the church, were coming to meet her carrying torches and candles and singing God's praises. Taking Clare with them they returned again to Santa Maria degli Angeli and kneeling before the altar she made her vows, and Francis cut off her hair and put on her the cross-shaped habit of the Order. She was with them when they sang the first mass of Holy Monday and from it she drew strength to face the persecution, the poverty and suffering that she knew were coming. The epistle and gospel, the sixty-third chapter of Isaiah and the fourteenth chapter of Mark, must have seemed like a special gift to her. "Who is this that cometh from Edom, with dyed garments from Bozrah? This that is glorious in His apparel, travelling in the greatness of His strength?" What could any suffering of hers be compared with the sufferings of the Divine Hero? And He would be with her through it all and at the end would be her Prize. "In all their affliction He was afflicted, and the angel of His Presence saves them . . . Thou, O Lord, art our Father, our Redeemer, Thy name is from everlasting." And when the gospel was read she heard the story of the woman who brought her treasure to Christ, "an alabaster box of ointment of spikenard, very precious", and broke it and poured it out, and He accepted her total giving with love and compassion.

Mass ended and now it was the dawn, perhaps a chilly one, the lights had gone out, and what was Clare to do next? Francis had not a convent in one hand and a community of nuns in the other with which to endow her, and the kindly Bianca, who had helped them so gallantly up till now, must go home. It is open to question whether Francis, who lived with such child-like faith and trust for the moment only, had given much thought to this morrow, or even any thought at all, Christ in the Gospels having explicitly commanded otherwise. However, whether from aforethought or on the inspiration of the moment, he took Clare to the Benedictine convent of San Paola at Bastia, a quiet place at the edge of the forest where two streams met, and asked the nuns to take care of her until he could find a home for her. Then he went away and Clare was left alone to face the coming storm.

It did not take her family long to discover where she was and they came next day, deeply angry, to take her home. She fled to

the church, and when they threatened to take her away by force
if she would not come willingly, she uncovered her shorn head
and clinging to the altar cried out that she belonged to God alone
now and they could not take her away. She was so strong, so
sure, that she convinced them. Till the end of her life Clare could
always convince people that she was right. She could subdue even
Popes to her will, so queenlike was she in her authority. And
perhaps the Lady Ortolana, her mother, remembered that this child
was Clare the "shining one" and suddenly understood that this
was her daughter's destiny. And so they left her before the altar.

A few days later she left San Paola and went to the convent of
Sant' Angelo in Panzo, not much more than a mile from Assisi on
the slopes of Monte Subasio and fairly close to her father's castle of
Sasso Rosso, and here a little later she was joined by her sister
Agnes who had run away too because she could not bear to be
without Clare. Agnes was only fifteen, not such a resolute character as Clare but strong enough to know that where Clare went
she must go and what Clare did she must do too, so dearly did she
love her. But a second runaway child was more than the family
could endure and this time an expeditionary force of twelve male
members of the house of Scefi rode out from Assisi and up the
mountain to the convent, bringing with them into the story the
comedy that is never far away. The jingling clattering arrival of
the cavalcade terrified the nuns, and sent the two girls running to
the convent chapel for refuge, but the twelve men trooped in
after them and stood round them where they clung together
before the altar. At first, as the chapel was holy ground, they
moderated their voices and struggled for a sweet reasonableness.
But to Agnes nothing was reasonable except that she should stay
with Clare and with Clare there to strengthen her she did not give
in. Then one of them, perhaps the girls' brother Boso, lost
patience, grabbed hold of Agnes by her long hair and pulled her
out of the chapel and the convent into the open air, where they
could all express themselves without the restraint that had been
imposed upon them by the holiness of the place where they
had been before. Clare remained on her knees before the altar,
praying to God to save her sister, until above the noise that her

relatives were making she heard Agnes's voice crying out to her for help and knew that they were trying to take her away. Then she too ran out of the convent and overtook them on the mountain side. Agnes was lying on the ground and the legend says that through the power of Clare's prayer she had become so heavy that the men could no longer carry her. Perhaps the truth is that she fought so hard that they could no longer hold her without hurting her. Clare came flying down upon them, took Agnes in her arms and commanded her menfolk to go home. And they went home, baffled and defeated by the calm imperious strength of this extraordinary girl.

Clare and Agnes stayed with the nuns at Sant' Angelo for a year, a time of patient waiting, solitude and prayer, and then the kindly Benedictines of Monte Subasio once more presented the Order with a "place". They gave San Damiano, the church and little house, to be the first convent of the Second Order, and Clare and Agnes came home rejoicing.

The Second Order of the Poor Clares increased as quickly as the First Order of the Friars Minor. Almost at once other women came from Assisi to join the two sisters, one of the first being Bianca Guelfucci, and after the death of Clare's father the Lady Ortolana and her daughter Beatrice came too; and so five ladies of that noble family were together in the Order. Agnes remained with Clare at San Damiano for seven years and then, as other houses of the Poor Clares were springing up all over Italy and needed women who were already experienced in the life of prayer and poverty to guide them, she was sent, at the age of twenty-two or twenty-three, to be abbess of the convent of Monticelli near Florence. She lived there for more than thirty years, and through all those years she never saw her adored Clare. The parting must have been anguish to the two sisters, but when they took their vows of poverty, chastity and obedience they had known and accepted the suffering that obedience might bring. When Clare was dying Agnes was allowed to come to her and the two were together again, and the next parting was short, for Agnes outlived Clare by only three months and was buried near her sister. In the convent and church of Santa Chiara at Assisi two precious relics are preserved. One is the casket containing the curling fair hair that Francis cut off when Clare knelt before the altar of Santa Maria degli Angeli on the night of Palm Sunday, and the other is the skull of Agnes. It is very small, suggesting that Agnes was a little creature, and that those thirty years of being an abbess without Clare to help her stand for one of the unknown heroisms of this world.

II

Of all the Franciscan holy places San Damiano is the least changed. A great church now encloses the Portiuncula and the little church of Santa Maria degli Angeli cowers down inside it, as though terrified by all the grandeur piled on top, but San Damiano still stands under the open sky, simple, humble and holy as it always was. You can still see, almost unchanged, the chapel where Clare and her sisters knelt in adoring love before the crucifix that spoke to Francis, and the worn stone staircase outside the chapel door leading to the sisters' dormitory, stairs where Clare went up and down for over forty years, and the refectory where they ate their simple meals. Celano says of San Damiano, "This is that happy and holy place," and here, more than anywhere, the pilgrim of today can feel near to the man and woman whose holiness still so enlightens the earth, can reach back through the centuries and make some contact with them. Here it is not hard to imagine the life of the sisters as it was so steadfastly lived right through the years until the death of Clare. It was modelled as closely as possible upon that of the brothers, except that the Second Order was an enclosed Order and the sisters might not leave the precincts of their convent. With them, as with the brothers, prayer came first, the saying of the offices and the hidden costly discipline of contemplative prayer, and intercession, that supported their labours for the sick. As they could not leave San Damiano they could not nurse the lepers as the brothers did but other sick people were brought to them at San Damiano to be cared for. They mended the clothes of their sick, patched the habits of the brothers and spun the thread for the altar cloths and corporals which they made for the brothers to distribute among the poor churches of the district. They worked hard within their enclosure, nursing, spinning, weaving, sewing, cooking and cleaning, and looking after their vegetable garden. When the food produced by their garden was not enough the brothers went questing for them, and they ate at the table of the Lord with the same joy and thankfulness that Francis had felt when he sat down with his first platter of scraps of food and found it was a sacrament.

Yet in all this it is probable that there was an element of tragedy for Clare. She had not wanted to be an enclosed nun. She had great strength of character, high courage and a love of adventure, and she had wanted to do as the brothers did and carry the love of Christ to the dark places of the earth, to the poor and the wicked in their squalor and misery, to the prisoners, the lepers and the heathen. She was a woman who would have found herself understood by Elizabeth Fry and Florence Nightingale, but she was born before her time, in which the choice was between marriage or enclosure, and her longing to serve Christ adventurously seems not to have been understood even by Francis. But she was utterly obedient to Francis from the beginning to the end, accepting the rule he had devised for her as the will of God Himself and finding her peace in the perfection of obedience. Only once was there an outbreak of passionate longing that shows how hard to bear, at times, the frustration must have been. When she heard of the heroic death of the Franciscan missionaries in Morocco she cried out that she must go out there and be a martyr too, and Francis had hard work to restrain her from breaking her enclosure and setting out at once, as Teresa of Avila had done as a little girl.

She obeyed, turning back again to her own private venture of heroic prayer. For if she had to be an enclosed nun hers was no ordinary enclosure. Like Angela of Foligno a little later she set to work to strip herself of every smallest comfort, even those things which most people consider necessities, that she might take poverty to her heart as entirely as Francis had done and be set free to have nothing but Christ and be nothing but the thrall of Christ. Her bed was a pallet and her pillow a piece of wood. But she slept little, for like Francis she had trained herself to be as abstemious over sleep as over food. When compline, the last office for the day, had been said, and the sisters had gone to bed, she stayed on alone in the chapel, kneeling before the crucifix and praying the "crucis officium", the prayers in honour of the cross of Christ which Francis had arranged and taught her. When she left the chapel she would go softly, like a mother to her nursery, to the dormitory where her nuns lay sleeping to see if all was well with them, and if the night was chilly she would spread an extra covering over the delicate ones that they might not catch cold. Though she held them to their strict discipline she had for them the same exquisite tenderness that Francis had for the brothers and all her maternity was poured out upon them. It was she who woke them in the morning, lit the lamps and rang the bell for early mass.

As her holiness grew so did the power of her prayer. Mysteriously, as the years passed, her light shone out, and without anyone but God knowing quite how it was happening she became a great power in the world. Her prayers were asked for, her advice sought, not only by her beloved poor but by queens, popes and cardinals; for it was one of the paradoxes of the Franciscan movement that although vowed to poverty and pledged to the service of the poor and suffering, it took the rich by storm. Perhaps it laid such siege to their hearts because Francis, and his sons and daughters taught by him, saw no difference between the rich and the poor. "A man's worth," said Francis, "is what he is in the sight of God and no more." But if he thought no better of a man because he had a fine castle and fine clothes neither did he, like so many reformers, think the less. He wooed the rich for Christ with exactly the same gentle love as he wooed the outcasts, and they responded as readily. So with Clare. She turned from nursing her sick to answer the letters of Queen Agnes of Bohemia and Queen Elizabeth of Hungary, and sometimes it was a poor beggar who came knocking at her door, and sometimes it was the Pope, and all alike were the children of her love and prayers. The great Cardinal Ugolino wrote to her with humble love: "Although I have always felt myself to be a poor sinful man, now that I have become acquainted with the pre-eminence of your merits, and with my own eyes have seen the austerity of your religion, now, I say, I know for sure that I am not in a state to die: I am so weighed down by the burden of guilt and have offended so grievously against the Lord of the whole earth, that I can never hope to be gathered to the company of the elect unless by your prayers and tears you obtain for me forgiveness of my sins." The strength that her prayers were to Francis he knew, perhaps, but no one else could know.

Her loyalty to him was unshakeable. At no time, either during his lifetime or after his death, when changes that were contrary to his wish and will were taking place in the First Order, would she allow any lessening of the austerity of the Rule of the Second Order. Francis had laid down evangelical poverty as its foundation stone, and she would have no other. Four Popes in succession begged her, now that the times were changing, to accept a little property, but she would never give in. Pope Innocent IV managed to stand out against her determination for some while but though she was ill and dying she beat him in the end. Her reply to an offer to release her from her vow of poverty was, "Holy Father, free me from my sins, but not from following our Lord Christ." Two days before she died she received and kissed a parchment bearing the Pope's signature and securing for the Poor Clares of San Damiano the right to live to the end as Francis would have wished.

Clare lived for twenty-four years after the death of Francis, and for much of this time she was ill for she too had worn out her body with austerities. She was ill when the army of the Emperor once more came down upon them, laying waste the valley of Spoleto and besieging Assisi, and Saracen archers surrounded San Damiano. The nuns, terrified, ran to Clare, but though she was so ill she was not alarmed. She had herself carried to the door of the convent that she might be the first to bear the brunt of what might come, and she sent some of the sisters to the chapel to fetch the silver and ivory ciborium that held the Host. Then kneeling before the Host she prayed aloud. "Doth it please Thee, O my God, to deliver the defenceless children whom I have nourished with my love, into the hands of these beasts? Protect them, good Lord, I beseech Thee, whom I at this hour am not able to protect." And when she had prayed she heard the Voice say to her, "I will always be your guardian," and she got up from her knees confident and unafraid to comfort her nuns. The Saracens changed their minds about breaking into San Damiano and took themselves off elsewhere.

Towards the end of her life, when physical activity was over for her, she would lie in her tiny garden sewing, surrounded by her flowers, for this one Franciscan luxury, flowers, she did not deny herself. These first Franciscans, with their wholesome common sense which protected their austerity from the morbidness which crept into the mortification of so many saints, never turned their backs on anything that spoke to them of God's love and care and beauty. Birds and flowers, trees, sunlight and water, were not luxuries but the Word of God. Her little garden was only a terrace four paces long but creepers grew over it and in it she planted lilies, roses and violets that they should speak to her of the purity, love and humility of Christ. Her life of enclosure is described by Celano in words that bring this garden vividly to mind. "Here she found shelter from the storm of the world, and here she remained as long as she lived, shut up as it were in a dungeon for love of Jesus Christ. Here, in a hole in the wall like a most fair dove, she made herself a nest." From this little place there is a wonderful view. One can see Rivo-Torto, the Portiuncula, the winding roads, the olive groves and the distant blue mountains. Probably there was not a day of her life that she did not come here and look out towards the dwelling-place of Francis, for whether his physical presence was there or not it held his spirit. The nature of the love that this man and woman felt for each other has been a source of worry to some of their biographers, who do not seem to have been content to leave it where they themselves left it, in the hands of God. Francis always spoke of the nuns of San Damiano as "the ladies", but Clare herself he called Christiana, and there we have it in a nutshell. Everything in the lives of both of them was so subordinate to the love of Christ that it could have no existence apart from Him.

Clare died on August the 11th, 1253, the Feast of San Ruffino the patron saint of the cathedral, when she was sixty years old, comforted in her dying not only by Agnes but by three old men who had loved Francis as dearly as she had, Brother Leo, Brother

Alinari

ST. FRANCIS SPEAKING TO THE BIRDS

Giotto

Angelo and Brother Juniper. Celano writes of her death with simplicity and beauty. "It seemed that her agony was to be a long one, and during those last weary days of labour the faith and devotion of the people increased more and more. Nay, every day, and many times a day, prelates and cardinals came to visit her for all men were thoroughly convinced that this dying woman was in sooth a great saint. And strange to say, although during the last seventeen days of her life she was unable to take any kind of food, the Lord comforted her with such fortitude that all who beheld her were strengthened in the service of Christ." When she was exhorted to patience "she made answer with a a stout heart, 'From the day when I first knew the grace of our Lord Jesus Christ through His servant Francis no pain has seemed grievous to me, no penance hard, no sickness difficult to bear.' And when the Lord took pity on her, and was knocking, as it were, at the gate, she desired to have the assistance of priests and devout men, and that they should tell her the story of Christ's passion, and amongst them that came to console her was Brother Juniper, that mighty hurler before the Lord, who used to hurl from his very heart the words of the Lord red-hot . . . Then she blessed all who had been kind to her, women as well as men, and she blessed, too, all the monasteries of poor ladies, present and to come. The rest—who can tell it without weeping? There were present then two of the holy companions of Blessed Francis. One of them, Angelo, with his own eyes streaming with tears, was striving as best he could to comfort the weeping sisters; and as for the other, Leo, he knelt down and kissed the couch on which the dying saint was laid . . . But Blessed Clare was communing thus with her own soul softly: 'Go forth, Christian soul, go forth without fear, for thou hast a good Guide for thy journey. Go forth without fear, for He that created thee hath sanctified thee, always hath He protected thee, and He loveth thee with the love of a mother.' And when one of the sisters asked her to whom she was talking: 'I am talking to mine own soul,' she said; and truly her glorious Guide was not far off, for presently, turning to one of them, she said, 'Can you see the King of Glory Whom I see?' . . . Thus was the passing of Blessed Clare . . . Her holy soul went forth and,

K

exulting in its freedom, soared on the wings of gladness to the place which God had prepared for it."

III

There is a story in *The Little Flowers of Saint Francis* of Francis and Clare together, and though it would seem to be a legend, for we are told that Clare never left the precincts of San Damiano, it none the less tells the truth about them both. The story tells how she longed to share a meal with Francis, and when he came to visit the sisters she would beg him that they might eat together, but he would not grant her wish. Then the brothers remonstrated with him for his severity. It was because of his preaching, they said, that Clare had forsaken the world, and could he not let her have her wish in this? So Francis yielded and said he would arrange a little feast for her at the Portiuncula. The day came and Clare with one of her nuns came out from her convent, and was met by the brothers and brought into the church of Santa Maria degli Angeli, as they had brought her on the night when she ran away from home, and before the altar where she had made her vows she knelt and prayed. Then, "her salutation to maid Mary given", she was led to the feast, which was laid on the bare ground. As this was a feast and not a mere meal perhaps there was a salad of herbs and vegetables from the garden, as well as bread and water. Francis at the first dish was overwhelmed by the thought of God's bounty, and began to speak of His love so wonderfully that they were all caught up into prayer. Everything was forgotten except God, they sat there adoring Him and the light of heaven streamed out from the wood so brightly that the people of Assisi, looking down from the city, thought the Portiuncula and the trees around it were on fire and ran down the hill to the rescue. They found no fire but only the two saints and their companions sitting around the untouched meal, rapt in contemplation of the glory of God.

If the climax of the story was suggested to its writer by the message to Clare's mother, "You shall bring forth a light whose rays shall enlighten the earth," no story about Clare and Francis could have a more satisfying ending.

THE THIRD ORDER

Seeking Thy honour in all things and with all our strength, by
spending all the powers and senses of body and soul in the service
of Thy love and not in anything else; and that we may love our
neighbours even as ourselves, drawing to the best of our power all
to Thy love.

Writings of Saint Francis

I

WHEN Francis arrived at Ancona after his unsuccessful attempt
to go as a missionary to the infidels, worn and tired and perhaps
dispirited by failure, he did not know that the providence of
God would use this failure to bring great things to pass. Because
he returned to Ancona just when he did, in the spring of 1213,
he received the gift of the mountain of Alvernia, and in the
divine pattern of things that gift played its part not only in his
own life but also in the creation of the Third Order. He could
not know this but he was accustomed to see in the circumstances brought about by any honest attempt to serve God,
even if the attempt had seemed to end in disaster, an indication
of God's further will for him. He had failed, and like a little
child running after his father had fallen headlong, and now he
must pick himself up and set his feet once more in the footsteps of
his Lord. So from Ancona he set off at once on a preaching
mission and found himself some while later in the foothills of the
Apennines, on the borders of Tuscany. Here he heard that at
Montefeltro in the mountains there was to be a tournament in
celebration of the knighthood of a young kinsman of the Lord of
Montefeltro.

A tournament in the mountains in the spring, with the lists set
in the meadows full of flowers, the singing of the troubadours at
evening in the great castle, the dancing, and all the grace and

colour of a knightly occasion made an irresistible appeal to
Francis. The troubadour he had once longed to be was not dead
in him, merely transmuted into the *jongleur de Dieu*, and he decided at once to take his own light heart and the song in his
soul up the mountain to Montefeltro. As he trudged up the
steep road towards the castled village on its high rocky ledge,
he could see the castle itself towering up against the brilliant blue
sky with banners flying from the tower and trumpets ringing out
their welcome from the walls. All the ways up to the castle were
thronged, for this was a great occasion for the countryside. From
all the castles that crowned the hilltops of the neighbourhood gay
cavalcades had ridden forth, the knights in armour followed by
their young esquires, each with that little round buckler of a page
upon his arm that once Francis himself had carried, the women
wearing the tall stiff head-dresses, and the brilliant gowns with
jewelled girdles that were *de rigeur* upon festive occasions.
Perhaps as the lovely ladies swung by in their litters Francis
remembered Clare in the dignity and beauty of her youth, sitting
in the cathedral at Assisi listening to his preaching, and his thoughts
reached quickly out to her where she was now, praying before the
crucifix at San Damiano, dressed in the habit of his Order. Or a
knight riding past would remind him of his son Angelo, or the
fine patrician bearing of some nobleman of his beloved Ruffino,
and he prayed for them all. There were humbler folk upon the
road too, pedlars, minstrels and mountebanks, and within the
shadow of his hood Francis's bright eyes sparkled with delight
and interest. And also with love. Many must have turned to
smile at the little trudging friar in his grey habit, and then as their
eyes met his deep clear voice rang out with, "God give thee
His peace." How he must have longed to gather them all into
God's kingdom and perhaps even then, though the time was not
yet, his thoughts were busy with all those men and women for
whom life in the world was God's will but yet whose hearts were
hungry for some sort of discipline upon their lives, some inner
dedication that should give purpose and sanctity to what they did,
and must do, in the world.

When they came to the castle he mingled with the crowd there

and at some time during the festival he found himself in the courtyard. Probably they were holding a minstrels' contest, for that
would have drawn him more surely than anything else. When it
was over he knew that he must speak to them all and climbing up
on some raised place he begged that there might be silence for him
for a little while that he might speak. It was the kind of request
that he seldom had to make twice, for the very tones of his voice
compelled attention and probably word had already gone round
that Francis of Assisi was here. They gathered around him,
minstrels, knights and ladies, their faces upturned towards him,
smiling at him, amused and touched by his diminutive figure,
eager face and bright eyes. He took as his text two lines of a
minstrel's song, perhaps one that had already been sung in the
courtyard.

"So great is the good I have in sight,
In every hardship I delight."

He preached to them of the saints of God who had thought
no price too great to pay in penance and discipline, counting
even death itself a little thing, if they could attain at last to the
vision of God. Here in this beautiful castle in the mountains he
painted for them a picture of the heavenly country, the green
pastures and still waters that are on the other side of the cross, and
no doubt then as always he uncovered the hunger in their hearts so
that they knew that all the beauty about them, every treasure they
possessed, was like so much dust running through their hands if it
did not bring them nearer God.

When his sermon was over, and he had climbed down and was
mingling with the crowd again, a noble and brilliant figure
approached him, bowed to him and asked if they might talk
together. Francis must have been used by this time to these
aristocrats who fell so readily into the net of his preaching, and
with a sense of the unfolding of a familiar pattern he smiled at
the Lord Orlando dei Cattani, Lord of Chiusi in Casantino, and
said, "Right willingly, but this morning thou must do honour to
thy friends and dine with them and after thou hast dined we will
confer together." The Lord Orlando consented to this and

later in the day they met in some quiet place and sat and talked long together; perhaps until the sun was low in the west and the valleys below them were filled with golden mist. But the interview did not follow quite the usual pattern, for the Lord Orlando wanted Francis to strengthen him not to forsake the world and join the Order but to live the Christian life within the world, a task which seemed to him the harder task of the two, and when the interview was over and the strength he needed had been given to him he said he wanted to give Francis a gift, and the gift he offered this little friar vowed to poverty must have taken his breath away. For he wanted to give him a mountain which he owned. Francis must have listened in astonishment as this mountain was described to him. It was Alvernia in the Apennines, close to the Lord Orlando's own castle of Chiusi. It looked down upon the plain of the river Arno, that was ringed about with mountains, and beautiful with its mulberry trees, olives and vines, wheat fields and meadows. The lower slopes of Alvernia were clothed with woods of chestnuts and oaks, and then pine, fir and larch, full of birds. Above the woods were bare rocks with chasms in them. At the summit of this mass of rock was a plateau where once again the woods grew, and the Lord Orlando thought this plateau, from which a man could look out and see half the sunlit hills of Italy, would be a perfect place for prayer and contemplation, and he offered it to Francis for the use of his Order. Francis accepted the gift.

II

He went back to the Portiuncula and sent some of the brothers to Alvernia at once but he did not yet go himself, for he had come to a turning-point in his life and he wanted to be at the Portiuncula to pray about it. His life shows a recurring rhythm of solitary prayer leading up to flashes of light, in which the will of God was made known to him in such a manner that it was as though the sun shone out suddenly from behind a cloud, followed by a period of intense and happy activity: an echo of the mystic's way of purgation and illumination, followed by union and a return to the world to work there for God in power and joy. We see it in his days of solitary prayer in the woods about Santa Maria degli Angeli, followed by that flash of insight when he heard the Gospel for Saint Mathias's day and knew God's will for him and set out instantly and joyously to preach at Assisi. Then again when he climbed up to the solitary place above Poggio-Bustone and was alone there in misery because of his sin, and there came to him the assurance of forgiveness and the vision of the growing company of the knights, and he hurried joyously back to the brothers and led them to Rome. And so it is with him now. He went "into the wood" and stayed there alone with his problem, praying to God for help and guidance.

The failure of his missionary journey, followed by the gift of Alvernia, had made him wonder if God did not want him to continue as a missionary and was calling him to the life of prayer only. He had always believed that contemplative prayer must support the labours of the Order, and now he wondered if it was his part to leave the missionary work to his sons and be their Moses on the mountain, Alvernia his Horeb, his arms held out in supplication for the battle down below. "Lord, what wouldst Thou have me to do?"

As always, he was too humble to think that he alone, by himself, was capable of knowing certainly God's will for him. *The Little Flowers of Saint Francis* says, "He had no opinion of himself or of the virtue of his prayers; and wishing to know the will of God he sought to learn it through the prayers of others." And also it seems probable, when we think how great was the gift of prayer that God had given him, that the life of the contemplative was what he would have chosen for himself if he had not put the will of God before his own, and that hidden longing made the decision harder for him. So he sent for Masseo and told him all his trouble and asked him to go to Clare and to Sylvester and ask them to pray that God would reveal to them His will for His servant. Masseo tramped off, to Clare at San Damiano and to Sylvester who was praying in one of the caves of the Carceri, and then back again to each to know their answer, and Francis waited for him at the Portiuncula. When Masseo returned, tired and hot,

Francis would not ask for the answer until he had looked after him, treating him with all possible honour as the messenger of God. He knelt before him and washed his feet, prepared a meal for him and served it. Only then did they go "into the wood" where Francis kneeled down, put back his hood and crossed his arms upon his breast to hear God's will for him. Clare and Sylvester had both received the same answer to their prayer for guidance. Francis's vocation was to go forth into the world and preach the gospel; for the grace of the vocation was not given to him for himself alone but was for the salvation of souls. If this was not what Francis had secretly wanted it was the will of God, the thing that he adored, and the moment it shone out upon him he was full of joy and cried out gladly, "Let us go forth in the name of God."

He set out at once and his mood of joy is shown in his choice of companions, the cheerful and eloquent Masseo and Angelo, gay and courteous. They tramped away through the woods from the Portiuncula, south-east in the direction of Cannara. It was summer with the sun fierce and wonderful, the harvest fields looking ready to burst into flame, the whole scene vital and strong and gay. From this glowing life in Francis himself and his companions, and in the world about them, there came two sermons so full of power that in their different ways they are as alive today as they were at this joyous time when Francis preached them. His utter delight in doing the will of God got into them and made them deathless.

Francis, Masseo and Angelo could see Cannara as they tramped along for it was only two miles' walk from Assisi. It was a walled city with a gate in the centre of each side and a tower at each corner. On one side its walls were washed by a river and a moat encircled it with drawbridges and gates, and there were trees near. It was set in a country of trees and water, such as birds love, and Francis found its narrow streets hot and stuffy when he came to them, and called to the people who were thronging around him to follow him outside. "Good people, good people, God give thee His peace! Come out to the fields where it is cool under the trees." Where he led he was always followed, above all today when he was so brimming with the joy of doing the will of God, and the whole population of the little town, men and women and children, streamed over the drawbridge after him and out into the fields, and Cannara was left empty like Keats's little town of the peaceful citadel.

Out in the fields Francis preached to the people of the kingdom of God, and he preached with such power and joy that he swept them right off their feet and they all begged to be allowed to join the Order straight away. Francis tackled their enthusiasm with his usual wisdom. What they asked for was impossible. They had their work to do in the world, work that was God's will for them, and he on his side could not go round Italy depopulating all the towns. Yet neither could he discourage their ardour for God's service. He told them to go back to their homes, and love and serve God there, and be patient, and he would think out some way of life for them that should combine deeper devotion and discipline in the service of God, and membership of the Order, and yet not separate them from those duties in the world to which God had called them. And the people of Cannara were content to wait, and their patience, in the fullness of time, became the foundation stone of the Third Order.

When Francis left Cannara he, Angelo and Masseo walked on towards Bevagna until they came to some fields where a multitude of birds had gathered, all very happy because of the harvest fields, the water and the trees. Francis also was happy and the sunlight on the glancing wings of the eager little creatures, their merry chattering voices, caught him up in delight. He loved all the creatures and had the gift of winning their trust and friendship, and today these birds delighting in the bounty of God so touched his heart that he could not pass on and leave them. He said to Masseo and Angelo, "Wait for me here by the way whilst I go and preach to my little sisters the birds," and he went on into one of the fields where the birds were all about him on the ground, and to his delight they were not frightened of him. The ones on the ground stayed where they were, even though his habit touched them as he moved gently among them, talking to them, and when they heard his voice the ones in the trees came flying down and settled themselves around him, and Francis said, "'My little sisters the birds, ye owe much to God, your Creator, and ye ought to sing His praise at all times and in all places, because He has given you liberty to fly about into all places; and though ye neither spin nor sew, He has given you a twofold and a threefold clothing for yourselves and for your offspring. Two of all your species He sent into the ark with Noah that you might not be lost to the world; besides which, he feeds you, though ye neither sow nor reap. He has given you fountains and rivers to quench your thirst, mountains and valleys in which to take refuge, and trees in which to build your nests! so that your Creator loves you much, having thus favoured you with such bounties. Beware, my little sisters, of the sin of ingratitude, and study always to give praise to God.' As he said these words, all the birds began to open their beaks, to stretch their necks, to spread their wings, and reverently to bow their heads to the ground, endeavouring by their motions and by their songs to manifest their joy to Saint Francis. And the Saint rejoiced with them. He wondered to see such a multitude of birds, and was charmed with their beautiful variety, with their attention and familiarity, for all of which he devoutly gave thanks to the Creator. Having finished his sermon, Saint Francis made the sign of the cross, and gave them leave to fly away. Then all those birds rose up into the air, singing most sweetly; and, following the sign of the cross, which Saint Francis had made, they divided themselves into four companies. One company flew towards the east, another towards the west, one towards the south, and one towards the north; each company as it went singing most wonderfully."

Francis stood watching them and he never forgot those cross-shaped wings. When years later upon Alvernia his Lord came to him it was as the crucified Seraph that he saw Him, with wings of power that filled the sky. He went back to Angelo and Masseo awed by what he had seen and aware that he had moved a little nearer to his God. After he had kissed the hand of the leper, and knelt before the crucifix in San Damiano, he had moved forward to a place where he could see Christ in all men, and all men in Christ, and love for men had become sweet and easy to him. Now it was the same with the creatures. He had always loved them for their beauty and endearing ways but now his love had grown so much deeper that later it would be said of him, "Francis beheld in each creature the goodness of God perfectly, and therefore he was moved by a particular and heartfelt delight and love for all creatures."

Francis, Masseo and Angelo tramped on, stopping at the hour of vespers to say their office in the fields, and if Angelo and Masseo were not quite recollected in their responses it was because the words of Francis's sermon still rang in their minds and they still saw his habit brushing gently against the fearless birds. They remembered what they had seen and told of it, and the story of that sermon lived on. It is the best known story in *The Little Flowers of Saint Francis* and is the subject of the most famous of Giotto's frescoes in the church of San Francisco at Assisi. It is a story of power because it was born of the joy that Francis felt in the doing of the will of God.

III

Joy carried Francis through the whole of that triumphant preaching tour. All the way through the valley of Spoleto, and later in the Marches of Ancona, the people flocked to hear him preach to them of the kingdom of God. And so, tired and happy, he came back in the hot late autumn to the Portiuncula, but not to rest there, for he could not forget the infidels whom he had failed to reach. They tugged at his heart and he made a plan to travel through Spain and Morocco and preach to the Moors. He chose a few companions, among them Bernard da Quintavalle, and set out again, walking with such an eager stride that his companions could scarcely keep up with him for "he seemed like one intoxicated in spirit". But the strength of his frail little body was never quite sufficient to support his zeal for God's service, he had spent himself, and when he reached Spain he fell ill and could not go on. As soon as he was strong enough he went home, for he saw in his illness another indication of God's will; the plight of the infidels still tugged at his heart, but the time was not yet.

But Francis never allowed illness to prevent him preaching the Gospel. Perhaps in this illness, perhaps in another attack of fever two years later, he dictated his "Letter to all Christians" which afterwards formed the basis of the Rule of The Third Order. Lying on his straw pallet he had no visible congregation to inspire him but the eyes of his spirit saw the vast concourse of all Christian people, men and women who like himself were trying to follow in the footsteps of Christ, but whose pilgrimage through this world was beset with temptations, with cares and anxieties that were like choking weeds about the flower of their faith. Forgetting the heathen for a while his heart yearned over them. He remembered the lords and ladies riding to the castle of Montefeltro, and the Lord Orlando bowing before him and asking for his help. He remembered the people of Cannara asking if they might join the Order, and the promise he had made them. He remembered Christians living in crowded cities, and he knew how evil pressed upon them, and he remembered the multitudes of the toiling peasants who were often too tired to say their prayers. They wanted help. He called Leo to him, and while he talked to them Leo's accomplished pen sped over the parchment.

The letter opens by saying that Francis, "the servant of all", is sick, and so this letter comes as a messenger in place of his bodily presence. Then it passes on to a remembrance of the poverty of Christ; for that was what they all so desperately needed, that poverty of spirit that would enable them to move with detachment among the luxuries, the anxieties and the evils that beset them. "The Word of the Father, so worthy, so holy, and so glorious. He being rich above all, willed nevertheless, both He and His most blessed Mother, to choose poverty." The letter went on to map out a rule of life. Christians were to remember the glory of the Blessed Sacrament, to repent of their sins, to confess them and to receive God with a pure heart and a chaste body. They were to visit churches frequently and to reverence the clergy, to fast at the appointed times, to be disciplined, self-denying and obedient, observant of the counsels and precepts of Christ. They were to love God, to praise Him and pray to Him both day and night, to love their neighbour as themselves, to be merciful and humble servants of all, and they were to be generous and to give alms because alms "washed the soul from the foulness of sin". Towards the end of the letter comes a great cry of delight that Christians should have such a Father, such a Brother as our Lord Jesus Christ. "O how glorious and holy and great it is to have such a Father in heaven! . . . O how holy and how beloved, pleasing and humble, peaceful and sweet and lovable and above all things desirable, to have such a Brother Who laid down His life for His sheep and prayed for us to the Father saying: Holy Father, keep them in Thy name, whom Thou hast given Me." The letter ends with a blessing. "And all, both men and women, who shall receive these things kindly and understand and send them to others for an example, if they persevere in them until the end, may the Father the Son and the Holy Ghost bless them. Amen."

A few years after the sermon at Cannara the Third Order was in existence, based upon this letter, but with more specific rules added to its broad outline of Christian living. It was open to all Christians, men and women, married or single, and its aim was to enable them to approximate their lives as closely as possible to that of the brothers and sisters of the First and Second Orders, while remaining in the world and carrying out there the secular duties to which they believed God had called them. Noblemen such as the Lord Orlando, who was one of the first whom Francis admitted to the Order, did not renounce their hereditary duties, they continued to administer their estates as before, but they did their work looking to God, regarding even the smallest duties as having their place in God's pattern, and when the needs of those dependent on them had been met they gave all their surplus money to the poor. It was the same with the merchants, who pledged themselves to carry on their businesses with strict integrity, renouncing all money which had been dishonestly earned in the past and keeping for themselves in the future nothing that was not needed for their sustenance. They dressed austerely and ate sparingly, holding themselves aloof from the luxury that was one of the evils of that as of any age. The men did not carry arms, they were pledged to peace, and they were absolved by the Pope from taking the legal oaths which bound men to fight for their party whether the cause was just or unjust. They became a great power for peace in the quarrelsome Italian republics and, as their numbers grew, in Europe also. But there was nothing negative about them, or they could not have called themselves Franciscans. They lived their lives joyously, in no spirit of condemnation, and they did not think they had done their duty to the poor merely by almsgiving, they loved and served them, bringing them into their houses and caring for them when they were sick and spending themselves for them in every way they knew.

The Third Order, called the Order of Penitence, increased as rapidly as the First and Second, working always for peace, justice, honesty and love. It lived on through the generations, a spiritual power the strength of which it is not possible to estimate, and lives still, and has numbered among its penitents some of the greatest servants of God that the world has known, kings and queens, poets and artists, men and women whose names ring like music in our ears today, such names as Christopher Columbus, Saint Louis of France, Elizabeth of Hungary, Angela of Foligno, Petrarch, Roger Bacon, Duns Scotus. Another penitent was Giotto, who painted the frescoes in the church of San Francesco at Assisi. It is probable that he came to Assisi as a pupil of Cimabue, whose paintings also glorify San Francesco, and whose portrait of Francis in the lower church shows us the little man with the humorous suffering face that our own imagination has pictured for us. After the death of Francis the brothers of the Order would often present dramatized scenes from the saint's life in their convents and churches, and the famous frescoes suggest that Giotto had seen some of these dramatic performances at Assisi, for there is much about them that suggests the medieval stage. They are fresh, dramatic and lovely, with a naturalness about them that was something new in the stylized art of Italy and was the direct outcome of the simplicity and naturalness of Francis himself.

Two great poets wore the habit of the Third Order, Jacopone da Todi and Dante Alighieri. Francis inspired not only a new school of painting but a new era in poetry. His *Canticle of the Sun* was the inspiration for Jacopone's verse and of that of the Italian poets, including Dante, who followed him. Jacopone was born in the strange old town of Todi probably in 1230, four years after the death of Francis, a man of wealth and ambition who found no place for God in his life until in middle age he passed through a time of such suffering and stress that the proud structure of his life collapsed beneath him and he became for a short while almost insane. Then from the ruins of it all God took him to Himself, leading him to find shelter with the Franciscan family, first in the Third Order and later in the First, and to become the greatest poet of his age, expressing the Franciscan spirit in his verse as perfectly as Giotto in his paintings. Like Francis himself he was aflame with the love of God. It has been said of his poem *Amor de Caritate* that it is the counterpart of Francis's mystic crucifixion, an expression in words, as that in flesh, of the miracle of the union of the soul with God. Saint Bernadine of Siena believed that Francis himself, not Jacopone, had written it. The influence of Francis upon Dante was lifelong. He was educated at the school of the Franciscan Friars at Santa Croce and buried in the habit of the Third Order by the monks of Ravenna. A story told of him says that at a time of suffering in his life he came one night to a lonely convent in the Apennines and knocked at the door. The brother who opened to him saw a stooped and grey-haired man standing in the shadows and asked him what he wanted, and Dante answered, "Peace!"

These great names of kings and queens and poets lend lustre to the Third Order, but there were thousands of humble men and women whose unseen and selfless lives were its bones and its strength. One of these was named Lucchesio. He was a native of Tuscany and lived at Poggibonsi, not far from Siena. He had been a rich merchant but when he joined the Third Order he gave all his superfluous wealth to the poor, keeping nothing for himself but his house, his garden and his donkey. He had a beautiful wife whom he dearly loved, Bona Donna, who was with him heart and soul in all that he did for the love of God. Together they kept their house as a hospital for the poor, cultivating their garden that they might grow food for them. All who came to them were made welcome and tenderly nursed and cared for, and not content with this Lucchesio would ride out to the fever-stricken Maremma and seek out the sick there and take care of them. Sometimes he would bring them home with him, and Bona Donna would see him approaching the house with one sick man on his back and another on the donkey. For many years these two toiled together for Christ, and then Bona Donna fell sick, and when Lucchesio saw that she was dying his grief was too great to be borne. Perhaps like so many husbands and wives they had often said to each other, "We will go together," and that while he knelt by Bona Donna's bedside, as she received the last sacraments, Lucchesio prayed that it might be so, and received the assurance that his prayer was answered, for he whispered to Bona Donna, "Wait for me," and calling back the priest he asked that he too might receive the last sacraments. Then he held his wife's hand and comforted her through her last agony, and when it was over he made the sign of the cross over her and lay down beside her, calling with love upon Jesus, Mary and Francis, and so followed her.

It is fitting that among all the unknown stories of the knights of the Third Order this one should have been handed down to us, for in their love for God, for His poor and for each other these two were typical of the chivalry.

PART THREE

THE KINGDOM

Chapter One

THE RICH

O Love, Thou fire divine, of laughter spun;
   Love that art smile and jest,
   Thou giv'st us of Thy best,
Thy wealth unmeasured that is never done.

Love, that art bountiful and courteous,
   Great gifts Thou dost divide,
   Thy table's long and wide:
How welcome is Thy servant in Thy house!
              Jacopone da Todi, *Lauda* LXXXI

I

FRANCIS would have trembled in horror and dismay if anyone had suggested to him that he moved through his life on earth as a prince among men. Yet it is true. The values of the kingdom of heaven are a complete reversal of those of the world, yet the kingdom is a mighty one and it has its princes. The spiritual ascendancy over the souls of men that is possessed by a man who is both holy and humble is one of the most satisfying of historical facts. Saint Bernard of Clairvaux striding from one end of Europe to the other in his tattered habit, fierce and lean, pouring out the vials of his anger upon wicked kings and erring popes, launching a crusade by the sheer glory of his eloquence, could not have been unaware of the power he wielded, though he ascribed all things to God alone, but Francis dominated rich and poor alike without having any idea of what he was doing. The little friar in company with the great men of his time is a fascinating spectacle. He moves amongst them quietly and humbly, a small lark among the peacocks, and most of us know about them only in so far as they were dominated by his loving humility.

In the year 1215, soon after Francis had been turned back by illness from his second attempt to reach the infidels, he travelled to Rome. Pope Innocent III had summoned a General Council and Francis as the founder of a religious order was commanded to be present. All the leaders of Christendom were there, representatives of kings and princes, heads of religious houses and universities, cardinals, bishops and archbishops. In all their glory and magnificence they thronged into the church of Saint John Lateran upon Saint Martin's Day, to hear the Pope's inaugural sermon, and with them went the barefoot man in the grey habit whom Innocent in his dream had seen holding up this same church upon his frail shoulders. The Pope's dream had not shown him the tottering Saint John Lateran filled with this congregation of the princes of the world and of the Church, but they had been there all the same. Francis upheld them now as he sat unnoticed in the most obscure corner he could find and prayed for them all, and for the Pope. There is no doubt that he knew, in the hushed moment when Innocent mounted the pulpit steps and stood and looked out over the congregation, that the great Pope was a dying man. Francis always knew these things about people and he would have prayed with all his loving selflessness for Innocent the man, now while despite his illness he must preach this sermon, in the weeks of suffering to come and in the agony of death.

The Pope knew he was dying and it was because he knew it that he had brought this great congregation here before him. Time was short and he had much that he wanted to say to them while he could. He took as his text the words of the dying Christ to His disciples, "With desire I have desired to eat this Passover with you before I suffer," and then with passion and power he spoke to them of his two great longings; that before he died he might see a great crusade rescue the holy places from the infidels, and that he might see a purified Church lead a Christendom that had sinned back to God in penitence and peace. He wished that he might see these things, but if it was not God's will for him, "not my will, but God's, be done."

He spoke powerfully to every man in the great congregation but perhaps to none more directly than to Francis, whose soul he set on fire with one of those moments of illumination that with

him were always the precursor of heroic action. He felt about the
crusades very much, but not quite, as did all Christian men of the
Middle Ages. Theirs was an age of faith, and the Church was
supremely important to them. Within her they found salvation
for their souls, and by her were the ignorant taught, the poor fed
and the sick cared for. She alone could control the greed of
princes and beyond her walls was only darkness and confusion.
She was the spiritual fortress of Christendom and the shrine
of the fortress was the land where Christ had lived, above all the
city that had seen His death and resurrection. Jerusalem, the holy
of holies, was held in the heart of every Christian man and woman
and the thought of its desecration by the infidels was something
that could hardly be borne, especially just at this time, when they
were still grieving over the loss of the Christian kingdom of
Jerusalem, brought to an end by Saladin only twenty-eight years
ago. For eighty-eight years the Christians had controlled the
holy places of Jerusalem and now they had been taken from
them. Richard Coeur de Lion had fought to get them back again
but his crusade had failed. All Christian men felt that it must be a
personal grief to Christ that the infidels held His earthly home.
But Francis felt something more than this, something peculiar to
himself, love for the infidels themselves. Where other Christian
men longed to rescue the holy places from the infidels, Francis
wanted to rescue the infidels for the holy places. Twice already
he had tried to reach them and had failed. Listening to the Pope's
sermon he was on fire to try again. When it was God's will he
would be a crusader. He had to wait five years before he had his
wish but he was always a man who knew how to wait.

He was no less stirred by the Pope's second appeal, the cleansing
of Christendom through the power of a penitent Church, for
"Repent ye!" was his own cry and the mission of his life. The
Pope based this part of his discourse upon the ninth chapter of
Ezekiel, where chosen men are called of God to go through the
city and cleanse it, and to their leader, God says, "Go through the
midst of the city, through the midst of Jerusalem, and set a mark
upon the foreheads of the men that sigh and that cry for all the
abominations that be done in the midst thereof." The sign that

was to be put upon the foreheads of the penitents was the sign Tau, the headless cross of the Old Testament that the Hebrew people put on their doors to save their firstborn in Egypt, the last letter of the Hebrew alphabet, the old form of which was a cross. According to tradition it was upon a Tau cross that Saint Matthew was crucified in Ethiopia. The sign Tau was thus the symbol of penitence, salvation and suffering, and to Francis with his love of symbolism it became very precious upon this Saint Martin's day and ever afterwards. From the hour of the Pope's sermon he took it as the symbol of the vocation of the Brothers Minor. With it he signed his dwelling-places, as the Hebrew people had done, and his letters too. Pacifico the visionary, in a dream that he had soon after this, saw it emblazoned in light upon Francis's forehead.

The crusade, when it came, failed, and the attempt to root out avarice from the Roman court also failed, but the subsequent adoption of the penitential brotherhoods into the organized system of the Church saved Christendom, and the two men who were to be the spearhead of the work of purgation for which the Pope pleaded were among his congregation; Francis of Assisi and Dominic Guzman, afterwards known to all the world as Saint Dominic.

This great man had come to the General Council to ask the Pope for permission to found a new Order of preachers. He too, obscure and unknown, had sat quietly in the church of Saint John Lateran and heard the sermon that had so stirred Francis. As Innocent made his great appeal for the cleansing of the Church he would have been equally stirred, for to this end had God called him. These two men in their shabby clothes, scarcely noticeable in the brilliant congregation, were destined to go down to posterity with their names linked together. They were utterly unlike but in the work that they were called to do they were complementary to each other. Francis and his Order were everywhere calling men to repent of their sins, and to follow in the footsteps of Christ in love and humility. Dominic wanted to found an Order of preachers who by defending the faith of Christ against the attacks of the heretics should cleanse the Church of heresy. The appeal of Francis was to the hearts of men, Dominic desired to cleanse their minds. He was at this time forty-five years old and had from his boyhood been stern and ascetic, a scholar and a preacher of sermons utterly different from those of Francis; reasoned, intellectual, hard-hitting expositions of the truth. Yet he had some Franciscan qualities. He was a man of peace and believed that the best way to stamp out heresy was to convince men's minds. And like Francis he was equally sure that men can be convinced of nothing unless the words of the man who reasons with them are the fruit of a dedicated life. The Order he desired to found would make war upon heresy with learning and holiness. And he loved the poor. Once during a famine he had sold his precious books to feed them.

And so it is not surprising that when a few days later these two met in the streets of Rome Dominic fell instantly under the spell of Francis, who embodied in his simple humble being the holiness, peace and love that Dominic adored. And he had had a dream the previous night. He had seen himself and a man he did not know presented by the Blessed Virgin to Christ, as God's messengers to the world. The man was Francis. Men were less inhibited in those days. They were not afraid to love each other at sight or to express their love. Dominic embraced Francis and said, "Let us stand together and no enemy shall overcome us."

In the following July Innocent III died at Perugia, and among the men who knelt by his bed was Francis. In his last agony most of those about him fled in terror, but Francis knelt on until the end. Did the great Pope see him there? If he did the last words that framed themselves in his conscious mind would have been the prayer of Francis, "The Lord give thee peace."

After the Pope had died disaster befell his body, a disaster that is somehow typical of the grim and terrible Perugia. For a short while the dead man was left unguarded in the night, and during that eerie time of darkness thieves crept into the death chamber and stripped the corpse of all its jewels. Francis, if he heard of it, was probably less distressed than many others.

The first of the Cardinals to fall under the spell of Francis had been the saintly Cardinal John of Saint Paul, who had befriended him when he had first sought audience of the Pope, but about this time he also died, and Francis must have mourned for him. Then he made another powerful friend, one whom he kept until the end of his life, Cardinal Ugolino, Bishop of Ostia, a relative of Innocent III. They met at Florence, when the Cardinal was sixty years of age and Francis was thirty-five. No two friends could ever have been a greater contrast to each other. The Cardinal, though old enough to be Francis's father, had far greater bodily vigour and comeliness. He was handsome, tall and strong, fluent and gracious, an able man of affairs and a scholar. Yet these two quickly learned to love each other. Cardinal Ugolino, like Cardinal Saint Paul, was an ascetic at heart and singleminded in his devotion to the Church. Even before he had met Francis he had reverenced the Brothers Minor and seen in them men marked with the Tau. And he was by temperament protective and affectionate so that the simplicity and frailty of Francis made an instant appeal to his good heart. Francis on his side saw in this disciplined, strong, warm-hearted man what he just now exceedingly longed for; a wise friend to give him strength and counsel in all the difficulties that beset him. For the Order was growing very fast. The first small company of the knights was now an army and as his sons multiplied so did his problems. Increasingly he turned to Cardinal Ugolino for advice.

The Cardinal, Dominic and Francis drew now into close friendship with each other. The Cardinal carried always in his heart the dying appeal of his kinsman Pope Innocent III, for the cleansing of the world through the purification of the Church, and he looked to Francis and Dominic for help. Dominic's appeal to Pope Innocent, made at the General Council, had been granted, and he had founded his Order of preaching friars. Cardinal Ugolino asked Francis and Dominic to come to him in Rome and opened his heart to them; he wanted to take bishops from the ranks of the two Orders for he thought that there was no better way of fostering holiness in the Church than through the leaven of Franciscan and Dominican bishops. But Francis and Dominic could not agree. They both believed that high office of any sort was contrary to the spirit of their Orders, that had been called by God to humility, and that only in obeying the will of God could they be of any service to the Church. They did not convince the Cardinal that they were right but as he could not convince them that he was right he had to yield for the moment and let them go.

They went out into the street together, and Dominic turned round impulsively and caught Francis's hands. The two men were so at one in their love of God and adoration of His holy will that Dominic had longed that their Orders should be one also. But Francis had known that this was not possible. The Dominicans were called to be scholars and in the intellectual sphere fighting men. In years to come they would be called "the dogs of God", so fiercely did they get on the scent of heresy and track it down. The Franciscans were called to poverty and in the thought of Francis a truly poor man must not possess the books that are essential to scholarship, nor the hunting instinct that is necessary even on an intellectual warpath. A lover of the Lady Poverty must be lowly in mind as well as station, gentle, peaceable, persuasive. And so he had said no, but with sadness that he must disappoint his friend. Now Dominic cried out again that he wished they could be united, but Francis shook his head. It was not good-bye between them but it was good-bye to the deeper intimacy that the union of their Orders would have brought, and Dominic felt something of the bitterness of parting. He begged that Francis would give him the cord that he wore around his waist. Francis hesitated, for he was scared by the reverence in the older man's voice. Then he unfastened the cord and gave it to him and until the end of his life Dominic wore the Franciscan cord under his Dominican habit.

The friendship between these two men, and between their Orders, is one of the great friendships of history. An artist and a poet have immortalized it. Andrea della Robia has portrayed the good-bye in the street. He shows the two saints standing facing each other, hands clasped, knowing that they must go their different ways but finding the parting intolerably hard. In the *Divine Comedy*, Dante writes of them together again in the glory of heaven. Dante and Beatrice, having ascended into the sun which is the fourth heaven, find themselves surrounded by a wreath of blessed spirits, the fourth family of God, whose glory passes description. Among them are Francis and Dominic, the two ordained of God to save the Church in her hour of need, so united that

> "he tells of both,
> Who one commendeth, which of them soe'er
> Be taken: for their deeds were to one end."

From within the glory their story is told by two of their sons, who share their joy, but such is the courtesy of heaven that it is Saint Thomas Aquinas the Dominican who sings the praises of Francis and his Order, and Saint Bonaventure the Franciscan who extols Dominic,

> "The loving minion of the Christian faith,
> The hallowed wrestler, gentle to his own,
> And to his enemies terrible . . .
> And I speak of him, as the labourer,
> Whom Christ in His own garden chose to be
> His helpmate."

And so the great circle of adoring saints, the helpmates of Christ, wheels about the sun,

> "Voice answering voice, so musical and soft,
> It can be known but where day endless shines."

Disappointed for the time being of his Franciscan and Dominican bishops, the Cardinal still believed it was the friars of the two Orders who would call the Church from worldliness to holiness, and believing this he wanted to make Francis known to the new Pope, Honorius. He thought it would be an excellent idea if Francis were to preach before Honorius and the Papal court, and Francis humbly consented.

But as the day fixed for the sermon drew near Ugolino was seized with panic. What would happen? Francis was, to say the least of it, unconventional, and men who yield every moment of their lives to the guidance of the Holy Spirit do sometimes behave in an unexpected manner. The Cardinal feared it would not be easy to contain Francis within the narrow path of custom and convention, and if he was not so contained what sort of impression would he make on the new Pope? Consumed with anxiety the Cardinal did his best. He suggested to Francis that it might be as well to think his sermon out very carefully beforehand, write it down and commit it to memory. Francis, who had hitherto prepared himself for preaching by hours of prayer and adoration, and then trusted to the Holy Spirit for guidance, humbly promised to do what the Cardinal wanted. He thought out his sermon, wrote it down and memorized it, but trusting to his own powers instead of in the Holy Spirit was not natural to him, and he was not happy.

As the appointed hour drew on the Cardinal was not happy either. Celano says, "The Venerable Lord Bishop of Ostia was in an agony of suspense, praying to God with all his might that the simplicity of the blessed man might not be despised ... trusting in the mercy of the Almighty, which never fails in time of need those who piously wait upon it."

Zero hour came and Francis, barefoot and shabby, stood before Honorius and his cardinals in all their magnificence, as once he had stood before Innocent and his cardinals. But then he had been confident and happy and had spoken out bravely, and now he was white and strained and the words would not come. Cardinal Ugolino redoubled his efforts, praying with yet greater urgency, but still nothing happened for Francis had forgotten every word of the carefully memorized sermon. The silence lengthened unbearably, and then, slowly, the strain began to grow less. Perhaps Pope Honorius had also begun to pray for Francis, for he was an old and holy man, "very simple and of much good will", a man so well able to understand Francis that it is surprising that Cardinal Ugolino should have worried so much about this meeting. He prayed, perhaps, and over the darkness that had fallen upon Francis there came the movement of the Holy Spirit. A little colour came into his face and his eyes began to glow as he remembered the God of love Whose servant he was. Racking his brains to try and remember his sermon he had forgotten God.

Now, the sermon forgotten, he remembered Him, and the remembrance filled him with joy and power. He began to speak of the love of God. He had said once to his friars, "So very high and very precious is the love of God that it should never be named save seldom and in great necessity, and with much reverence," but now he was so lifted out of himself with joy that the words poured from him with the passionate eagerness of a lark singing. Even his feet took wings and began to dance beneath him. To the old Pope it was as though fingers plucked at his heart strings and tears began to trickle down his cheeks, and several of his cardinals wept with him. They wept for the days when they had said with Saint Augustine, "He looked through the lattice of our flesh, and He spoke us fair, yea, He set us on fire, and we hasten on His scent." The years had hardened them, and they had lost their first fervour, but now through Francis they were captured again for Christ.

II

It was not only the princes of the Church who fell under the spell of Francis, men and women of the world, the nobility of Rome and their ladies, revered him too. The Lady Giacoma di Settesoli was one of Francis's greatest friends. Clare the contemplative and the practical, delightful Giacoma are the Mary and Martha of the story and they came into it at much the same time, for the year when Clare joined the Order was the year when Francis first met Giacoma in Rome. She was twenty-five years old then, and she came to him because she was in sorrow and perplexity. Her husband, Gratiano Frangipani, had just died leaving her with two small sons to bring up, and great wealth and large estates to administer, and though she was a woman of strong character she was in these first days of her grief and loneliness appalled by the prospect. Francis was able to comfort and strengthen her and she made a threefold resolve; to dedicate her life to the upbringing of her sons, the service of the poor and the worship of God, and splendidly, until the end of her life, she kept her vow.

When the Third Order came into being Giacoma joined it. She continued to administer her estates as before, and to bring up her sons to play the great part in the world that was waiting for them, but her own life became increasingly simple, humble and devout, and her house in Rome was always open to the poor and the suffering and all who needed her care. Francis delighted to visit her there. We picture her as capable, hospitable and vigorous. Francis called her Brother Giacoma because of her almost masculine strength of character, and mother of sons that she was she was evidently one of those women with whom men feel entirely at their ease, her motherliness laced with a certain astringency, a very great lady with the naturalness and selfless courtesy of all such great ladies. She seems to have been a good cook, for she used to make for Francis an almond sweet-cake that is still called after her, and it speaks volumes for her tact and diplomacy that she could actually induce him to enjoy good food.

Her sense of humour seems to have been equal to the demands he made upon her, even when he presented her with a lamb for a pet. It was his habit to buy lambs destined for the slaughterhouse, the purchase money generally being a cloak given him for his own use, though always on the understanding that he was not likely to keep it for long, and a blessing for the shepherd. That a creature symbolic of the sacrifice of Christ should be slain for food was intolerable to him, but it was a little difficult to know what to do with the lambs afterwards, especially as they grew rather quickly into sheep. One lamb Francis kept with him at the Portiuncula, and trained it to go into church with the friars. He told it to be "instant in the divine praises and avoid any occasion of offence to the brethren". When it heard the brothers chanting it would "bend the knee, bleating before the altar of the Virgin Mother of the Lamb, as though it would feign greet her". Another he gave to a community of nuns and a third was presented to Brother Giacoma. She trained it so well that if she overslept in the morning, and was in danger of being late for mass, it would butt at her and wake her up, and when she was dressed it would run along to church at her heels. As it grew older she turned it to practical use by shearing off its wool and spinning and weaving it into cloth. It was a habit made from the wool of this lamb that was Francis's shroud when he lay in state upon his bier.

After his death Giacoma left her Roman home and lived out the rest of her long life at Assisi, hospitable until the end, her house a meeting place for all the faithful friends of Francis. It was she who closed the eyes of Leo when he died. She was buried in the church of San Francesco at Assisi and her inscription reads, "Here Giacoma rests, a holy and noble Roman."

III

It has been said that the closer a man comes to God the more does he become himself. Absorption in the world can blunt a man, rub away the clear outline of his personality, but absorption in God makes him more of an individual. Pebbles lying in clear running water take on an astonishing beauty and shine like separate many-coloured jewels. Taken out of their element they look dull and much like each other and are not found again until they are put back where they belong. Francis, absorbed in Christ, was so strikingly individual that he has never been forgotten. From the final union with his Lord on Monte Alvernia he returned more himself than he had ever been. He took no colour from the world. In Rome he did not do as the Romans did. The most beautiful of all the stories told of him shows him being himself at a Roman dinner party.

His host was Cardinal Ugolino, in whose palazzo he was staying. Many knights and nobles were to dine with the Cardinal that night and Francis, as the hour of the feast drew on, saw the preparations that were being made. In the kitchen the cooks and scullions were sweating and toiling, preparing the food that they would not eat themselves, and in the banqueting hall other servants were setting the long carved table with the gold and silver dishes, bringing in the platters of wheaten bread, the flagons of wine and dishes of fruit and sweetmeats. Enough food was being prepared to save an army of poor men from starvation, and the light wines and the fresh fruit would have slaked the feverish thirst of many a leper. Francis remembered his brothers. Some had been toiling all day at hard tasks, to be rewarded at the end of the day, if they were lucky, with a handful of dried beans and a bit of rye bread. Others had been unlucky and tired out though they were had had to take their bowl and beg a few scraps from door to door, or else go hungry to bed. He did not need to remember, because he never for one moment forgot, the Son of God who had not where to lay His head, and he went secretly, none seeing him, out of the palazzo and away into the streets of Rome.

When the guests assembled he was not there and they had to go in to dinner without him, and the seat of honour next to Cardinal Ugolino, that had been reserved for him, was left empty. The distinguished guests, prelates, knights and nobles, took their places and presently the luxurious and beautiful entertainment was in full swing. The lights gleamed on the arras and on the splendid garments of the guests, the wine was poured out and the polite hum of conversation rose and fell. They did not see Francis when he first came in, moving soundlessly on bare feet, scarcely more substantial than a shadow in his grey habit. He went to the place prepared for him and sat down quietly, placing on the table before him what he had brought with him. He had been to the table of the Lord. He had been begging for scraps at the back doors of Rome, and it was these poor broken bits of food that lay now on the Cardinal's table. Silence fell, and the Cardinal was ashamed. Francis, unselfconscious and unaware of any awkwardness in the situation, ate a little of the food that was to him a sacrament of the bounty of God, and then, the old chronicler tells us, "he took of his alms and sent a little to each of the knights and chaplains of my Lord Cardinal on behalf of the Lord God", and one can imagine the exquisite gentleness and courtesy with which he did it. There was no more awkwardness. Deeply moved, each man took his scrap of food, the gift of God, with reverence. Some ate it but others put it by to keep in memory of Francis.

When the guests had gone the Cardinal took Francis into his own room and embraced him, but his hospitable heart was still grieved and he said to him, "Why, my most simple brother, hast thou done me this shame today, that coming to my house, which is the home of thy brethren, thou shouldst go begging alms?"

And Francis explained that he had done it for his brethren's sake, that he might set them an example of the humility and poverty to which he and they were vowed. And he said also that he had begged alms "in honour of Him who when He was Lord of all wished for our sakes to become servant of all, and when He was rich and glorious in His majesty became poor and despised in our humility."

And the Cardinal said, "My son, do that which is good in thine eyes, since God is with thee, and thou with Him."

Chapter Two

THE POOR

In a narrow heart God cannot bide;
Where the love is great, the heart is wide;
Poverty, great-hearted, dignified,
Entertains and welcomes Deity.

Poverty has nothing in her hand,
Nothing craves, in sea, or sky, or land:
Hath the Universe at her command!
Dwelling in the heart of Liberty.

Jacopone da Todi, Lauda LX

I

THOUGH Francis was at ease among the rich he was at home among the poor. He bore proudly, and will bear for all time, the title of El Poverello, the poor man. He had built up his own life, and the life of his Order, upon the foundation stone of poverty. His home was the homelessness of the Lady Poverty and his riches her dereliction. It is hard to grasp the passion of his dedication to poverty. It was as deep and strong as his dedication to Christ because in his thought they were never separated. It was Christ in the dereliction of the cross Who had taken possession of him in the church of San Damiano, the life of Christ that he shared in his poverty and Christ Himself Whom he served in His poor. And so he was determined that there must be no man anywhere who was poorer than he. If he was tramping along the road in the pouring rain, with perhaps a sack that someone had given him around his shoulders as an added protection, and saw a beggar coming along with nothing but his rags, that sack immediately came off him and was given to the beggar, for he said, "I think the great Almsgiver would account it a theft in me did I not give that I wear unto one needing it more." When he met poor folk

M

carrying burdens he would immediately take them on his own shoulders, though there can have been few of them who were not far more able to carry a heavy weight than he was. He was never known to refuse a beggar. When he was on the road and had nothing whatever to give, not even an old sack, he would tear off a bit of his worn habit and give that rather than say no, and these scraps of his garments were inestimable treasures to those who possessed them. They believed that through them healing came to their sick bodies; certainly healing came to their sick souls through knowing that there was a man in the world ready to pour out his very life for them, and feeling through that knowledge to a dim realization that that was what God had done.

Francis never stopped to inquire into the worthiness or other-wise of the poor for whom he spent himself, for only those who have some opinion of their own worthiness do that, and Francis had no opinion whatever of his. Once when he and Masseo were travelling home together from a preaching tour Masseo, teasing him, said, "Why after you? Why after you? You are not fair to look upon; you are not a man of parts; you are not of noble birth; why, pray, does all the world run after you?"

There is no doubt that Masseo knew the answer to his question perfectly well, or the Gospel phrase, "the world is gone after Him", would not have been ringing in his head, but he wanted to know how Francis himself accounted for his power over men. Was he aware of his own Christlike holiness?

"Would you know why?" answered Francis. "Because in all the world God has not been able to perceive a viler creature, and so He has chosen me to confound the nobility, the might, and the wisdom of the world, that people may know that all things come from Him, and not from the creature."

This was his honest belief, as it is of all saints, for the nearer a man comes to the terrible holiness of God the more fearful does his own sin seem in his eyes. And so Francis felt himself one with all sinners in his sin, as he was one with all poor men in his poverty, and like Christ he had a special love for those who were lost, the outcasts of society who with all their crimes are nearer to sainthood than the self-satisfied and the hypocrites. When he came to die he asked that he might be buried on the *collis infernus*, the hill outside Assisi where criminals were executed, that he might be one with them in his death, and it is there that the great church was built that holds his bones today.

He knew exactly how to win these outcasts. In the woods near one of the convents of the Order lived a gang of desperate men, who kept themselves alive by robbery and murder. Three of them, finding themselves hungry one day, presented themselves at the convent and demanded food. The brother in charge, though he was likely to be murdered for his plain speaking, confronted them with great courage and told them what he thought of them. What right had they, robbers and murderers, to come to a convent demanding food which had been given in charity to the servants of God? "You are not worthy of the earth which bears you," he said, "for you neither respect man nor the Lord who made you. Go about your business, and do not appear here again." A bully, withstood with pluck, often crumbles, and the thieves did not use their daggers, though they went away in great anger.

A little later Francis arrived, bringing with him a sack of bread and a little vessel of wine that had been given to him, and the brother, feeling a little pleased with himself, told him what had happened. But he was not commended, for this was one of those occasions when the fierce streak in Francis suddenly showed itself, and he lashed out at the brother as he had lashed out at Ruffino when he had failed in obedience. For this brother too had been disobedient. He was vowed to the service of Christ in His poor, and he had turned three hungry men from the door, men for whom Christ had died. The brother had perhaps enjoyed telling the robbers what he thought of them, but now he had to have a taste of his own medicine and stand humbly and patiently while Francis, at length, gave him his candid opinion of his behaviour and told him what he was to do to retrieve it. He must take the bread and wine and go, alone, through the woods and mountain passes until he found the robbers, and then he was to kneel before them and humbly confess his fault. He was to tell them that Brother Francis had sent them the bread and wine and begged them not to do evil any more, but to fear God and never again offend Him. And he was to say that if they would promise this Francis on his side promised to look after them and see that they never wanted food and drink.

These sons of Francis, though they might fail in obedience now and then, always retrieved their failure with startling courage. The brother did exactly as he was told, as Ruffino had done, though he must have been convinced that he went to certain death, and while he went on his lonely dangerous way Francis within the convent gave himself to prayer. It was for the robbers that he prayed, asking God to touch their hearts and bring them to repentance. The story as told in *The Little Flowers of Saint Francis* does not say that he prayed for the safety of the brother. Dearly though he loved them he never seems to have been concerned for the physical safety of his sons. The exaggerated importance which we in our day attach to the safety, comfort and pleasure of the body was something that he would not have understood. To him the body was only the cell of the soul. It was far more terrible to him that his son should have endangered his immortal soul by his harshness to three poor men than that he should die at their hands. But he understood, none better, the misery and clamour of a starving body, and he knew how often the crimes of poor men are rooted in that alone, and so, to win these men to God, he sent them food and offered them security.

And his wisdom won them. As they ate the bread and drank the wine, offered so humbly on his knees by the young friar who put his life into their hands with the gift he brought them, brokenly begging them to forgive him for his harshness, the same thing happened to them as had happened to the thief on the cross. They saw what they were beside the other. That this man should be kneeling before them in penitence for so small a fault made their own crimes seem suddenly hideous in their eyes. They said to each other, "For all these cruel deeds we feel no remorse of conscience, and no fear of God! And behold this holy friar who is come to us, for a few unkind words, which we merited most justly, has humbly confessed that he was wrong, and has brought us likewise bread and wine, with a most gracious promise from the holy Saint Francis. These men indeed are holy religious of God who merit His paradise, and we are sons of perdition worthy of the pains of hell. Let us go to Saint Francis; and if he gives us a hope that our sins may find mercy in the sight of God, we will do what he shall command to save our souls from the punishment of hell."

And so the young brother brought them to the convent and they came in to Francis in fear and trembling. "Father," they said, "because of the multitude of our sins we dare not look for mercy from God; but if thou hast a hope that He may have pity on us, we are ready to do what thou shalt order, and do penance for our sins with thee." Francis comforted them, telling them that the mercy of God is boundless. And so they trusted themselves to God's mercy and a little while later Francis, without the slightest hesitation, received three murderers into the Order.

II

As Francis grew progressively further from himself and nearer to God he saw men more and more as God sees them, with deep pity for their sin and profound and cherishing love for all that was good in them. There was no intolerance in him. He could be angry but he was never critical and never sarcastic. It was in no critical spirit that he had brought food from the table of the Lord to Cardinal Ugolino's dinner party, but in a spirit of pure love, and it was as a gift of love that the guests had received what he gave. For the rich and the poor alike seemed to understand him almost as well as he understood them. The saints are simple people. It is the condition of divided allegiance, doubt and compromise and the twists and turns of self-deception, that is complicated, not holiness. Francis had attained to what T. S. Eliot calls, "a condition of complete simplicity costing not less than everything," and everyone was entirely at home with him. And so it was no wonder they gave him such a tremendous welcome wherever he went, ringing the church bells, flocking out from town or village to meet him with palm branches in their hands, their priest leading them, the children crying, "*Ecco il santo! Ecco il santo!*" When

he had preached to them they would press about him, trying to
kiss or touch his habit, and they would bring their sick to him to
heal.

He was not eager to heal, though he had the charismatic gift in
high degree. He did not refuse, for healing the sick was a part of
his apostolic obedience, but he would draw back from healing if
he could do so without harshness. Like Bernard when he fled
from the reverence of the people of Bologna he was terrified for
his humility. The charismatic gift is a spectacular one and he
knew well that those who possess it must be always on their guard
against spiritual pride. The men of those days adored a miracle
worker but Francis would never work a miracle just to make them
listen to him, indeed he would do all he could to distract their
attention from any power of his that was at all unusual. Once
when he was preaching a wild young donkey came into the
market-place where he stood with the people about him and began
running around and frightening them. "Brother donkey," said
Francis, "stand quiet and let me preach to the people," and
brother donkey immediately stood still, put his head between his
legs and was silent. "And blessed Francis, in order that men
might not take notice of a miracle so stupendous, began to say
comic things to make them laugh."

And no doubt he healed as well as preached with gaiety, for he
never did anything in a spirit of solemnity but always with that
joyous courage that is in itself a healing gift, so infectious is it
when we meet it in the saints. It was said of him that it was not
possible for anyone "to be in such trouble of mind that all the
clouds would not depart and the sky be clear again at his bright
words". There are many stories of his healing and they include
the casting out of evil spirits and the raising of the dead. One of
the most delightful is that of an old woman who pushed her way
to him through the crowd when he was preaching at Gubbio and
"with a miserable and woebegone face" showed him her useless
crippled hands. He took them and held them in his own and
they were restored to her again. Overcome with joy she hurried
home and put her hands to instant use, making a cheese-cake for
Francis. Then with delight and pride she brought it to him, the

firstfruits of her restored usefulness. Francis did not normally allow himself to eat anything so luxurious as a cheese-cake, but he was not going to disappoint her, and so to her joy he took a piece and ate it, and told her to take the rest home to feast her family.

Francis healing a child was something that those who witnessed it must have treasured in memory for the rest of their lives, for his own childlikeness would have made of it a heavenly occasion. At Tuscanella a small boy lay paralysed in his little bed. Francis prayed, blessed the boy, lifted him up in his arms and set him upon the ground, "and in the sight of all the boy straightway rose whole in the name of our Lord Jesus Christ, and began to walk hither and thither about the house."

There was one healing of a child which was of importance to Francis himself. In the year 1221 he was in the little mountain town of Bagnorea when he saw a young woman coming towards him with her dying child in her arms. Speechless in her grief she knelt down and laid her little boy at Francis's feet. As soon as he saw the child Francis's face lit up with joy and he cried out, "*O buona ventura!*" Then he prayed for the child, blessed him and gave him back to his mother. Francis, when he cried out, "Good luck!" must have had foreknowledge of the future and communicated something of what he knew to Maria dei Ritelli, the boy's mother, for like Pica Bernadone she realized that her son belonged in some special way to God and she dedicated the boy to Him. She called him Bonaventure and as soon as he was old enough he became a Franciscan. After the death of Francis the Order passed through many troubles but new hope came back to it again when Bonaventure became its Minister General. He was a man of great personal beauty, a poet and scholar but holy and humble too. He instituted the angelus, the bell that rings three times a day to call the world to remember the Mother of God. He was so true a son of Francis that stories told of him might have been told of Francis himself. Saint Thomas Aquinas, the saint who sings the praises of the Franciscan Order in Dante's *Divine Comedy*, once came to visit Bonaventure, caught a glimpse of him in his cell where he was writing his life of Saint Francis, and praying as he worked, and withdrew without disturbing him. "Let us leave a saint to work for a saint," he said. Later he asked the Minister General how he found time to study. "My book is the crucifix," said Bonaventure. On hearing that he had been made a Cardinal he was seized with the same sort of terror as would have seized Francis, fled to a convent near Florence and hid himself there. But the papal nuncios pursued him and ran him to earth in the kitchen where he was doing the washing-up. They showed him the gorgeous cardinal's hat and he looked at it with dismay. He could not touch it with his greasy fingers but a tree by the kitchen door made a convenient hat-stand. "Hang it up on that tree," he said to a brother, "and show the nuncios to the parlour," and he continued with the washing-up.

The prologue of his beautiful *Legenda Sancti Francisi* looks back in memory to that day when his mother laid him at the saint's feet. He speaks of the devotion that he bears "to this our holy father, by whose merits and invocation I was (as I remember well) while yet a child, delivered from the jaws of death."

There was another child whose life Francis saved. He was once walking along the road that runs from Todi to Perugia, not far from the Tiber, when he met a woman with a basket of clothes on her head. Instantly he knew that something was wrong here, and he stopped the woman and asked her where she was going. "To the river to wash these clothes of mine," she said. "Nay, woman," said Francis sternly, "what thou carriest belongeth unto God. Set down thy basket and I will take charge of him." When Francis commanded people obeyed. The woman put the basket down and Francis lifted away the dirty linen and took into his arms the new born baby whom she had been going to drown in the river. Later he built a little house upon the spot where he had rescued the baby, and entrusted it to the care of charitable women. This was the first foundling hospital for the illegitimate children of the poor, and from this humble beginning has grown a great work accomplished for children through their own hospitals. There is another blessing that children owe to Francis, and that is the Christmas crib; but the story of Greccio belongs to another chapter of this book.

When we think of what he did for children, and how much he

must have loved them, it is sad that there are so few stories of
Francis with children. But the one we have in *The Little Flowers
of Saint Francis* shows us a child perfectly at his ease with Francis,
as though with another child, and more aware of the heavenly
country in which Francis lived than were the majority of his adult
contemporaries. In one of the convents of the Order a little boy
was living, and one evening Francis arrived to spend the night
with the brothers. As soon as compline had been said he went to
the brothers' sleeping place to get some rest, for he liked to get his
few hours' sleep in the early part of the night so that the hours after
midnight could be given to prayer. Now Francis was the little
boy's hero and he had made up his mind to watch him very
carefully and learn how to be a saint too, for saintliness, he
thought, could be learnt by observation. He was particularly
anxious to watch Francis when he was praying in the woods at
night, but the difficulty was to be with him there, for he had been
told that Francis always went secretly and alone to prayer. Then
he had a bright idea and when he had observed around the corner
of the door that Francis had fallen asleep he crept in and lay down
beside him. Then he took the end of the little cord that encircled
his middle and tied it to the cord that Francis wore. He thought
that when Francis moved he would quickly wake up and untie
the cord, and then creep out after him to the wood and see exactly
how saints behave at prayer. But things did not work out quite
according to his plan, for when Francis awoke he was in the first
deep sleep of his healthy childhood and did not stir. Francis,
finding himself tethered to the child, unfastened the knot gently
so as not to disturb him, and went softly from the dormitory,
waking none of the sleeping brothers, and "into the wood"
where a small cell had been built as an oratory. Some while after
the little boy woke up and found his bird had flown. But he was a
determined child, who meant to be a saint, and he did not allow
himself to be discouraged by this temporary thwarting of his plan.
He too arose and made his way to the door that led to the wood.
It was open and he went through it and followed the path that led
to the oratory. Presently he heard voices and saw a light shining
through the boughs of the trees. He crept cautiously nearer and

it was not moonlight but the light of the other country in which the saints live and move and have their being, even while their bodies still inhabit this world, though the light of it is seen so seldom by themselves. Children see it occasionally, and are aware sometimes of the great ones who have been purified, and of terrible pacing angels who have never sinned. The little boy, creeping as near as he dared, saw their figures in the light and heard the music of their speech. Though he had the innocence of a child he was too young to bear it, and Francis, returning some while later to the convent, found the small and apparently lifeless body lying across the path. He picked the boy up in his arms, found to his relief that he was not dead, carried him back to the convent and put him to bed. Later, when he was awake and recovered, the saint and the little boy had a talk together in some private place and the child told Francis what he had seen. This, Francis said, was to be a secret between them, and he asked the boy never to speak of what he had seen until he himself should be dead. The child promised, thrilled with the thought of sharing a secret with Father Francis. He grew up a very valiant son of the Order, growing daily in God's grace and in deep love for Francis, and he kept his promise. Not until after the death of Francis did he say what he had seen.

Chapter Three

THE CREATURES

Let the heavens and the earth praise Him, the Glorious, and every creature which is in heaven and on earth and under the earth, in the seas and all that are in them. Let us praise and exalt Him above all forever.

Writings of Saint Francis

I

POPE PIUS XI wrote of Francis, "The herald of the great King did not come to make men doting lovers of flowers, birds, lambs, fishes or hares; he came to fashion them after the Gospel pattern, and to make them lovers of the cross." This is a warning which most of us need, so prone are we to think of Francis only as the happy troubadour singing God's praises over the hills and through the valleys, as the storyteller who could keep the crowd rocking with laughter at his jokes and as a man who so loved animals, birds and flowers, that he would preach to them and talk to them as though they were his human friends. We dwell on this sunny side because it seems to us easy and happy and turn aside from the other because it is grim and difficult. We would rather not think of the penitent who scourged himself until the blood ran down, of the man who was not ashamed to go weeping through the world for the passion of Christ, of the fasting and the night-long vigils in darkness and cold. We would like to think of poverty in terms of spiritual freedom and sunny days in the woods, not in terms of hunger, lice-infected rags, pouring rain, lepers, disease and death. The dark side of the picture presents a challenge it is not easy to meet, and we are not altogether sure that we wish to be made into lovers of the cross.

But having acknowledged ourselves cowards, sodden with comfort, anxious to escape if possible even a twinge or two of shame, it is permissible to go back and think of Francis with the creatures, because though his mastery of them is a happy and pleasant thing to think of there is nothing easy about it. Like his gift of healing it is the fruit of holiness in its three aspects of selflessness, obedience, and that deep reverence for God which grows out of true penitence.

In his book *The Problem of Pain* C. S. Lewis draws an imaginative picture of man before the fall, man with his whole being centred upon God, not upon self, consciously in control of every part of himself, all his functions and all his powers, because his whole consciousness reposed on God. "Wholly commanding himself, he commanded all lower lives with which he came into contact . . . for man was made to be the priest and even, in one sense, the Christ, of the animals—the mediator through whom they apprehend so much of the divine splendour as their irrational nature allows." The saints, who through their costly discipline and fiery love for God have almost attained again to this primeval blessedness, show us something of what man was meant to be, what he might be again if he could turn back from self to God. Marvellous powers and energies are in us all but they are stifled and overlaid by the mud of self. Once that is washed away they are liberated and the man who enters into the enjoyment of them is not so much abnormal as normal; now at last he approximates a little nearer to what he was meant to be.

Francis himself ascribed all his powers to obedience. When a man gives himself to live in obedience to the will of God the power of God enables him. "Though we are commanded to do things beyond our strength," said Francis, "yet will holy obedience give us power to do them." In his *Salutation of the Virtues* he wrote, "O holy obedience, thou confoundest the will of the body and the flesh, thou takest the body and makest it to obey the spirit and to obey a neighbour and all the animals and wild beasts, so that these too can be free with man, as far as God permits it." This passage draws a wonderful picture of the brotherhood of creation as it ought to be, all bound together not only in obedience to the God who made them but in obedience to each other because the Creator Himself dwells in every created thing. Saint Bonaventure says of Francis, "His all-embracing love for every creature set forth a new picture of man's estate before the fall. When he thought of the first beginnings of all things he was filled with overflowing charity, and would call the dumb animals, however small, by the names of brother and sister, forasmuch as he recognized in them the same origin as himself."

Through penitence, and its awareness of the great gulf that separates sinful man from the awful holiness of God, Francis had attained to a deep and adoring reverence for God, and it was because of this reverence that he loved the creatures so much. Not only were they God's handiwork but they had all of them some attribute that lifted his thoughts to God. He could never bear to put out lanterns or candles because they reminded him of the Light of the World, and when he washed his hands he chose a place where the water that fell would not be trodden by his feet, for water was to him a symbol of penitence. When he walked over stones he walked in reverence for love of Him who is called the Rock, and he would never allow a whole tree to be cut down for firewood because Christ died upon a tree. The Three Companions say, "We who were with him used to see him rejoice, within and without as it were, in all things created." Celano says, "This happy traveller . . . exulted in all the works of the Lord's hands, and penetrated through these pleasant sights to their lifegiving Cause and Principle. In beautiful things he recognized Him who is supremely beautiful; all good things cried out to him, 'He who made us is the Best.' Everywhere he followed the Beloved by the traces He has impressed on all things; he made for himself of all things a ladder whereby he might reach the throne."

Francis would have echoed the words of Saint Augustin, "Thy whole creation speaks Thy praise . . . that so our soul rises out of its mortal weariness unto Thee, helped upwards by the things Thou hast made and passing beyond them unto Thee who hast wonderfully made them; and there refreshment is and strength unfailing."

No wonder the animals loved and obeyed him, as entering deeply into their being and their life he made himself their brother in obedience and their servant in reverence, a mediator of the love of God to them as he was to the sick and poor with whom he identified himself. He understood as few have done that this is the meaning of redemption. To grieve for the suffering, to pray for them, to relieve them out of one's own affluence is something, but not redemption. The redeemers huddle with the homeless under the dark arches where they sleep at night, wear their filthy rags with them, starve with them, sicken of their diseases with them, remembering always that God Himself could only redeem the soul of the penitent thief by bleeding and dying beside him. In something of the same fashion it would seem that by sharing the temporal existence of the creatures a man can bring them to share in some sort in his own heavenly life. We shut up animals in cages that we may observe their habits but Francis slept out in the open with the beasts, as fearless of them as they were of him because his sharing of their life made brotherhood between them. We watch the birds through field-glasses but he had only to sit still in the woods to have them perching on his shoulders and knees and outstretched hands. All the stories of Francis and the animals show him sharing their life of danger and hardship that they might share his life of worship, obedience and compassion.

At the Portiuncula there was a fig tree by Francis's little cell of wattle and daub and in this tree there lodged a cicada. The man and the small creature lived side by side in neighbourliness, and when the cicada started her merry chirpings in the mornings Francis would rouse himself to sing the divine praises. "One day he called her," says Saint Bonaventure, "and she, as though divinely taught, lighted upon his hand. He said to her, 'Sing, my sister cicada, and praise the Lord thy Creator with thy glad lay.' For eight days she came and went at his bidding, singing when he told her to. Then he said to the brothers, 'Let us now give our sister cicada leave to go, for she has gladdened us enough with her lay, stirring us up these eight days past unto the praises of God.'" He gave her leave and she flew away.

Francis the gay troubadour was especially happy with the birds and of them all his favourite was the lark because "sister lark hath a cowl like a religious". The killing of birds horrified him and he wanted the Emperor to pass a law "that no man shall take or kill sister larks, nor do them any harm", and he wanted another law passed that should compel men to feed all the birds and animals on Christmas Day. The creatures were nearly always well behaved with Francis, even the swallows of Alviano who were so noisy over their nest building that the sermon Francis was trying to preach could scarcely be heard. Nest-building swallows are generally very intent on their own affairs, yet when Francis called to them, "My sisters, the swallows, it is now time for me to speak," they were promptly silent till his sermon was finished. But there was once a robin who misbehaved himself. At the Portiuncula a cock and hen robin used to come every day and take crumbs from the table for their chicks, and Francis made them welcome and offered them grain as well. This was a good home for chicks, the parents thought, and when they were out of the nest they "offered their chicks to the brethren, as having been reared at their cost; and having made them over, did not appear in that place any more". The chicks behaved well for a time, shunning all lay folk and professing themselves nestlings of the brethren only, and then the biggest got above himself, persecuting the little ones and driving them away from the food that he might have it all to himself. Francis, saddened, feared he would come to a bad end, and so he did. "The disturber of his brethren went up on a vessel of water to drink, and immediately fell in and was drowned."

Another story is told by Thomas of Celano, and concerns a leveret who would run to Francis as chickens run to the shelter of their mother's wings, and could hardly bear to be parted from him. "Once when he was staying at Greccio, one of the brethren brought him a live leveret that had been caught in a snare; and when the blessed man saw it, he was moved with compassion and said, 'Brother Leveret, come to me. Why didst thou let thyself be so deceived?' And forthwith the leveret, on being released by the brother, fled to the holy man and, without being driven there by anyone, lay down in his breast as being the safest place. When he had rested there a little while, the holy father, caressing him, let him go, so that he might freely return to the woodland. At last, after the leveret had been put down to the ground many times, and had every time returned to the holy man's bosom, he bade the brethren to carry it into a wood which was hard by."

Most famous of the animal stories is the tale of the wolf of Gubbio. Towards the end of his life, when Francis had become too ill to walk from place to place, he would ride on a donkey, with one of the brothers walking beside him. He was journeying one day from the monastery at San Verecondo to Gubbio, and at evening came near a forest through which he must pass to reach Gubbio. Some peasants working in a field close by looked up and saw the familiar and beloved figure of Brother Francis on his ass, with an old sack flung over his shoulders to keep out the cold, and the brother walking by his side. They saw that he was riding towards the forest and they called out to him to stop. "Tarry with us tonight, Brother Francis," they entreated him, "for the day is far spent and yonder forest is full of fierce wolves, who will rend thee and thy comrade, and assuredly devour thine ass." But Francis, unperturbed, called back to them, "What evil have I done to brother wolf that he should wish to sup on brother ass ? Good night, friends, and God bless ye." And he rode on into the forest, the brother with him. It is sad that we do not know who this brother was, for the names of all these men who accompanied Francis on the more dangerous of his adventures should surely be written in letters of gold. It was generally only one brother who was with him, and the poor man was not perhaps always endowed with Francis's sublime indifference to wolves or martyrdom. Yet they always went on tramping faithfully beside the donkey.

Francis and the unknown brother emerged in safety from the forest and came to Gubbio, to find the little town in a state of panic. It was bitterly cold and the wolves were hungry. There was one great wolf in particular of whom they went in ceaseless dread. He hunted alone, so fearless and savage with hunger that he came right up to the walls of the city, carrying off animals and children and not afraid even to attack armed men. Gubbio was in a state of siege, grief-stricken and terrified, and all the trouble was poured out to Brother Francis as soon as he arrived. Full of compassion he said he would go out and talk to the wolf, who was known to be not far away in a stony lair. At this there was an outcry but frail and ill though he was he persisted. Signing himself with the cross he walked out from the city gate, a few friars with him and the citizens of Gubbio following. The citizens did not get very far; they preferred to view the little drama from the dress circle. The friars went on with Francis and then halted. *The Little Flowers of Saint Francis* says that they feared to go farther, but it seems more likely that Francis told them to stop and wait for him, for failing to go farther was never a Franciscan failing. He went on alone and presently encountered the wolf. As the creature ran at him Francis made a great wide sign of the cross and cried out, "Come hither, Brother Wolf; I command thee, in the name of Christ, neither to harm me nor anyone else." The wolf recognized his redeemer. He was in danger of death from the cold and the gnawing hunger in his belly. This man, coming to him in his stony wilderness, was also in danger of death. They were together in danger. He crept to the man's feet and lay down there, and for them both the danger was past. Francis talked to the wolf. He knew, he said, how hungry he was, and that it was hunger alone that had made him so wicked. He promised the wolf that if he would make peace with Gubbio, and do no more harm there, the citizens on their side would keep him supplied with food so that he should not again have to suffer this hunger. "But if I obtain all this for thee," said Francis, "thou must promise on thy side never again to attack any animal or any human being; dost thou make this promise?" The wolf sat up on his haunches and bowed his head, and Francis said, "Brother Wolf, wilt thou pledge thy faith that I may trust to this thy promise?" And putting out his hand "he received the pledge of the wolf; for the latter lifted up his right paw and placed it familiarly in the hand of Saint Francis, giving him thereby the only pledge which was in his power".

Then Francis commanded the wolf in the name of Christ to follow him, and together they went back to Gubbio, Brother Wolf trotting along beside Francis as meekly as a lamb. In amazement and joy the people at the city gate parted to let them come through, and Francis and the wolf went up through the

N

steep streets of the city while young and old, men and women and little children followed them in procession to the market-place. The great wolf walked very sedately, head down, tail between his legs, for he was very sorry for his sins. He was so big and strong that one snap of his jaws would have demolished the little man beside him, but the power resided in the little man. Then Francis talked to the people. He told them that if they would promise to feed Brother Wolf until the end of his days he on his part would promise not to hurt them any more, and the people with one voice promised. Then Francis turned to the wolf and said, "Brother Wolf, dost thou promise to keep the compact, and never again to offend either man or beast, or any other creature?" And the wolf knelt down, bowing his head, and, by the motions of his tail and of his ears endeavoured to show that he was willing to hold to the compact. Then Saint Francis continued: "Brother Wolf, as thou gavest me a pledge of this thy promise when we were outside the town, so now I will that thou renew it in the sight of all these people, and assure me that I have done well to promise in thy name;" and the wolf lifting up his paw placed it in the hand of Francis.

Brother Wolf lived for two years in Gubbio, very gentle and courteous. He went from door to door for his food, living at the table of the Lord like a true Franciscan, and the people received him with a courtesy equal to his own and fed him gladly. In all that time no dog barked at him and he did no harm to any living creature. The people loved him dearly because his gentleness reminded them of Francis. The creature who had yielded himself in obedience to his redeemer had become very like him. Then Brother Wolf died "and the people of Gubbio mourned his loss greatly".

There are certain persons who have considered the veracity of this story open to considerable doubt, declaring Brother Wolf to have been no wolf at all but a bandit whose ferocity had earned him the title of wolf, yet two historical facts support it. It is true that Gubbio was afflicted by a plague of wolves at this time, and in a very old church in the city, San Francesco della Pace, the skeleton of a large wolf was found reverently buried.

Chapter Four

THE CHAPTER OF MATS

Show me your cloister, asks the Lady Poverty of the friars.
And they, leading her to the summit of a hill, showed her the wide
world, saying: This is our cloister, O Lady Poverty.

Sacrum Commercium

ON earth the great days cannot, and may not, endure. "This is
too good to last," we say, and at our happiest we are often most
afraid. When a great man is at the height of his power then it is
slipping from him. When physical beauty has come to the peak
of perfection decay has set in. The mystery of spiritual survival,
not only of the souls of men but of anything that in its earthly
flowering has caught some reflection of the shining of God, is
something we must believe in if we believe in God at all, since all
beauty is a part of Him, but is as much beyond our comprehension
as He is Himself. We only know that relinquishment is one of the
laws of our being, and that we must submit to it, since it is our
only pathway back to God. We journey out from Him gathering
to us one after another of His gracious gifts, and we journey home
putting them back one by one into His hands. It should not be so
difficult for us, for we know where they are, but even for the saints
there is one sort of relinquishment which can be like the bitterness
of death. When they have to stand back and see the work they
have done for love of God being apparently corrupted or destroyed even they can hardly bear it. It had not been too hard for
Francis to give up all the earthly treasures, youth and health with
all their attendant joys, home and security, he had not even
waited, as most of us do, for time to take them from him, he had
flung them away himself that he might embrace the poverty of
Christ. But in their place had come treasure of a different sort; the
poverty of Christ itself, the glory of the Order in its spring
flowering, the love and devotion of his sons, and these had meant

more to him than all he had flung away. Now there was to be
loss of a more searching kind, a relinquishment so hard that he
would not be able to accomplish it for himself. The years were
coming when the Order, that was to him as his own being, would
fall away from its first beauty, would turn back upon the journey
to God and want again a measure of the power and security it had
relinquished. The poverty of Christ would no longer be acceptable to all his sons. Many of the brothers would forsake him, not
as man but as leader, because the path to heaven that he was
treading was too hard for them. The agony of Francis, his Gethsemane and his Calvary, had not come yet, but at the Chapter of
Mats there appeared over the horizon a cloud that foreshadowed
the coming sorrow.

Apart from the cloud it was an occasion of rejoicing, holding
within itself all the special Franciscan beauty, and to it there came,
as though in homage to Francis, all those over whom he would
have been so astonished to know that he reigned; the rich, the
poor and the creatures. The Franciscan chapters were at this time
held twice a year, at Whitsuntide and Michaelmas, and of the two
the Whitsun chapter was the more important and was attended
by every friar who could get there. The Whitsun chapter of
1219, called the Chapter of Mats because of the vast number of
thatched huts built for the housing of the brethren, followed the
accustomed pattern. From all over Italy the brothers, about five
thousand of them, converged upon the Portiuncula, tramping
barefoot over the mountain passes and through the woods, happy
in the thought of this family reunion, of participating in the conventual mass in Santa Maria degli Angeli, seeing the beloved face
of Father Francis and hearing him preach. Many of them were
young novices who had never seen him or the Portiuncula and
their expectation was tinged with excitement. What was he like,
this little man who had brought all Italy under his spell? What
would life be like at the Portiuncula? They had been told that
they would have both peace and liberty there. Though a multitude of men would be living in their huts in the woods they
would speak only in low voices and there would be long hours of
prayer and quietness, as well as the glorious tumult of all of them

praising God together. When they met in assembly to discuss the affairs of the Order the youngest novice might get up and speak out his heart and be respectfully and courteously listened to, for none was more important than another, and the concern of one would be the concern of all. They would see all the great men of the Order as well as Francis himself; the first men, Bernard and Giles, Sylvester and Angelo, Ruffino and Leo, and though they would not see them they would know that Clare and her sisters were kneeling in prayer for them in the chapel at San Damiano. And it was early summer. The vines were green, the birds were singing and the young brothers had not a care in the world. Men working in the fields stopped and called out a cheery greeting as the grey-clad friars tramped by, and many voices cried back to them, "God give thee His peace!" As well as the brothers other poor men were making their way through the forest to the Portiuncula, beggars and those who were sick and lame. They would find healing and comfort there and hear the brothers singing the praises of God. All Umbria felt a thrill of pride because it was the time for the Whitsun chapter, for the fame of the Order was spreading through Europe now and the country of its origin sunned itself in its glory. Assisi was especially proud for Francis was its own son. The city was preparing a surprise for him at this chapter, a gift which it hoped would give him joy.

The rich as well as the poor were coming to the Portiuncula this year, though they would not tramp barefoot. Cardinal Ugolino was to preside at the chapter and on Whit Sunday he would ride from Perugia with a retinue of nobles and princes of the Church, all of them sitting easily upon fine horses, their many coloured cloaks and surcoats making a river of colour threading through the woods.

And the reason for this vast concord, the focal point of it all, was a tired little man who was also making his way barefoot through the woods, limping a little because it was the end of a long journey. Francis had been away on a preaching tour and was only now coming home to the Portiuncula. With a lifting of the heart he came to the space where the trees thinned out, and saw the gable of Santa Maria degli Angeli and the quick-set hedge.

And then he saw something else and could hardly believe his eyes, for a large stone building stood near the little church. It was the surprise that the people of Assisi had prepared for him, the chapter house they had built so that whatever the weather the deliberations of the brothers and their distinguished guests could take place comfortably. But Francis did not know this. All he knew was that this was not the poverty of Christ. His Lord had preached at street corners, in the fields or in a little boat rocking on the lake, and had prayed at night on the bare mountain side, His head wet with dew. The rain had drenched Him, and the wind had tanned His skin and caught at His garments, for He had not had where to lay His head. The heart of Francis, that had been near to breaking, was suddenly hot with that fierce anger that could at times take hold of him. He strode into the enclosure and called to some brothers, no doubt the hefty Masseo, Leo and Ruffino and other faithful sons, to come and help him. With them he climbed up to the roof of the fine new chapter house and began to hack and tear it to pieces, flinging the wooden laths down to the ground. The sympathy of all the brothers was not with him, and a messenger was sent hastily to Assisi. Francis had not got far with his furious demolition when burgesses and knights came running down the hill and into the enclosure. "Father Francis," they cried, "this building is not yours; it belongs to the city." And they were upheld by the brother who had been chosen to be seneschal of the chapter, an Englishman called de Barton. Francis stopped and looked down at them, deep sadness and his habitual courtesy taking the place of the rage that had consumed him. "If this house is yours I have no wish to touch it," he said, and he climbed down from the roof. There was nothing else he could do but he had not accepted the gift, for in order to save it the giver had had to take it back.

The cloud passed and the next day, Whit Sunday, was full of joy. When a messenger arrived to tell Francis that Cardinal Ugolino was coming the brothers went out in procession to meet him. The two processions met in the woods, the rich men from Perugia and the poor men from the Portiuncula, and the difference between them so touched the Cardinal that he got down from his horse, took off his rich cloak and his shoes and walked behind the brothers barefoot to the church. There he sang mass, Francis assisting as deacon. The little place could not hold the vast congregation, but outside in the cathedral of the woods the brothers knelt rank upon rank on the grass and among the flowers, their deep voices lifting like a wave in the Sursum Corda, rolling through the forest in a storm of praise in the *Gloria in Excelsis*. Francis in his place in the little church, shaken by that most moving of all tremendous sounds, a great multitude of worshipful men singing together, must have remembered the dawn of that day ten years ago, when the old priest of San Damiano had said mass for him alone; and now God had added to him all these sons.

When mass was over he came out of the church to an out-of-doors pulpit to speak to them, and they gathered in as closely as they could, for it did not appear possible that the voice of such a frail little man could reach very far. Yet when he turned and faced them, and began to speak, "his voice was powerful, sweet-toned, clear and sonorous", and as always, "he saw the greatest concourse of people as one man; and to one man he preached most carefully, as if to a multitude." The one man who had served the mass ten years ago had become this vast army, and yet this multitude of men was still one man in the sight of God, the Franciscan Order. To it he preached and each man heard his sermon as though it were for him alone. His text was a minstrel's chant.

> Great things we have promised,
> But greater are promised to us;
> What we have promised let us fulfil,
> To what we are promised let us look forward.
> A brief delight and punishment for ever;
> A little suffering and glory infinite!

Then he preached to them of the life to which they had pledged themselves, the life of love, humility, obedience, penitence, prayer, service and poverty, recalling them to their first vows and their first fervour. He begged the five thousand men to have no care for their bodily needs at this chapter, but to give themselves wholly to prayer and praise, and God would feed them as he fed the birds and the creatures. Now, and for all the rest of their days, they were to cast all care upon "the good Shepherd and Nurse of soul and body, our Lord Jesus Christ the Blessed".

The days that followed were happy and carefree. The brothers slept in their little huts of branches, with mats of reeds for roof, lying on straw with stones for pillows. They spent their time in prayer and praise, and in caring for the sick and poor who came to them for help. Cardinal Ugolino was moved to tears by the sight of their quietness and devotion and exclaimed, "Truly this is the field of God; this is the army, and these are the knights of the Lord." But he did more than weep. Putting on the Franciscan habit he made himself one with them and tried to help them in their works of mercy. But in caring for the poor he lacked their experience, and in washing the feet of a beggar he was not very successful in getting the dirt off. The beggar, unaware that the brother kneeling humbly at his feet was a cardinal, exclaimed, "Go on your way and let someone come that understands this!"

Francis's faith that his five thousand would no more go hungry than did those five thousand men who followed Christ into the wilderness, and were fed with the loaves and fishes, was justified, for the creatures came to the Chapter of Mats, bringing food for the brothers. From Perugia, Spoleto, Foligno and Spello came trains of horses and donkeys with carts and panniers laden with bread and wine, beans and cheese, the frugal food that the people of Umbria knew the brothers liked best. For God had put it into their hearts to see that the brothers did not go hungry, and until the end of the chapter they furnished the table of the Lord with all that was needed.

Yet in spite of God's care for them, and Francis's appeal to them on Whit Sunday, there were those at the chapter who were afraid of the future, and they appealed to the Cardinal to support them in their desire for a more practical way of life. Once again the fine stone building that Francis had attempted to pull down cast its shadow; it stood for what they wanted, just that minimum of shelter and security that were possessed by the other great Orders.

The Cardinal listened to what they had to say and afterwards repeated it to Francis, who heard him out and then took him by the hand and led him to the brothers assembled in chapter. Then only did he speak, crying out upon them all in anger and sorrow. "My brethren, my brethren, the Lord called me by the way of simplicity and humility, and this way hath He shown me in truth for me and those who will believe and imitate me. And therefore I would that ye name not to me any rule, neither of Saint Augustine, nor Saint Benedict, nor of Bernard, nor any way or form of living, but that which was mercifully shown and given me by the Lord. . . . But God will confound you through your wisdom and knowledge, and I trust in the sergeants of the Lord that God will punish you by them, and that you will yet return to your state with reproach, willye, nillye." He was so passionate in his grief that he silenced them. They were ashamed and could say no more, and it was perhaps out of this shame that there grew the decision that was taken at this chapter. The Order decided to send three missions to the infidels. Three bands of brothers were to set out for Morocco, Tunis and Egypt. It was an immensely courageous decision, and we have seen already how fearful was the martyrdom that awaited the brothers who went to Morocco. The leader of the mission to the Moslems in Egypt was to be Francis himself. The moment he had longed for had come. It was four years since he had listened to the Pope's sermon in Saint John Lateran, and he had waited patiently for the hour that God had appointed for him, and now it was here at last and he was to go on the crusades.

Chapter Five

THE CRUSADES

O Love, forever glowing and aflame,
  Kindle Thy warriors' hearts,
  And turn their tongues to darts,
To pierce each soul that hears Thy sacred name.
                    Jacopone da Todi, *Lauda* LXXXI

I

THE crusade that Pope Innocent III had inspired, and did not live
to see, was now in full swing and the armies of Christendom were
in Egypt. Francis must have been on fire to join them for some
while, only held back because the will of God was not yet
clear to him. As we have seen, the movement of events about
him was for him a clearer indication of God's will than his own
feelings, which he profoundly distrusted. Now the spontaneous
decision of the whole Order that they must go to the infidels had
settled the matter, and lifted him up on a wave to see the far
horizons to which he must travel before them as their leader. For
that he should stay behind while they went forward to martyrdom
was unthinkable. On a former occasion, arguing with Cardinal
Ugolino as to whether or no he should share the missionary
journeys of the brothers, he had said, "My Lord, much shame will
it be to me if, having sent others of my brethren into far countries, I
myself do not share in the hardships and troubles that await them."

From the practical point of view this was hardly an expedient
time for Francis to leave Italy, for with him out of the way the
brothers whose way of thinking was symbolized by the new stone
building would have a freer hand, but expediency was not a thing
he considered when the will of God was clear to him, and in this
particular decision he showed a high and heavenly wisdom. What
a man does is far more compelling than what he says. A man who
talks about his convictions may be politely listened to, but the

man whom other men follow is the man who offers himself to die for them. If Francis had stayed at home and argued with the discontented brothers about the cross of Christ he might have postponed for a few months the changes in the Order that later took place, but a great chapter in his life would have been missing, the chapter on martyrdom, and we shall see later that it was through his union with the suffering of Christ and not through his arguments that he saved the Order. Actually he did not suffer martyrdom on the crusades, but without the crusades there might have been no Alvernia, for it was the consummation and acceptance of his offering of himself to die for Christ in Egypt.

Undoubtedly he wanted to die at the hands of the infidels and hoped that he would. Saint Bonaventure says he "yearned to offer himself up as a living sacrifice unto the Lord in martyr flames, that he might pay back somewhat in his turn unto Christ Who died for us." It needs a hard stretching of the imagination to realize that this was his outlook upon life. In his time he had shared the normal desires of men, he had wanted to make a success of his life, to achieve something, to be liked and loved, and the high peak of his youthful dreams had been some heroic action that should make him famous. But his outlook had changed and gone into reverse. He made no more claims upon God, clamoured for no more gifts. Saturated through and through with the love and bounty of God, drenched in it as a man is drenched in the sunlight that pours down upon him, he longed only to pay back something of what he owed. He would have been the first to realize the absurdity of his longing, and to laugh at it, for what can a gnat do for the sun? Nothing at all except stretch himself out in the sun's flames to die. "Greater love hath no man than this, that a man lay down his life for his friends. Ye are my friends . . ." In those words of Christ is a statement that cuts both ways. If God and man are friends then each can die for the other and for both calvary is the peak of being and the point of union. And so Francis's whole being strained after martyrdom, and when later he was told of the death of the brothers who went to Morocco he was overcome not by remorse or sorrow but by pure joy.

However absorbed Francis might be in God he never forgot his sons. The small fiery chariot of his concern for them was always with them, chasing to and fro, as the brothers had seen it in their vision at Rivo-Torto. Before he left them he did all he could to arrange for the smooth working of the life of the fraternity while he was away. He appointed two brothers to govern the Order in his absence, Brother Matthew of Narni who was to live at the Portiuncula and receive the novices, and Brother Gregory of Naples who was to travel through the provinces "to console the brethren". They were men in whose loyalty he trusted and in whose hands he thought he could safely leave the welfare of his sons.

Twelve brothers were to accompany him to the east, among them Peter Cathanii, Barbaro, Illuminato, who once had been Lord of Rocca Accarina in the valley of Rieti, and Leonard, who also was of noble birth. These were four staunch friends, a fact that lends colour to the story that he himself did not choose the twelve, for it would have been very unlike him to cushion himself for martyrdom with the company of those he loved the best. According to the story he called a child to him and told the boy to choose twelve men out of the many who wanted to be with him. The presence of this child among the brothers, the fact that the choice was entrusted to him, suggests that the Order had been deeply moved, and perhaps strongly influenced, by something that had happened in the April of the year in which Francis had made his first unsuccessful effort to reach the infidels. A shepherd boy of Vendôme, impatient at the tardiness of the grown-ups in freeing the holy places, had preached a crusade to his companions, crying out that if men would not free the sepulchre of Christ then children would. Followed like the Pied Piper by a stream of children he had marched down to Marseilles, and was only halted there by the impassable sea and the refusal of the grown-ups to find them ships. The story of the children's crusade was something that would have sunk right into the very heart of Francis. Perhaps the small boy who walked up and down before the company of grown men lined up for his consideration, choosing one here and one there, counting up twelve on his ingers, was a shepherd boy, a sheepskin over his shoulders and his shepherd's pipe slung around his neck.

Once more Francis and his friends set sail from Ancona, traveling with a convoy of crusading transports by way of Cyprus to Acre on the Syrian coast. It was a voyage of about six weeks. One can picture them standing on the deck of the transport watching for their first sight of the Holy Land, their hearts beating, hardly sure at first whether the dim shapes they saw on the horizon were clouds or the mountains of Israel. When they came nearer and saw the coastline, and knew it for the coast of Galilee, then surely Francis's voice rang out, leading them all in a joyous *Te Deum*. Slowly the ship drew in to the little town of Acre among its date palms, Acre that had been called Accho Ptolemais in the days when the Phoenicians had sailed from it to the Tin Islands of the west. From the hills above Nazareth the boy Jesus could have seen the blue sea and the ships sailing from Ptolemais. It has been said that Joseph of Arimathea sailed with the Phoenicians and that on one voyage Christ the Son of God sailed with him. Francis and the brothers landed, bemused by memories, and by the thought that Nazareth was so near, and at Acre to welcome them was Brother Elias, Minister-Provincial of Syria, who was in charge of the Brothers Minor who were already in the Holy Land. But they could not stay at Acre. The transports had merely put in there because it was the military base for Damietta. Having greeted Elias and the brothers they sailed on down the coast to Damietta at the mouth of the Nile, where for a year and a half the chivalry of Christendom had been suffering and dying before the walls of the city and had not breached them yet. It was imperative to the success of the crusade that Damietta should be captured, for it was one of the gates of Egypt, and Egypt was the heart of Saracen power and influence. With Damietta in their hands the crusading army would be half-way to possession of the holy places.

To find himself in the crusaders' camp must have been a great experience for Francis, for all about him were the dreams of his boyhood come to life. Here in their bright pavilions dwelt princes of the Church and of the world, knights and nobles from nearly every country in Europe, with their men-at-arms, their minstrels, their destriers, their sumpter mules, their hawks and their dogs. The camp was brilliant with flying pennants, escutcheons and banners emblazoned in scarlet and azure and green. Francis, making his way through the lanes of glittering colour, listened to many voices chattering in a babel of Spanish, French, German, English and Italian, heard the songs of the soldiers, the ring of the trumpets, the clang of hammer on anvil. And at night, when it was quieter, he listened in delight to the music of the lutes and viols and the songs of the troubadours, stealing out into the darkness from the glowing pavilions where the princes, knights and prelates were feasting. He watched the lifting pennants in the torchlight and the lights out at sea, where the Venetian fleet was riding at anchor, and sometimes he wandered away from it all into the stillness of the night and looked out over the desert, faintly lit by the glory of stars in the sky, and breathed the breath of the east, and knew that this was Egypt. And then the lights at sea, the camp behind him, vanished from his consciousness, and he heard nothing but the faint rustle of the wind in the date palms close to him, saw nothing except the little donkey plodding through the desert, the man with weary bowed shoulders walking beside it, a woman in a blue cloak upon the donkey's back with her baby in her arms.

When he came back to the busy camp again he was confused and distressed by the contrast between that vision and this. For it had not taken him long to discover that only outwardly was this chivalry that of his boyhood's dreams. There were a few Galahads here; he saw them kneeling at mass, their young faces rapt and absorbed when the cup was lifted. Sometimes he saw a bearded Charlemagne, or the eyes of Roland met his with a smile of recognition in them. There were some holy priests among those who followed in the trains of the bishops and abbots, and many good fellows among the rough men-at-arms. But in this army of the cross there was also much of the riff-raff of Europe, here for loot. The drunkenness and vice of the camp appalled Francis and nearly broke his heart. He was not surprised at the bloodshed and disaster that had marked the progress of the siege, and when he heard that the commanders of the army were planning what they hoped would be the final assault on Damietta he knew it would not succeed. Such sin as he saw about him could not fail to pull down upon itself the inevitable aftermath of pain and death. He was in great fear for these men but as always he was practical. What could he do? He could preach repentance and Christ crucified to the sinners about him, and he could do his best to prevent the attack upon Damietta.

The first was the easier task for he loved sinners and knew how to talk to them. Dissolute nobles, worldly clergy and the jailbirds and bandits in the ranks alike listened to the little man, at first with kindly amusement, later with attention. He put the fear of God into them and if they were not too hardened he broke their hearts. There were many repentances. Presently it was not only the Galahads who knelt at mass but rank upon rank of men who presently would meet their death as the penitent thief met his, with good hope of Paradise because they had repented of their sins. It was said of Francis at this time, "He is so lovable that he is worshipped by all." Here too in this camp Francis had his kingdom.

But he was not successful in preventing the attack upon Damietta. It was not often that he shrank from any duty, but though martyrdom held no terror for him he was not at all happy at the thought of going to the commanders of the army and telling them the attack would fail. They would be sure to laugh at him. "If I tell them disaster will happen to them," he said to one of the brothers, "they will think me a fool; yet if I remain silent I shall not escape the judgement of my conscience. Tell me, therefore, what think you I should do?" The brother replied with humour, "Less than nothing is it for thee to be judged of men; for it is not now that they will begin to call thee a fool."

So Francis went bravely to the men in command and gave his warning, and they laughed at him, and on August the 29th, 1219, with trumpets sounding and banners flying, the great army marched forward to defeat and death. Throughout the progress of the battle Francis was in such agony of mind that he could not bring himself to watch it. Twice he sent one of the brothers up to a high place to watch and bring him news, and twice the brother returned to say he could not see how things were going. Then Francis sent him a third time and he came running back with fearful news; the army was retreating, defeated and broken. When the remnant returned it was found that the crusaders had lost six thousand men captured and killed, and among the latter was almost the whole chivalry of the knights of Spain, who had fought with heroic grandeur.

For a while Francis and the brothers had their hands full ministering to the wounded and the dying, and then, out of all the tragedy and pain, came the moment for which Francis had been waiting, the chance to do what he had come to do. A truce was called that the dead might be buried and negotiations opened. Both sides wanted a pause in the fighting. The Sultan because he hoped the discouraged Christian army would take itself off altogether, and the crusaders because they were waiting for reinforcements. Now was the time for Francis to cross over to the enemy lines and preach to the infidels.

Characteristically he decided to go straight to the Sultan. All Francis's ideas had this bold simplicity, the ideas of a man who is either quite mad or supremely sane. The Sultan was the representative of his people and the symbol of the Moslem faith. Where he led his people would follow and if he were captured for Christ his people might very well be captured too. This was common sense to Francis, and he went to the Papal legate who was with the army and asked for permission to go and preach to the Sultan. As soon as the legate had recovered a little from the shock of the request he reminded Francis that the Sultan had offered a golden ducat per head for every martyred Christian. But at this Francis's face lit up with joy and the legate capitulated. With such men as Francis there was nothing else to do. Saints, geniuses and lunatics are alike hard to withstand, and Francis probably seemed to him a mixture in equal parts of all three.

Francis chose Illuminato for the supreme honour of accompanying him to probable martyrdom. The Moslem tortures were well known. Decapitation would only be the *coup de grâce* of a long process. In that black hour there was nothing to tell Illum-

Alinari

ST. FRANCIS AND THE SULTAN

Giotto

inato that he would be Bishop of Assisi in his eighties and die in his nineties. His heroism was supreme and that of Francis cannot be compared to it because Francis wanted to die a martyr's death. But he did understand the feelings of his companion sufficiently to give him a little comfort as they set out together. A couple of lambs ran across their path and he said cheerfully to Illuminato, "Put thy trust in the Lord, brother; for in us that saying is fulfilled: Behold I send you forth as sheep in the midst of wolves."

The sight of the lambs must have taken the thoughts of both back to the shepherd boy who had preached the children's crusade, and the other little boy who had gone up and down the ranks of the brothers picking out the twelve who were to come with Francis to this nightmare country. How flat it was, flat beneath the pitiless blue sky, a wasteland of reeds and lagoons and sand, no trees except the palms. They were far from the forests of Italy, from her mountains and musical ravines, and from Assisi upon her hill. They were far from home and every step they took brought them nearer to that grim crouching old city of Damietta, and the camp of the victorious army of the Sultan Melek-El-Kamil. They were crossing the wasteland that divided Christendom from the dark heathen world at the thought of which men trembled, two little plodding figures who never looked back at the crusaders' camp that was receding farther and farther away behind them. Their bare feet left light tracks in the sand that lasted for a while and then disappeared as the desert wind stirred over them. The sounds of the Moslem world came out to meet them, high shrill cries in an unknown tongue, weird singing, a hot breath of scents that were alien and frightening. They went on. They reached the fringes of the camp and saw it all before them, terrible, rich and strange. Then they were over the rim of the heathen world and swords flashed about them. They were set upon, seized and captured. The terrible new world closed over their heads and they disappeared.

The wonderful story becomes mysterious and uncertain with their disappearance. They were in the saracen camp for some time, they emerged from it alive after much suffering, and their mission was on the face of it a failure. These are the bare facts but

o

around them there is woven a web of stories that may be factually true, or may not, but are at any rate true to the fact of Francis. They show him courageous, quick-witted and ready to endure any agony to save a soul for Christ. The joyful thing about all the stories of him is that whether they are proved fact or unproved tradition they all show us Francis and for that reason all ring true.

At first Francis and Illuminato had to suffer rough handling from the Moslem soldiers. Possibly they were beaten, perhaps they were kept in chains for a few days. That they were not killed was most likely because the soldiers thought them mad, and Allah bids men spare the mentally sick. They could not understand the lingua franca and so Francis could not talk to them. All he could do was to cry out through all they did to him, "*Soldan! Soldan!*" And the soldiers, not knowing what to do with these lunatics, brought them to the courtiers about the Sultan, who were able to talk to Francis and ask his business. He said he had come to preach the gospel of Christ to the Sultan. Ferocious though these men could be they were not without chivalry and courtesy and they spared this strange little man who had so trustingly put his life in their hands. Possibly they were touched by him, beaten and weary, with bruised flesh and torn habit, and yet so bright-eyed and eager and so apparently unconcerned by his danger and physical plight. They spoke of him to Melek-El-Kamil and the Sultan said that he would see the two Christians. Perhaps he thought talking to them would pass an idle hour entertainingly.

The story tells us that he made amused preparations for the audience. He ordered a carpet covered with crosses to be spread on the ground, saying, "If he treads on the cross I will accuse him of insulting his God; and if he refuses to walk on it, I will accuse him of insulting me." Then he came to his great pavilion, surrounded by his emirs and courtiers, soldiers and nubian slaves, and seated himself there. Colour glowed about him, the crimson and blue of the arras, the robes and jewelled turbans of the men in attendance. There was a point of brightness here and there as the subdued light struck fire from a great ruby or a curved scimitar.

There was a hush of expectation, and then the two poor tattered friars were brought in.

Francis saw nothing of the splendour about him, he saw only the dark bearded face of Melek-El-Kamil the infidel, a man for whom Christ had died and yet who did not worship Him, and compassion for him surged up in his heart. The light of his love leaped into his eyes as he met the amused and wary glance of the infidel, and he went quickly towards him over the carpet studded with crosses. At once the Sultan pulled him up, taunting him with having trodden under foot the cross he professed to adore. Francis's retort flashed out instantly, one of his perfect answers. "You should know," he said, "that our Lord died between two thieves. We Christians have the true cross; the crosses of the thieves we have left to you, and these I am not ashamed to tread upon." The Sultan was delighted. Francis's quick wit had won him a hearing, and he listened attentively while the battered little Christian preacher talked to him about his God. He spoke with such love and conviction that he touched the heart of Melek-El-Kamil. He was oddly drawn to the little man and when their eyes met he felt a bond between them. When the sermon ended and Francis stood silent before him, trembling with eagerness and exhaustion, he spoke gently to him. He asked him to stay in his camp awhile that they might talk together again, and he gave orders that the two friars were to be courteously treated.

The days must have passed strangely for Francis and Illuminato. They prayed and said their offices in some quiet place, talked as they could with the men who looked after them, ate the strange food and listened to the alien noise of the great camp all about them. Perhaps they ventured to walk about the camp a little, saying to one and another, "God give thee His peace!" At evening they would have heard the cry of the Muezzin, "There is one God, Allah, and Mohammed is his Prophet!" And when the faithful turned towards Mecca in prayer they would have prayed also, making large slow signs of the cross, their faces turned towards Jerusalem. And Francis talked with Melek-El-Kamil and failed to win him for Christ.

The Sultan liked to talk with Francis, and was so charmed by him that he wanted him to stay with him always. "Willingly," said Francis, "if you and your people will be converted to Christ." But the Sultan only smiled and shook his head. He was moved by all Francis's pleadings, infinitely attracted by the man himself and by his faith, but the head of the Moslem world, whatever his private doubts and longings, could acknowledge only one God, Allah, and Mohammed as his Prophet. To bring Melek-El-Kamil and his people to Christ, to bring peace to the world, Francis would have done what he said; he would have offered his life for this man and stayed with him always. That offering was refused but there remained the other. He could offer his death. He offered himself to undergo the barbarous Moslem ordeal by fire. "If you hesitate as to the merits of the law of Mohammed and the faith of Christ," he said to his friend, "command that a great fire be lighted, and I together with your priests will enter into the fire that you may know which is the more worthy and true." The Sultan, who had observed the most revered among his priests quietly leaving the pavilion at this point, said smilingly that he doubted if any priest of his would accept the challenge. Francis replied, "Then if you will promise for yourself and your people to come to the worship of Christ if I come out of the fire unhurt, I will enter the fire alone. But if I am burnt up, impute it to my sins, and if the Divine power protects me, acknowledge Christ to be true God and the Saviour of all."

But the Sultan refused the test. Had he accepted it there would have been an uproar among his people, and Francis would have lost his life. He refused and there was no more that Francis could do except ask for permission to return to the Christian camp. It was granted and the two friends said good-bye to each other with sorrow in their hearts. "Pray for me," said Melek-El-Kamil, "that God may deign to reveal to me that faith which is most pleasing to Him." It was Pilate's cry of "What is truth?" the cry of the heathen world feeling blindly for God's hand in the dark.

And so Francis and Illuminato left the Moslem camp and once again the two little figures plodded through the wasteland of sand

and rushes and water towards the pavilions of the Christians. They had failed. Neither converts nor martyrdom had been granted to them. The taste of failure was bitter but no doubt Francis was well used to it. His biographers record only his successes but there must have been occasions when his prayers failed to turn a sinner from his sin, or when a sick man on whom he had laid his hands went from him only to die. But his humility would have taken the worst sting from the pain. For who was he? Only a miserable manikin who had offered himself to be used or not used, to die or not to die, just as God wished. It was the willingness that mattered, not the success. The willingness was all. But *The Little Flowers of Saint Francis* is not content to leave the matter there, and if the story that it tells of the death of Melek-El-Kamil is legend it is a legend that stands as a symbol for some unknown truth. For God the great Husbandman wastes nothing. Every prayer, every task of love, all pain of mind or body borne for His sake, is gathered into the storehouse whose wealth pours out unceasingly for the salvation of souls. Melek-El-Kamil would never have forgotten Francis and the memory would have wrought upon him.

According to the legend Francis promised Melek-El-Kamil that he would at last be a Christian, for when he himself had died he would send two friars to baptize him into the faith of Christ. "Free thyself from every hindrance," he said, "so that when the grace of God arrives thou mayest be well disposed to faith and devotion." The years passed and the great Sultan lay dying. Francis himself had been dead for many years but Melek-El-Kamil had not forgotten his words. He commanded that guards should be set in the passes, and if they saw two brothers in the Franciscan habit they should bring them to him at once. At the same time Francis appeared to two of the Brothers Minor in a vision and told them to go to the Sultan. They set out at once, were brought to him by his guards and found him still living. "Now I know of a truth that God hath sent His servants to save my soul," he said. And so the Sultan Melek-el-Kamil was baptized and died a servant of Christ.

II

It was typical of Francis that he never thought he had done enough. After his experience in the Saracen camp, the beatings and the chains and the long strain of his fight for the soul of Melek-El-Kamil, no one would have thought the worse of him if he had taken a little rest and allowed himself the pleasure of giving way to feelings of discouragement and depression. But the luxury of moods, and leisure in which to indulge them, had with Francis gone the way of other luxuries. Christ had told His disciples to say, "We are unprofitable servants. We have done our duty." Obedience to the astringency of that command had cleared a lot of rubbish out of his spiritual system. His mission to the infidels had failed, but when one door shuts another opens and when he got back to the Christian camp he set himself instantly, with redoubled vigour, to the task of preaching Christ to the Christians.

The result was many new recruits to the ranks of the Order. A French bishop who was with the crusading army wrote at this time, with a certain annoyance, "Rainier, the Prior of Saint Michael, has gone into the Order of the Friars Minor. Colin, my English clerk, has gone into the same Order, and so has Master Michael and Dom Matthews to whom I had given the Rectory of Holy Cross, and I am having a task to keep Cantor and Henry back." That shows no picture of discouragement. Francis was at his habitual work of setting others alight from the torch of his own soul.

The expected reinforcements arrived and in November the crusaders once more attacked the Saracen army. This time they broke through and Damietta was captured after a heroic defence of over a year. Within her walls they found horror and tragedy, for starvation and plague together had done their deadly work. An enemy at their mercy, the ending of the long strain, had their usual demoralizing effect upon the victors and the Christians forgot the pity of Christ. All the baser elements in the army were held in check sufficiently for a triumphal entry into Damietta upon the Feast of the Purification, and then discipline broke down and the army of the cross disintegrated. In spite of the fall of

Damietta it was obvious that this crusade was doomed to failure, and small companies of dispirited men began one by one to leave the demoralized army. What Francis felt when he saw the stricken city, and when he saw how so-called Christian men can behave when all that is evil in them is let loose, can be measured by the fact that after the fall of the city he too went away. He was accustomed to the sight of suffering, he was accustomed to the company of bad men, but not to a hell like this. He did what he could but the evil was so great that it tossed him aside like a straw and he went away overwhelmed by grief. Moods of self-pity and depression he had renounced, and the renouncement had set him free for something far deeper, a sharing of the redemptive agony of his Lord when He wept over the fall of Jerusalem. To that point now had his life come in its conformity to the pattern of the life of Christ.

He sailed for Acre and with him went a number of priests who had joined the Order. Arrived there he was again greeted by Brother Elias and introduced to a young novice, Caesar of Speyer, who had been preaching the crusades in Germany and had become so unpopular with the relatives of the men whom he had inspired to join the crusading army that he had had to escape to Syria. He was a man after Francis's own heart, a fine theologian but possessing also the humility and simplicity that Francis loved to see in his sons. Welcoming the young Caesar into the Order must have been a joy to Francis just now when he was so broken-hearted. He did not rest long at Acre but almost instantly set out to visit the neighbouring Christian communities and preach to them.

And then he disappeared. While he was in the camp of Melek-El-Kamil the Sultan's brother Conradin, the Sultan of Damascus, had given him what was probably the most precious gift he ever received in his life, a free pass to visit the shrines of the Holy Land. Without this he could not have done so, for although the Moslems allowed Christian pilgrims to visit the holy places they made them pay for the privilege and Francis, a poor man, could not have paid. He had so worked and suffered and prayed to win the infidels for Christ that it seems only fitting that this gift should have been made to him by one of them. And so, carrying them in his heart, he set out to visit the places where his Lord had lived and died. Francis, even less than most saints, has been allowed no privacy. The most intimate details of his dying and his death are common property, and as he liked to squander himself this would not have worried him over much. Yet there is one part of his life of which we know nothing. He went to the Holy Land, he was there for several months and he came back again, but he does not seem to have spoken of his time there even to Leo for "we that were with him" made no record of it. It is as though Christ hid him beneath His mantle during those months, and they remain a secret between Francis and his God.

Yet we can imagine, if we will, the course which his journey may have taken. His first visit to Acre had been no more than a pause in the voyage to Damietta and there had been no time for an inland journey. But now he could go where he would and probably his first journey was to Nazareth, and because he was a pilgrim perhaps he allowed himself the pilgrim's scrip and staff and bottle of water, and wore the scallop-shell of Saint James of Compostella fastened to his habit. Like Sir Walter Raleigh's pilgrim he would have needed something else:

> "Give me my scallop shell of quiet,
> My staff of hope to lean upon,
> My scrip of faith, immortal diet,
> My bottle of salvation,
> My gown of glory, hope's true gage,
> And thus I'll take my pilgrimage."

In Nazareth, mountain built, the great plain of Jezreel below, the snow-covered mountain ridge of Mount Hermon to the north, looking upon olive and vine terraces, Francis would have felt at home, for this home of Christ's boyhood was not unlike the home of his own boyhood, Assisi. He must have walked about it shaken with joy, knowing that the beauty he looked upon was the same loveliness that Christ had seen and loved. He saw the same unchanging country sights, the carpenter at work in his arched shop opening on the village street, the women drawing water at the well, the yoked oxen, the shepherd leading his sheep, talking to them in their special language, a lamb on his shoulder.

When he left Nazareth it would have been to travel through Galilee in the springtime, his bare feet walking the very paths that his Master had followed, through the fields bright with red anemones, the lilies of the field, and the white narcissus that is the rose of Sharon. He would have stood by the lake of Galilee and watched the fishermen mending their nets, their small boats rocking at anchor, and heard the slap of the water against the hulls and known that Christ had heard it too. He would have gone up into the hills at night and prayed there, the hood that he had drawn forward over his face wet with the dew. He would have travelled up to Jerusalem slowly, footsore and tired and hungry at times because through all these months his only means of subsistence would have been the table of the Lord, but scarcely aware of hardship, only aware that every step he took was in the footsteps of Christ. He would have seen the barren savage mountains, so different from the wooded ranges of his Italy, but with such wonderful changing colour on their bare slopes that it was as though flowers clothed them, as they clothed the fields. He would have climbed the arid, sun-scorched Mount of Fasting, and prayed in the cave there where it was said that Christ had prayed. He would have seen Him everywhere, by the camp fire at night, seated among the pilgrims, muleteers, rogues and vagabonds who crowded the caravanserais, talking to them and telling them stories, sitting beside a well to rest, asking a woman for a drink of water, calling to the bright-eyed brown-skinned children to come to Him that he might bless them. Above all, wherever the blind beggars and the cripples stood by the wayside crying for help, and in the wild places where the lepers wandered, Francis would have seen Him. And wherever he saw Him he would have followed, as he had always done. He too would have sat among the vagabonds, and laughed and played with the children, and anything he had about him he would have given away, a scrap of bread from his scrip or a bunch of anemones that he had picked. His love, his prayers, his healing hands would have been at the service of whoever needed them.

It must have taken him a long time to reach Jerusalem but the turnings of the way brought him at last to where he could see her throned upon her hill, the Holy City beloved of Christ. He would have fallen on his knees beside the way, oblivious of the busy traffic of the high road and of the dust that the camels kicked over him as the caravans went by. His habit was itself dust-colour and he would have been scarcely noticed, so small and insignificant was he, so much a part of the landscape wherever he was. Had anyone caught a glimpse of the illumined face within the hood they might have turned around and looked again, but he always kept his face well hidden when he prayed. He stumbled to his feet and went on, perhaps a little shakily, for at some point on his journey he had contracted the malaria from which he suffered until the end of his life, and a disease of the eyes which caused him much pain and in the end blinded him. But any pain or weakness from which he suffered would have given him added joy, for it was something to offer Christ in the city where He Himself had endured so much.

Francis mingled with the crowd and entered Jerusalem through one of the gates in the towering tawny walls. The hospice for pilgrims that his beloved Charlemagne had founded in the eighth century had been destroyed but he would have found another and gone out from it day by day to visit the holy places. He saw the house of Mary, mother of Mark, in which Jesus had celebrated the Last Supper, the same house in which He showed Himself to His disciples after His resurrection, and the house of Pentecost, where tradition says the Blessed Virgin lived until her death. When the Christians who had been in hiding in the mountains came back to Jerusalem after its destruction they had found the house in ruins and had rebuilt it as a place of Christian worship. During the crusading period it had been a convent of Canons Regular, and just over a hundred years after Francis saw it, when the guardianship of the holy places was entrusted to his own Order, it became for a while a Franciscan convent, its church containing the Chapel of the Last Supper, its garden looking out over Jerusalem.

Francis so often knew the future. Perhaps in vision he saw his sons kneeling in prayer in this place, tending the lamps and serving the altars in the Church of the Holy Sepulchre and at Bethlehem, tending the flowers in the Garden of Gethsemane. What joy it would have given him. He could have asked of God no higher honour for his sons. He went to Bethany. He saw the moonlight falling through the olive trees in the Garden of Gethsemane and knelt and prayed beside the rock of the agony. He walked step by slow step, many times, along the Way of Sorrows, though perhaps at no time did he manage to see it very clearly, not because of his coming blindness but because he was still not ashamed to go weeping through the world for the Passion of Christ.

The Way of Sorrows ended in a door in a wall and inside was the courtyard of the great church that held the Chapel of Calvary and the Chapel of the Holy Sepulchre. The church that the Emperor Constantine had built had been destroyed. The church that Francis saw had been built by the Crusaders, and part of it still stands today. To keep vigil there must have been for him an experience so deep that it is scarcely surprising that he seems never to have spoken of it. In the centre of the crusaders church, with its roof of cedar wood, was the Chapel of the Holy Sepulchre. Some distance away, and fourteen feet higher than the rest of the church, was the Chapel of Calvary, built over the hill of Golgotha. Francis, when he had slowly mounted the eighteen steps that led to it, would have found a marble chapel with a central column supporting a pictured vault, altars, and lamps burning. There was also a rock, and men said that the hole in it was the socket-hole of the cross. Here he would have prayed, oblivious to all around him, aware only that he was on Calvary, kneeling at the foot of the cross.

When he came down the steps again to the main body of the church, to go to the Chapel of the Holy Sepulchure, he would have entered first the dim Chapel of the Angel and looked with awe upon the stone there, for they said the angel of the resurrection had sat upon it. The opening into the rock tomb was very small, so that a man must stoop to creep inside, and the windowless chamber could hold no more than three or four men kneeling together before the altar which covered the place where the body of Jesus had lain. Here too Francis prayed. It was the custom during crusading days for young men to be knighted in the rock tomb. After their vigil they would receive the accolade kneeling before the altar. Francis as a young man had longed for knighthood. Now, kneeling where the young knights knelt, he too kept his vigil as a knight of Christ.

Francis was at Bethlehem for Christmas. It is only five and a half miles from Jerusalem and he walked there in the track of those first three pilgrims from a far country, the three kings. He passed the well of the star, where it is said that they stopped to drink, for they had lost the star and they were weary, but stooping over the water they saw it shining again within the well. Perhaps he stopped there too, to refill his water-bottle before he went on to white-walled Bethlehem among its cypress trees. It was another little hill-town such as he loved, and as in Nazareth he must have felt he had come home. He walked up the narrow streets and saw the old houses of Bethlehem built over the caves in the limestone rock where the animals are stabled. He asked for the birthplace of Christ and they showed him a low door in a strong wall. It was such a small door that only a child could go through it without bending his head, and had been made so to prevent the infidel from riding in on horseback and slaying the Christian worshippers inside. But Francis would have seen it as a symbol of Christ's humility, who bent His head so low that He might pass under the low lintel of our human flesh, and of the humility asked of His followers, who cannot enter the kingdom of heaven unless they in their turn become as little children. Francis bent his head and went through the low door into the austere and splendid church that Constantine had built when he became a Christian. He went down the flight of steps from the choir to the cave beneath the church and kneeled down in the small place at the heart of the world where Christ was born.

There was another place where he would have prayed that Christmastide, before he went back to Jerusalem, and that was a certain spot in an upland valley where it was said the shepherds had been watching their sheep when they heard the angels singing.

Shepherds still kept their sheep there, for it was an immemorial sheepfold.

The time came when Francis had to start the return journey to Acre. The last day arrived and he said good-bye to Jerusalem on earth. There was another one, and she filled his thoughts as he set out on the last stage of his pilgrimage, for within her walls dwelt all that he loved. "When shall I come to appear before the city of my God?"

As he travelled in the Holy Land Francis would often have seen the deserted castles of the crusaders on the hills and his heart would have been sore for that lost Christian kingdom of Jerusalem. Yet he would have found the chivalrous Saladin a man after his own heart, for he gave away all his wealth to those in need and died so poor that the money for his funeral had to be borrowed. As his humble funeral procession passed through the streets of Damascus men broke down and wept, and said that a saint had left the earth, even as they would say to each other as the funeral procession of Francis passed through the streets of Assisi. It is strange to think how alike in spirit these two men were and how few years separated them in this land that was holy to them both.

But there was one crusaders' castle which was still in full glory and probably Francis saw it, for it was on the main caravan road along the sea coast, the road that the Roman legions had tramped, which the crusaders had followed and that was the Pilgrim's Way to Jerusalem. This was Athlit, the last castle to be held by the crusaders in the Holy Land. Its great walls towered up among the rocks on the Mediterranean shore, where the waves creamed in over the golden sand. It was held by the Knights Templar, and the banner of the Order flew from its battlements. It may have been one of the last vivid memories that Francis carried with him as he came again towards Acre. And so the great experience, the greatest of his life excepting only one other, drew to its close, and by it he had been strengthened for his own Gethsemane and Calvary, that were waiting for him at home in Italy.

But it is all conjecture. All that he did, all that he thought, is his secret.

PART FOUR

THE POWER AND THE GLORY

Chapter One

THE RETURN

How much interior patience and humility a servant of God
may have cannot be known so long as he is contented. But when
the time comes that those who ought to please him go against
him, as much patience and humility as he then shows, so much
has he and no more.

Writings of Saint Francis

I

FRANCIS came back to Acre and was welcomed by the Minister
Provincial, Brother Elias, Caesar of Speyer and Peter Cathanii.
With them was a young lay brother, Stephen, who had come out
from Italy to find Francis, bringing much news for him. He told
him of the martyrdom of the brothers whom the Order had sent
to Morocco. Francis had longed die in this way himself but he
felt no jealousy, only infinite gratitude to God who had allowed
to his sons His highest honour of martyrdom. "Now I can truly
say I have five brothers," he said. He or they, what did it matter?
The Order was one. But Stephen had other news. The brothers
at home who were Francis's closest friends had sent him out to
find Francis and beg him to come home and save them. He had
been away too long; so long that at home they had wondered if
he was dead. His disloyal sons had thought they could do what
they liked now and his loyal sons had been in grief and despair.
This was the beginning of a trial harder for Francis to bear than
the rack or the fire and he must have known it as he quietly told
Stephen to tell him all that had happened. Physically he was in
poor shape now to stand up to the shock and grief of betrayal, but
his spirit was steady and calm for he had prayed beside the rock of
the agony and its strength was in him.

   The news could hardly have been worse. The two men to
whom he had entrusted the government of the Order in his

P

absence, his two friends, Matthew of Narni and Gregory of Naples, had betrayed the trust he had placed in them. They had put themselves at the head of the discontented brothers, and at a chapter meeting over which they had presided they had imposed upon the Order a new set of Constitutions which were totally at variance with the Rule that Innocent III had ratified, the Rule which all the Brothers Minor had vowed to keep, the command of God which made them what they were. The loyal brothers who had refused to consider themselves bound by the new Constitutions had been persecuted by the two Vicars-General. Some of them had been driven out of the Order altogether and Stephen had had to escape from Italy secretly without the knowledge of the Vicars.

The new Constitutions were admirably devised for preparing the knights of God to forsake the Lady Poverty and play a distinguished part in the affairs of the Church. The Franciscan missionaries were no longer to go out carrying their lives in their hands, objects of ridicule and potential martyrs, they were to carry with them letters of protection from the Pope and the Order was to do no work that had not received legal sanction. The small families of brothers that Francis had favoured, as fostering brotherly love and holiness, were to be superseded by much larger communities of men, living not in small hermitages and rustic "places" but in well-built convents. These convents were to possess libraries so that the Brothers Minor might become the equals of the other religious orders in learning and scholarship. Discipline was to be enforced by a bewildering number of rules and regulations, replacing the few simple precepts of love that had been based upon the gospel of Christ.

When Francis was told of it all many memories must have passed through his mind, memories of his Lord and Master and of the old happy days of the Order. No legal sanctions had protected Christ and His apostles from martyrdom and no stone walls had housed them, keeping out wind and rain and beggars. Christ could have been the greatest scholar the world has ever known, but He said good-bye to the scribes in the temple at Jerusalem and went home to Nazareth with His parents and was subject unto them. He could have been a great man among the princes of the world but He chose His friends among the outcast and the poor. Francis remembered the sunshine of the spring day when Bernard had given away all his wealth to the poor. There would not have been such joy in the square that day if he had been building a library with it. He remembered Pacifico crying out to him, "Take me away from the world and give me back to God," and he had been able to do it in a matter of minutes, not after a year's novitiate. He remembered nights sleeping out under the stars and the friendliness of the birds and the flowers and the creatures; the friendliness of a poor man when you shared your last crust with him, both of you huddled together on the leeward side of a haystack on a cold night. No doubt the new constitutions were full of wisdom and common sense, and rules much like them regulated the lives of the other orders. But the Brothers Minor were not other orders. They had been called by God to embrace the poverty and suffering of Jesus Christ their Lord, for the salvation of sinners for whom He died.

Perhaps Francis said little at first to the anxious brothers, but later, when they were seated at table for their meal, and the parchment bearing the new constitutions was put into his hands, his eyes lighted upon the sentences regulating what the Brothers Minor were to eat, or not eat, upon this day or that. He read that the brothers were not to quest for meat even on days which were not fast days, and that they were to fast on Mondays as well as on the days prescribed in the rule. There was meat on the table now. Francis looked at it and then he looked at his old friend Peter. "Messer Peter, what shall we do?" he asked.

"Ah, Messer Francis," replied Peter with a touch of fire, "do as you think well, for authority is yours."

"Then we will eat what is set before us according to the gospel," said Francis. And they ate meat.

As soon as it was possible, probably in the following September, Francis sailed for Italy and with him were Peter Cathanii, Caesar of Speyer and Elias, to help him and uphold him in his need. He trusted Elias and there is no doubt that that extremely able man was a great comfort to him at this time.

They reached Venice and stayed there for a few days, for Francis was not well, and when they set out for home he was too weak to walk and they had to find a donkey for him to ride. The brother who tramped beside the donkey was Leonard, who had set sail with Francis and now was home with him again, and today he showed himself not quite worthy of the donkey brotherhood. If they had been in danger he would have been worthy but the trouble today was not wolves or brigands but sore feet and hurt pride. He had been a great man in the world, with horses and servants at his command. He uttered no word of complaint but his aristocratic temper was fretted by stones in the road and the remembrance of past glory. "In the world," he thought to himself, "my people would not walk beside the Bernadone, and here am I compelled to trudge behind his son whilst he rides." He had forgotten that saints can read thoughts. Francis stopped the donkey, dismounted and said courteously, "Take my place, brother; truly it is not becoming that I should ride whilst thou, who art of noble stock, should have to walk on foot."

Leonard, overwhelmed with sorrow and shame, knelt down at Francis's feet.

They went on to Bologna and here the storm broke. The Minister Provincial of Lombardy, Peter Stacia, was a Doctor of Law of the University of Bologna. When he had joined the Order he had sacrificed his academic fame for the love of Christ, but deep in his heart learning had remained his first love. When Francis disappeared in the east, and the changes began to take place in the Order, the old love flamed up again. The Dominicans had opened a school at Bologna and why should not the Brothers Minor do the same? He collected money and built a House of Study which he proclaimed to be the property of the Order. Franciscan scholars flocked into it, and in his eagerness he forgot that years before Bernard of Quintavalle had been sent here to witness to the humility and poverty of Christ in the midst of the intellectual pride and intolerance of Bologna, that he had been stoned in Bologna's market-place, and later had fled because the people did him too much honour. Probably in the thrill of it all he scarcely realized that he had broken the Rule of the Order, to which he had promised obedience as to God, three times over. He had collected money, which no Franciscan might touch, he was holding property in the name of the Order, and the life which he and the brothers were living within the convent was no longer the life of evangelical poverty and simplicity to which they were vowed.

Francis, arriving at Bologna ill and anxious, was faced with this thing, and became for a short while a man whom it is difficult to recognize as Francis, a man fierce, intolerant and even pitiless. All the gentleness and humour of that, "Messer Peter, what shall we do?" that seems to us the true Francis, was lost as the harsh streak that was in him burst out like the pent fires of a volcano. Yet that harshness was Francis too. The serenity of the saints is not necessarily something they are born with, but the fruit of struggle. Robert Bridges says of them, "Their apparent grace, is won by discipline of deadly strife." The control is hardly held and can break when a man is tested beyond his strength. Francis was confronted with the disloyalty of his own sons to the ideal to which he had given his life at a time when he was physically exhausted, and it was too much for him. It is a comfort to think that even the saints can at times be betrayed by the weakness of the body.

Francis cursed Peter Stacia with that father's curse of which every Italian of the Middle Ages lived in dread, and of which he himself had been so terrified. He ordered the brothers who were living in the convent to leave instantly. Some of them were ill but though he was usually so gentle with the sick he had no mercy on them. They had to get out of bed and go. He himself would not enter the place but took refuge with the Dominicans, and it was left to a Dominican to plead with him to be merciful and to tell him that the brothers were grieved and sorry, and willing to make any reparation that he demanded. The fierce anger began to leave Francis and he demanded no penance from them except that of not going back to the convent.

Then he left Bologna. During all the sorrows of the few years of life still left to him, though he would yield not one inch of ground and kept his personal integrity intact until the end, he never again lost his temper or tried to bludgeon his sons into obedience. It would seem that the harshness in him was purged by the sorrow and shame he endured after he left Bologna. The depth of his penitence is seen in the humility of what he did next. He did not go home but set out on the donkey through the wintry weather for Rome. He had had a dream which expressed his thoughts at this time, and seemed to give him guidance for the future. The Three Companions tell us of it. In his dream "he beheld as it were a little hen that was black and had feathered legs with feet like a tame dove, and she had so many chicks that she was not able to gather them under her own wings, but they went about in a circle round the hen, beyond her wings. Then, waking from sleep, he began to think about this vision, and forthwith perceived by the Holy Spirit that he himself was intended under the parable of the hen. And he saith: 'I am that hen, small of stature, and by nature black, and ought to be simple as a dove, and on winged affection of the virtues to fly toward heaven. And unto me the Lord of His mercy hath given and will yet give many sons, whom I shall not be able in mine own strength to protect. Whence behoveth me to commend them unto Holy Church, the which under the shadow of her wings shall protect and govern them.'"

The outbreak at Bologna, and his penitence after it, had made him see himself as a greater sinner than ever, by nature black. He ought to have been gentle as a dove with his erring sons and he had been angry and intolerant. He was not fit to look after them any more, and there were so many of them now, so strong and self-willed, that he could no longer control them. When he had had only a few sons he had been able to gather them all under his wings, now he could not, for "they went about in a circle round the hen, beyond her wings". Stronger, broader wings than his must cover them now. It is one of the mercies of God that true penitence after sin can bring a man even nearer to Him than he was before he sinned, and so Francis on this humble heart-broken journey would have felt very close to his Lord, and remembered His cry, "O Jerusalem, Jerusalem . . . how often would I have gathered thy children together, even as a hen gathereth her chickens under her wings, and ye would not!" Christ too had known this sorrow of having the children circling beyond the wings.

If when he reached Rome Francis followed his usual custom he went first to Saint Peter's tomb and prayed there, his mind full of memories of the day when he had brought the first little company of the Brothers Minor to see the Pope. Now he was once more going to see the Pope but because he had too many sons he had to go alone. He was too ashamed, too humble, to ask for an audience and be received with the honour that would have been accorded to the head of the Order of the Brothers Minor, but went to the corridor outside the Pope's room to wait until he should come out. He was too tired to stand so he sat down on the ground. At last the door opened and the Pope came out, and Francis greeted him with the words, "Father Pope, God give thee peace!"

The old and holy Honorius III who loved Francis replied gently, "God bless thee, my son," and waited to hear about the trouble. Francis explained his need. The Pope, he said, was so busy and so great that the poor could not always have access to him. He wanted Honorius to appoint some wise man who would be a father to him and the Order in the Pope's place, and to whom he could turn for counsel and guidance. "Whom do you wish that I should give thee, my son?" asked the Pope, and Francis replied, "Give me the Lord Cardinal of Ostia." And so Cardinal Ugolino, as the representative of the Pope and the Church, took the Brothers Minor under his wing and became Protector of the Order.

Francis could have asked for no better Protector for by his very nature the Cardinal was well fitted to do what could be done to heal the differences between Francis and the rebellious brothers. He understood both sides, for they represented the two sides of his own character. He was scholar and diplomat and able administrator, but he was also a humble man of God. As a scholar he sympathized with those brothers who demanded that they should be allowed to study and use their minds for God. He thought it was a legitimate demand. If a man of intellect does not use it he wastes the gift of God. And scholars must have books. As an administrator he realized that an Order numbering thousands of men could not live at the table of the Lord in quite the old manner without becoming a burden on the lay fraternity, and that the sick and old of a perpetually growing company of men would increase in number too and would have to have adequate care. He could see no way out of it except the raising of money to build convents that should include libraries and infirmaries. And the larger the number of men the stricter must be the discipline and the more careful the novitiate. In the nature of things it seemed to him that the changes had to come and that his task was to try and help the Order to preserve through them all, as far as was possible, the Franciscan spirit of simplicity and humility and love. And as well he had to try and protect Francis from too much suffering, for with all his heart he loved him and sympathized with him. If there would be many in the days to come who would not understand the attitude of Francis to inevitable change he would not be one of them. His own humble devotion to his God would enable him to realize that Francis was quite unable to separate Jesus Christ, the poor man crucified, either from His poverty or His crucifixion, and that from this fundamental inability grew his conviction that men called of God to follow Christ in the way of the Gospel could not be separated from them either. A Brother Minor must be utterly poor and utterly crucified or he was not a Brother Minor. In the worldly nature of things there had to be compromise but in the heavenly nature of things Francis could not accept it and remain Francis. That was the dilemma, the old tormenting dilemma of how to live in two worlds at once.

The Cardinal was in Rome during the winter of 1220 and he and Francis met and talked together of the difficulties, and from their discussions grew two decisions of the Cardinal's that well illustrate his double sympathies. Peter Cathanii, Francis's faithful friend and loyal son, was to take the place of Matthew of Narni as Vicar at the Portiuncula, so that Francis should have the comfort and support of his presence there, but before the next Whitsun chapter the Cardinal wished Francis to revise the Rule of the Order and bring it more into line with the inevitable changes that the passing years had brought. Then they said good-bye and

Francis journeyed home to the Portiuncula, and as the news of his return spread quickly from one mountain hermitage to another, where the sons who had been faithful to him had hidden themselves from persecution, joy leapt up like the flames of spring. Their father was not dead. He was alive and he was home again and now all would be well. Spring was coming and up in the mountains under the melting snow the grass was green.

But the spring brought sorrow to Francis for on the 10th of March Peter Cathanii died. For his old friend he would have rejoiced, for Peter had lived long enough to come back from the crusades and for the last time see the Portiuncula in the spring, but not long enough to grieve for the sorrows that were coming. For himself it was irreparable loss. Never again would he be able to say, "Messer Peter, what shall we do?"

II

Perhaps it was some comfort to Francis that Peter Cathanii's successor as Vicar at the Portiuncula was the able Elias, for Elias was a man who knew how to keep his own counsel when it was expedient to do so, and Francis did not know yet that the sympathies of the man whom he had chosen to bring home with him from the east, to help him, were with the enemy. Elias has been called the Judas of this story, but that is surely to blacken him too much. His chief likeness to Judas seems to be in the puzzle which he presents, for his complex baffling character has produced many divergent judgements from those who have studied his extraordinary career.

Elias Bombarone was born at Beviglia, a small village about three miles to the north-east of Assisi. His mother was a woman of Assisi, his father a mattress maker. They were very poor and it is said that Elias had the wizened little body of a man who in childhood has gone hungry, but in compensation he had great force of character, a keen intellect, and an ambition that was perhaps a result of the bitterness of that early poverty and deformity. Like Francis he had his dreams, but when Francis was dreaming of knightly chivalry Elias was dreaming of power. He wanted power and he was a man to get what he wanted, for he was willing to toil and sweat for it. Apprenticed to his father he made mattresses by day and studied by night, to such purpose that while still only a boy he had moved to Assisi and was teaching in one of the schools there. Judging by his later character he was gracious and charming to the boys who did what he wanted and brutal to those who opposed him; but there would have been few of these, so great was his power over others. Whether he met Francis at this time we do not know, but he was not in Assisi for long. Somehow, by some means, poor as he was, he managed to get to Bologna and studied in the famous schools, where he did brilliantly. He became a notary but he also studied the arts and experimented in alchemy. His interest in science, and his skill in it, brought him to the notice of the Emperor Frederick II and they became friends.

In the year 1211, when Elias and Francis were both twenty-nine years old, they met at Cortona. It is a beautiful city on a mountain top, girdled by Etruscan walls. Far down below is Lake Trasimene and from the city to the lake a stream tumbles down a great gorge, densely wooded with lime trees, chestnuts, oak and ilex, with caves in the cliff rather like the caves of the Carceri. In these scenes of beauty, in the springtime, the two men met, and Elias became a Franciscan. At first sight that is the most extraordinary thing about him, for the lowliness of the Brothers Minor was something that cut right across his ambition, alien to the sort of man that he was. The explanation would seem to lie in Francis himself. Before he met Elias he had been spending the forty days of Lent on an island in Lake Trasimene. It is said that he took with him two loaves and ate half of one of them. He would have liked to have eaten nothing, like his Lord in the wilderness, but in his humility he did not dare to presume upon equality with Christ. He spent those forty days of suffering and prayer alone with God and from this tremendous experience he went to Cortona worn and exhausted but fulfilled with the joy of his Lord, his face shining with it, the breath of heaven's peace about him, and met Elias. And Elias loved him. Possibly he had never loved anyone before, and never did again. It was a case of, "thy people shall be my people, and thy God my God". Elias was a religious man and naturally ascetic, so to those who did not know him well it would have seemed that there was nothing to prevent him from following Francis all the way. The obstacle lay in his love of power, that was curled like a snake about the roots of his being. His gifts were rooted in it, his great intellect, his fine powers of drive and imagination, the affectionate pleasure he took in managing the lives of others. He could relinquish such worldly goods as he had with no trouble at all, but he could not uncover his snake that Christ might slay it for him for he loved it more than Christ. He could not do the one thing needful. And so in the end his pride wrecked his life and, worse still, it caused incalculable suffering to Francis whom he loved. That was his tragedy.

Naturally he climbed swiftly in the little world of the Brothers Minor, as he would have done in any world. He was only about thirty-five when he was made Minister Provincial of Syria. From being Vicar of the Portiuncula in place of Peter Cathanii it was only a short step to becoming Minister General of the Order in place of Francis, and from the point of view of organization and discipline he was an extremely fine Minister General. After the death of Francis the Order split into two, like a river dividing into two great streams, the friars of the Strict Observance remaining loyal to the ideals of Francis and living the old life of poverty in the hermitages and humble "places", and the rest, the Conventual friars who were Elias's men, carrying on in their convents, schools and hospitals the great works of learning and of mercy which his energy inaugurated. But after the death of Francis there was a change in Elias. His love for Francis had sweetened and softened him, but when the gentle influence was gone he was, in his own words, "left in the very midst of night", and a cruel despotism grew out of his pride. He scourged and imprisoned the friars who opposed him, even those whom Francis had loved the best, even Leo; though if it is true that Leo in a rage smashed the urn in which Elias was collecting offerings of money for the building of San Francesco, then Leo was not blameless. Even his own men had to suffer from his violent temper and his despotism, and the men of learning and ability whom he had attracted into the Order were not of the gentle temper of the early Franciscans. Francis's recipe for perfect joy would not have appealed to them at all. At last they could stand Elias no longer and they cast him out. He resigned and Pope Gregory IX, who had once been Cardinal Ugolino and his friend but who had by this time suffered much from him, accepted his resignation.

He went straight to his old friend the Emperor Frederick, the Pope's enemy, and entered his service, and Gregory IX retaliated by excommunicating the Emperor and Elias with him. Elias worked for the Emperor until Frederick died, and was his trusted ambassador, but all the while, defiantly declaring himself still a Franciscan, excommunicate or no, he wore his habit and cord. After the Emperor's death he went back to Cortona, where he had first met Francis, and high up in the clouds at the summit of the city he built a convent and church which he called San Francesco. Here he lived proudly, called the Lord Elias by the Ghibelline burghers of Cortona and a band of friars who had thrown in their lot with him, and here at last he died.

But the defiance and the pride were not the whole of Elias, there was another man in him besides the despot, the gentle and tender man who had loved Francis and had been loved by him. We see a glimpse of the other Elias in a story told of Agnes in the early days of the Order. When she was sent to be Abbess of Monticelli at twenty-two years old, and was sick with grief at parting with Clare, she wrote, "Bid Brother Elias come to comfort me in Jesus Christ often, very often." Father Cuthbert points to two buildings which Elias created as representative of the two men in him. They are San Francesco at Assisi and the Celle of Cortona. San Francesco, comprising the two churches, the papal palace built for Gregory IX and the great convent, oppress by their scope and grandeur, but the Celle, the little hermitage that Elias built in the wooded ravine above the stream, where he must often have walked with Francis, is simple as his gentleness to a homesick girl, and as humble as his first love for Francis.

Is it not possible to see in San Francesco at Assisi not only a monument to the pride of Elias but to his remorse too? His cruelty to Francis during the last years of his life was something of which he was perhaps scarcely conscious at the time, for though he was trampling on all that Francis stood for he was also caring very tenderly for his bodily welfare. But when Francis died he would have seen it for what it was and there is no misery like knowing too late how cruel you have been to those you love. Elias spared neither labour, money, strength nor imagination in the rearing up of that great monument to the memory of the man he had loved, but still it was too late and the place seems to reflect something of the coldness of his grief. But the little Celle reflects the happiness that he had with Francis in the days when they were young together at Cortona.

The letter that Elias wrote to the Order in the first flood of his grief when Francis died is, like the Celle, the best in him and the cadence of pure poetry is in its opening sentences. "The thing I feared has come to pass, for me and for you. Far from us has gone the consoler, and he who carried us like lambs in his arms has set forth a pilgrim into a far country . . . The beloved of God and men has entered the mansions of exceeding light." And the letter is signed, "Elias, sinner."

At the end the humility of Francis conquered. Through all the years of his passion and pride as Minister General, at the Imperial Court, as the Lord Elias of Cortona, the pure flame of his love for Francis must have burned on hiddenly within him. When he was old and ill and could no longer stride abroad on his great enterprises, and perhaps was too weak to dominate those about him as he had done, his pride began to crumble. In the convent high up above the Etruscan ramparts of Cortona, cloud-shadowed, the world fallen away, he would sit alone, and when the great winds were still he could hear the ripple of the water in the ravine far down below. The Celle was there and the air was fragrant about it. He would be for a while back in the past, living in the days when he had been a beloved son of Francis, one of the gay and gallant brotherhood. He would be once again kneeling with them in Santa Maria degli Angeli, joining in the chanting of the deep voices all about him, or walking with them up the steep path to Assisi, where all the bells were ringing on a feast day. Or he would take some trouble of his to Francis the consoler, and they would go together "into the wood" to pray about it. Suddenly a harsh sound would disturb him, the banging of a shutter in the rising wind, and he would be back in the desolate convent of Cortona. It was cold and he was alone. Those of his true brethren who still lived did not speak of him now for he was excommunicate.

The thought of his excommunication weighed upon him intolerably and he would sit for hours together beating his breast, murmuring the same words over and over again. "Alas, how great a sinner I have been and am, and how vainglorious! Spare me, O Lord, and enter not into judgement with Thy servant. Spare me, O Lord, spare me!" The days of his bitter penitence went on and on until at last there was no more pride left in him. And then, shriven and at peace, he died. His grave is still to be seen at Cortona, but no one seems to disturb its loneliness.

III

All this was far in the future on the day of the opening of the Whitsun Chapter of 1221. On that day Elias as the Vicar of the Portiuncula welcomed the brethren to this happiest of meetings with all the graciousness and charm that made him so popular with so many. For to all the three thousand men tramping in to the Portiuncula this was a truly joyous occasion. Francis was alive. They had feared their father was dead and now here he was, older and frailer, but alive. Those who had been persecuted in his absence, and had felt like mariners riding out some frightening storm, felt now that it was all over and they were safe in the harbour of the Portiuncula. They crowded around Francis with joy and thanksgiving. Even those who disagreed with him thanked God for his safety. For now and through all the coming troubles there was never a man who wanted to get rid of Francis. They loved him far too well. What they wanted was that he should be amenable to progress. And if there were a very few who did not love him they still wanted him as the figurehead. They were well aware that his enormous prestige was of incalculable value to the Order.

Cardinal Ugolino could not be present at this Chapter, but another cardinal presided and a bishop sang the mass on the opening day, Francis assisting as deacon. Then he preached. At the Chapter of Mats his text had been a minstrel's song, but now it was not a hand swept over the harp strings that set the tone for this chapter but the blast of a trumpet. His text was the first verse of Psalm 143, "Blessed be the Lord my God, Who teacheth my hands to fight", and ill as he was his voice rang out as strongly as ever. As they listened to his sermon the hearts of the reformers must have sunk heavily, for it was not the sermon of a man who intends to allow himself to be used as a figurehead. Francis had appeared amongst them once more not to acquiesce in progress but to lay the old foundation stones all over again.

The chapter awaited the reading of the rewritten Rule with trepidation. The young Caesar of Speyer had helped Francis with the work of revision but considering his record that was only an added reason for anxiety. The Rule was read and the worst fears of the reformers were realized. Nothing was changed, only emphasized. They were still grounded on the strict Gospel observance, still rooted in evangelical poverty. Two new regulations had been added to the Rule. Francis had said no harsh words at the chapter on the subject of the persecution suffered by the loyal brothers in his absence, or about the building of the convent at Bologna, but the new regulations were a worse blow to the reformers than if he had lost his temper all over again, for they made sure that such things should not be repeated with his permission. No brother, said the first regulation, was bound to obey a minister who laid upon him a command "contrary to our life or against his soul . . . because that is not obedience in which a fault or sin is committed". The second regulation forbade the collection of money for houses or "places".

When the reading was over the disappointed ministers tried to talk it over with Francis. One minister was particularly distressed because his books, he told Francis, were valued at fifty pounds, and what was he to do? Francis cried out passionately, "O you brethren who wish to be called Friars Minor by the people and to appear to be observers of the Gospel and yet in fact would have your treasure chests! But I am not going to lose the book of the Gospel for the sake of your books. Do as you will; but never shall my permission be made a snare to the brethren."

This now was to be his standpoint through the months that were coming. If they would not listen to him, would not obey him as they had promised the Pope that they would do, he was not going to coerce them. "I am not minded to become an executioner to punish and scourge them like the magistrates of this world," he said later. "My office is spiritual only, namely to overcome their vices and spiritually to correct them by my words and example." But he was not going to condone what they did, he was not going to allow them the hypocrisy of appearing to live as his obedient sons in the eyes of the world when they were no such thing. If they would not obey then they must go their way and he would go his. For himself, he would follow Christ in the way of the Gospel until he died.

The majority of the three thousand men present at the chapter probably remained unaware of the tension between Francis and the ministers until the time came to commission the brothers for their missionary work. Then they saw the change in him. He was so tired that he could not speak to them. Elias spoke to them in his place and Francis sat on the ground beside Elias, and when there was something he especially wanted Elias to say he tugged humbly at his habit, and Elias bent down and he whispered to him, for during all the heartbreaking arguments he had lost his voice as well as his strength. But not his passion for souls. He had been concerned about Germany ever since the Franciscan mission there had been such a failure. He thought they ought to try again. Sometimes he had seen bands of German pilgrims travelling to Rome, and the sight of them had deeply touched him. Tugging at Elias's habit he whispered to him about them. Elias, who had been bending down to him, straightened himself and spoke to the assembled friars. "Brothers, our brother says there is a certain country, Germany, where dwell devout Christians, who as you know often pass through our country, with long staves in their hands and wearing great boots; and they sing the praises of God and the saints as they go along, perspiring in the heat, to visit the

tombs of the apostles. But because when the brethren were sent
to them once before they were treated badly, our brother does not
wish to compel any brother to go thither again. Yet if any
inspired by zeal for God and souls, be willing to go, he will give
them a like obedience, nay, a more willing obedience, than he
gives to those who go to the infidels beyond the seas. Let those
who are willing stand up and draw apart."

Francis did not appeal in vain and the difficult chapter ended in
a sudden blazing up of the old authentic Franciscan spirit. The
assembled brothers regarded a second mission to Germany as
certain death, so fearful were the stories that the first missionaries
had brought back with them, and at this chapter many of them
had heard for the first time of the torturing and beheading of the
Moroccan martyrs. Nevertheless ninety men immediately
offered themselves with joy to die for Christ in Germany. The
old courage was still there, unchanged, and sent a thrill of delight
and pride through the whole packed assembly.

And then came a twist of the familiar comedy, like a quirk to
the tale of the grave and anxious proceedings. There was one
man, an Umbrian named Giordano da Giano, who had no desire
whatever to be a martyr, or even a missionary, but who like so
many of us liked to associate himself with courage so long as it
involved no personal commitment. He strolled over to the brave
ninety and moved among them, chatting affably, asking this man
and that man his name and birthplace so that he might boast in
years to come that so-and-so and so-and-so had been friends of
his, and he had been almost the last man at the chapter to speak
to them alive. But retribution awaited him for his questioning
brought him to the side of a brother with a singularly penetrating
eye. "Your name, brother?" he asked innocently. "Palmerio,"
replied the other, "and since you are here you too are one of us
and must go with us." And then he grabbed hold of Giordano
and would not let him go. In vain the poor man protested,
Palmerio held on, and at last Giordano said miserably that he
would ask Elias what he should do. Elias, appealed to, asked him
if he wanted to go? And here Giordano showed that he was a true
Franciscan after all. He had been trained to obedience and

selflessness and the words, "I don't want to," were words that he never spoke. He said instead, "I wish neither to go nor not to go." Elias said, "Then you had better go." And Giordano went.

Only twenty-five of the ninety who had volunteered were chosen for the German mission. They were led by Caesar of Speyer and were a notable band of men, courageous and merry. Thomas of Celano was one of them and also an adventurous brother who was later in his life to explore Tartary. The second mission to Germany was a success and no one was martyred. Giordano da Giano lived safely through it all, came home and wrote a book about it. He was exactly the type that thoroughly enjoys putting pen to paper.

Chapter Two

THE DARKNESS

The Cross hath lifted
Love, Heaven-gifted,
Never to let it go:
And the Cross shall take me,
Lift me, break me,
For all the world to know.

Jacopone da Todi, *Lauda* LXXXIII

I

FOR two and a half years Francis continued his active life with his Order, increasingly ill, increasingly heart-broken, humbly striving to meet so far as he could the demands his sons made upon him but never yielding to any that seemed to him contrary to the will of God as he saw it, and the vocation to which he believed himself called. Through it all he was courageous, patient and loving, but those two and a half years were his Gethsemane. He was not broken by them. A weak man breaks when his life's work is wrested from him and twisted to a semblance that is abhorrent to him, and when his dream has turned to what seems to him an ugliness. But Francis had never supposed that he owned anything, not even his work or his dreams, and in his ability to let go of them he was a strong man; strong too in the knowledge that nothing could take from him the power and glory of prayer and suffering, and that he would be able to offer these for his sons until he died.

After the chapter of 1221 Elias and his men laid incessant siege to Francis, and the manner of it, and Francis's response, are summed up in a story told in *The Mirror of Perfection*. A certain novice wanted to possess a psalter of his own, not one belonging to the community but his special property, and Elias, who had now been accorded the title and authority of Minister General,

said that he might have it. But he did not want to have it without
the approval of Francis and so he waylaid Francis and said to him,
"Father, it would be a great solace to me to have a psalter, but
though the General has conceded it to me, yet I wish to have it,
Father, with thy knowledge."

Francis answered, "Charles the Emperor, Roland and Oliver,
and all the Paladins and strong men, being mighty in war chasing
the infidels with much travail and sweat to the death, had over
them notable victory, and at the last themselves did die in battle,
holy martyrs for the faith of Christ; but now there are many who
would fain receive honours and human praise for the mere telling
of the things which those others did."

This fiery answer, which all writers, all Giordano da Gianos,
should take to themselves with shame, settled the young novice
for the moment, but a few days later, when Francis was sitting by
the fire, he came to him and spoke again of his longing for a
psalter of his own. Francis said, "After you have the psalter, you
will desire and wish to have a breviary. Then you will sit in your
chair, like a great prelate, and say to your brother: 'Bring me the
breviary.'" And taking up some ashes he spread them on his head
saying, "I am thy breviary, I am thy breviary," over and over
again, moving his hand round and round upon his head as
though he were washing it with the ashes. The novice was so
amazed and surprised that Francis had to comfort him. He told
him that he too had longed for books but he had prayed about it
and God had shown him that it was not His will. "There are so
many who willingly rise unto knowledge," he said to the novice,
"that he shall be blessed who makes himself barren for the love of
God."

But still the novice was not going to give in and some while
later, meeting Francis at the Portiuncula, he tried again, and
Francis, weary and heart-sick, yielded at last and said, "Go and do
concerning this what thy Minister tells thee." The novice,
triumphant, turned and walked away, but a moment later
Francis "called after him, saying: 'Wait for me, brother, wait!'
And he came up to him, and said to him, 'Turn back with me,
brother, and show me the place where I said unto thee, that thou

shouldst do in the matter of the psalter as thy Minister should say.' When therefore they had arrived at the place, blessed Francis kneeled before that brother, and said: '*Mea culpa*, brother, *mea culpa*, for whosoever will be a Friar Minor should have nothing except a tunic, as the Rule concedes to him, and a cord and breeches, and those who are forced by manifest necessity, sandals.'"

All the difficulties are in this story. The psalter stands for every-thing for which Elias and his men were fighting. They were determined to have their way but they wanted to have it with Francis's approval, and that was a thing they could not wring from him. The question of the books was for Francis an especially tormenting one. He knew, and said to the importunate novice, that if his sons spent more and more time reading and writing about the selfless deeds of others they would spend less and less time in performing them, and it was to the ministry of mercy that they were called. And he knew too that men who get too involved in studying books on the science of prayer lose the simplicity and humility without which they cannot pray them-selves. The scholarship of his age was a greedy thing. The men of the Middle Ages were intoxicated by the great world of learn-ing that had opened to those among them, the men of drive and ability, who could push their way in. But the majority, all the mass of the suffering peasants, were left outside. There were many humble and holy men among the scholars but there were more of the type of Elias, and they tended to form an aristocracy of scholarship. Intellectual pride was their besetting sin. It was this that Francis feared for his sons. A sense of superiority would separate them for ever from the suffering poor, and if that hap-pened they would be like salt that has lost its savour and would no longer be Brothers Minor. But he was not opposed to scholarship as such. He revered men of learning, and he so reverenced the written word that if he saw any scraps of paper with writing on them fluttering about on the road he would gather them up, just as he would have gathered up a flower or a butterfly that it might not be trodden underfoot. The writing spoke to him of the wisdom of God, as the flower and the butterfly of His beauty and grace. He who so loved the beauty of verse, the minstrels' songs, the cadence of the psalms, would have loved to possess books. "Brother, I likewise was tempted to have books," he said to the novice. He knew the cost of the sacrifice he asked of his sons, and suffered in asking it. "I am thy breviary," he said, but even while he spoke he put the ashes on his head in profound humility and performed the symbolic action of washing his head as though in the waters of penitence. God had called him to be an example of poverty to his sons, and had called them to obey and imitate him, but he knew his unworthiness.

II

Out of the ranks of the scholars in his Order there rose up one to comfort him. Anthony, the young priest who had prayed beside the tomb of the Moroccan martyrs, and left it to join the Order, had made himself "barren for the love of God". The brothers among whom he lived so quietly had no idea that he was a fine preacher and a man of wide learning. His early days in the Order were shadowed by a great disappointment, for his desire to preach Christ to the infidels had been frustrated. Like Francis himself at his first attempt he had been shipwrecked, and then he had been very ill. He came to the chapter of 1221 and was so gentle and withdrawn that when the brothers were being directed to the various provinces where they were to labour he was nearly overlooked altogether. Then the Minister Provincial of Lombardy noticed the humble young priest, thought he might come in useful and took him under his wing. He could at least speak Latin, and he would be able to say mass for the lay brothers in the hermitages. So Anthony was sent to live in the mountains, at San Paola near Forli, and was useful to the brethren there. He said mass for them and he delighted in unobtrusively doing all the hardest tasks he could find, and he prayed for long hours in the loneliness of the mountains, and no one took much notice of him.

Then one day at the convent at Forli there was something of an occasion. There was an ordination of priests there and some Dominicans, the dogs of God, were invited to be present as guests. Anthony and the brothers of San Paola were also there, and when the ceremonies were over they all had an evening meal together. When they had eaten the Father Guardian of Forli thought the time had come for edification and he asked one of the Dominicans to speak to them. But all the guests excused themselves. Perhaps as scholars and preachers they did not want to appear as though they were displaying superior powers before the humble Brothers Minor. But the Father Guardian still thought they should be edified and glancing round the assembled company his eye fell upon Anthony and he commanded him to address them. Anthony, like Ruffino before him on a somewhat similar occasion, implored that he might be excused, but the Father Guardian, scenting a faint whiff of the forbidden disobedience, insisted, adding kindly, as he saw the distress on the face of the humble young priest, that a few simple words as God should inspire him were all that was required. Anthony stood up and began to speak, and as his quiet voice gathered power a tingling silence held his audience, a silence held within the deep and holy quietness of the mountains where these men were assembled. It was one of the great moments of the Franciscan Order, one of those occasions when a sermon makes history. Anthony was in no sense displaying his great gifts of learning and eloquence, he was incapable of that, but his gifts were of God and under the guidance of the Holy Spirit he gave of them and of himself as well as he could. He finished and sat down in his humble place, glad it was over.

But now the obscurity he loved was no longer allowed him, for the new spirit that was in the Order believed in using genius in strategic positions. Also it would seem that it is so often the wisdom of God to place His most devoted servants exactly where they least want to be. Their gifts and their personal preferences run counter to each other, and the discipline of being used in a way that is not of their choice preserves their humility. Anthony, the mystic, would have chosen the quiet prayer-life of the mountain hermitages, but he was soon by the command of authority preaching up and down the countryside, pressed upon by the crowds who flocked to hear him, earning for himself by his fiery defence of his faith the title "the hammer of heretics". But he was also in the providence of God used for a gentler purpose, and one

more after his own heart. He made more endurable for Francis
the reopening of the House of Studies at Bologna and the found-
ing there of a theological school for the Brothers Minor. This had
been made possible by the diplomacy of Cardinal Ugolino, who
had declared the House of Studies to be the property of the Holy
See, not of the Brothers Minor to whom it was merely lent. The
scholars among the brothers did not mind to whom the house
belonged provided they could go back there, and though Francis
must have been deeply distressed there was nothing he could say.
It was the Portiuncula Chapter House that belonged to the citizens
of Assisi all over again. But Anthony was appointed lecturer at the
new school and he proved to Francis that a Brother Minor could
be a brilliant scholar and yet remain holy and humble.

It would be comforting to think that in these years of sorrow
Anthony gave Francis hope for the future, when the stormy years
of transition should be safely over, and that through this hope he
had foreknowledge of the Franciscan missionaries travelling to
every corner of the known world, and the harvest they reaped
there, and saw the thousands of men in the grey habit toiling
in the slums of all the great cities. He would have been so
happy to see their hospitals for lepers, the sick and the old, their
orphanages and asylums, and to know that down the centuries
whenever the plague broke out, wherever there was misery and
death, the beloved grey friars would always be there in the thick
of it. Such knowledge would have reconciled him to the scholarship of the Order, to the libraries and schools, the trained choirs
and the fame of Franciscan music. Whether he knew something
of these things or not he knew that Anthony was destined to be
one of the great men of his Order, for he wrote to him as
"Brother Anthony, my bishop". But even with Anthony at
Bologna he was ceaselessly anxious about the brothers there and
wrote to him, "It pleases me that you should read sacred theology
to the brethren so long as on account of this study they do not
extinguish the spirit of holy prayer as is ordained in the Rule."

He was several times at Bologna during these years and on the
Feast of the Assumption 1222 he preached to almost the whole
city, packed in the great piazza. His sermon was described in these

words by one who heard him. "I, Thomas, citizen of Spolato and Archdeacon of the cathedral church of the same city, studying at Bologna in the year 1220, saw Saint Francis preach in the square before the Little Palace, where nearly the whole town was assembled. He spoke first of angels, of men, and of devils. He explained the spiritual natures with such exactness and eloquence that his hearers were astonished that such words could come from the mouth of a man so simple as he was. Nor did he follow the usual course of preaching. His discourse resembled rather one of those harangues that are made by popular orators. At the conclusion, he spoke only of the extinction of hatred, and the urgency of concluding treaties of peace, and compacts of union. His garments were soiled and torn, his person thin, his face pale, but God gave his words unheard-of power. He converted even men of rank, whose unrestrained fury and cruelty had bathed the country in blood; many who were enemies were reconciled. Love and veneration for the saint were universal; men and women thronged round him, and happy were those who could so much as touch the hem of his habit."

It is not the picture of a broken man. The spiritual power, the fire and the eloquence are there unchanged.

III

"As is ordained in the Rule," Francis had said to Anthony, and it was this Rule that haunted them all. Francis believed it had been ordained by Christ, therefore he could not alter it. Elias and his following saw it as a great mountain blocking the road to progress. There was a new spirit in the Order now. Loss of unity had meant loss of peace and happiness. On all sides there were arguments and recriminations and a loss of discipline. Francis was blamed for it. The new men said the old Rule was far too difficult and heroic. It was impossible to keep and Francis by refusing to modify it was only encouraging indiscipline. His faithful sons blamed him for dealing too gently with his opponents and for allowing power to pass into their hands. His suffering and his patience irked them and they could not see that it was that alone which was keeping the Order from open schism. Great desolation fell upon Francis and he wondered if he was indeed to blame. He searched himself for sin. Surely he must have sinned very deeply that this confusion had come upon his sons. Sick and heartbroken he lost his joyousness and humour and began to suffer from scrupulosity. He wondered if his regular visits to Clare and her nuns at San Damiano had been wrong. He decided he must discontinue them, lest they be misconstrued, and he sent a message to Clare to tell her he felt he must not come again.

Clare thought she had never heard such nonsense, and she sent back a strong protest. The brothers, she said, had promised to look after their sisters in the Order. If Francis did not come any more to minister to the spiritual needs of herself and her nuns he was betraying his trust. She had her way, of course, as she always did, and once more he took the familiar path to San Damiano. But it was a sad meeting. When he came in among them he was not the Francis whom Clare and her sisters had known. They saw him emaciated, bowed down with sorrow, the old light gone from his eyes, his face bearing already the marks of incurable disease. He found that he could not after all talk to them in the old happy way. Instead he sat down on the ground and taking some ashes he sprinkled them around him and on his head. He struggled to speak but when the words came they were those of the *Miserere*, "Have mercy upon me, O God." His voice at least was unchanged and went steadily on. "A broken and contrite heart, O God, shalt Thou not despise." He finished the psalm and went away without another word. Doubtless when he had gone Clare and her sisters wept.

More and more now he withdrew into the lonely places in the mountains, that he might spend his days and nights in prayer. They had wrested his authority from him, many of his sons had forsaken him, but they could not take from him the power of prayer. And he was not entirely alone. The death of Peter Cathanii, and lately of Dominic too, had been among the sorrows of this time, but one or other of the faithful few was always with him, Leo his secretary, Bernard, Ruffino or Angelo. They could not understand the depth of his grief but they could love him and bear him company. Occasionally bitter lamentations broke from him, but not often. He found comfort during his last years, when he was so separated from the majority of his sons, in writing to them, and his letters contain no bitter words, only words of love and tenderness, pleading with them to keep the Rule, to be loving and humble and obedient. One letter which he wrote at this time may have been written to Elias, for it is a plea for love, humility and mercy, qualities which he knew Elias lacked. It opens gravely, "May the Lord bless thee. I speak to thee as best I can on the subject of thy soul." Then, after speaking of love and humility, it goes on, "and by this I wish to know if thou lovest God and me His servant and thine, to wit: that there be no brother in the world who has sinned, how great soever his sin may be, who after he hath seen thy face shall ever go away without thy mercy, if he seek mercy, and if he seek not mercy, ask thou him if he desires mercy. And if he afterwards appears before thy face a thousand times, love him more than me, to the end that thou mayest draw him to the Lord, and on such ones always have mercy."

The discontent which the brothers had felt over the revised Rule festered and the Whitsun Chapter of 1223 decided that Francis must be asked to rewrite it again. It seems probable that Cardinal Ugolino persuaded Francis that if he could rewrite it in a way that would be acceptable to them then it could be sanctioned by Pope Honorius and they would then have to obey. Francis did what they desired. Through these last years of his life he always did what they asked him to do, unless it went against his conscience, offering to them the humility and loving obedience that he longed to see again in them. He never demanded anything of other men that he did not give himself. He went away into the mountains above the valley of Rieti. Leo as always was with him, and one other brother, Bonizzi. He went to Monte Rainerio where far up the mountainside there was a lonely cavern, the sort of place that he loved. Below it were the woods and a rushing mountain stream and all about it a bird-haunted solitude. The mountain belonged to the Lady Columba, who had a house there. She welcomed Francis courteously to her mountain, sent food every day to the brothers, and left them alone. Though she comes only very briefly into the story she deserves her niche in history.

Francis, fasting and praying, set himself to his impossible task. All he could do was to alter the arrangement of the Rule, not its contents, that remained as before. He could neither add to nor take away from the commands of Christ. Incorporated in the first Rule, that now gave such dissatisfaction to the brothers, there had been that great burst of joyful praise. Francis omitted that now for the fountain of joy in him was sealed over with pain.

His days and nights of prayer and suffering ended, the Rule written out again by Leo to his dictation, he went back to the Portiuncula and put it humbly into the hands of Elias. And now a dark confusion falls upon the story and the only thing that emerges clearly is the almost unbelievable cruelty of Elias. For after a few days he came to Francis and told him that the Rule was lost. Who destroyed the Rule, at whose command, has never been known. That they were the same man is only a guess, though it seems a safe one. Francis cannot have believed what he was told but he accepted the statement quietly and travelled all the way back to Monte Rainerio with Leo and Bonizzi to write out the Rule again. But this time he was not left in peace, for Elias and some of the Ministers came after him, climbed up the steep mountain path to the cave where he was praying and told him they would not observe his Rule. "Make it for thyself and not for us," they said. Francis heard them with indignation and answered, "Let those who will not obey it go out from the Order." The ministers looked at each other, and went away confused and frightened.

There was only one thing for Francis to do now, finish writing out the Rule all over again and take it to Cardinal Ugolino the Protector of the Order. The Cardinal was in Rome, a long journey for a man as ill as Francis, but he set forth courageously. It was his last visit to Rome, the last time his mortal eyes saw the holy city on her seven hills. He had to leave Leo behind him, and it must have been a hard parting for them both, but he left a letter for him, a letter of quiet tenderness that evidently carried on some conversation they had had together. It seems to echo some quietness within his own soul, as though the shadows were beginning to lift a little. "Brother Leo, wish thy father Francis health and peace! I say to thee: Yes, my son, and as a mother; for in this word and counsel I sum up briefly all the words we said on the way, and if afterwards thou hast need to come to me for advice, thus I advise you: In whatever way it seemeth best to thee to please the Lord God and to follow His footsteps and poverty, so do with the blessing of the Lord God and in my obedience. And if it be necessary on account of thy soul or other consolation and thou wishest, Leo, to come to me, come!"

In Rome Francis and Cardinal Ugolino worked over the Rule together. If the Cardinal modified it in any way it was only slightly. It did not embody the changes that had been hoped for but it was not in him to hurt Francis any more. He lacked the cruelty of Elias when in pursuit of what he wanted. They took it to the Pope, and Honorius, so in sympathy with Francis and all he stood for, solemnly approved it on November the 29th, 1223.

Francis travelled back to the Portiuncula and gave it to Elias. There was nothing Elias could say now for the Rule had the papal authority. On the face of it Francis had won the battle and could say with Saint Paul, "I have fought a good fight, I have finished my course, I have kept the faith," but he was still intensely sad, foreseeing perhaps what skill Elias and his men would show in interpreting the Rule according to their own ideas.

And then God comforted him, for he heard again the interior Voice telling him not to be so distressed, but to lay all that he loved, his work, his Order, his sons, in the hands of his Master Christ and to leave them there. It is a touch of human weakness in Francis, making him akin to ourselves, that he had been forgetting that if he loved his sons so much God loved them infinitely more. He had done all that he could and now God would do the rest. "I will keep and feed them," said the Voice. "Be not therefore perturbed but work out thy salvation; for even if the religion should come to but three members, yet through My gift shall it remain unshaken." Kneeling in Santa Maria degli Angeli Francis realized that the great darkness of spirit in which he had been living for more than two years had been a temptation to despair, a temptation to doubt the love of God. He had been crying, "My God, my God, why hast Thou forsaken me?" when God had been there all the time. He wept. Then a great peace fell upon him. The time had come now to work out his own salvation by such an abandonment of himself to the will of God that he would hold back from nothing whatever that God wished to do in him and with him for the salvation of others. For he knew that salvation is never a lonely thing. There was never a soul saved yet whose salvation was not a sort of net of glory for the catching of other souls. His prayer now was that of the Mother of Our Lord in whose own church he was kneeling. "Be it unto me according to Thy word."

Chapter Three

MIDWINTER SPRING

O ye sinners, erring throng,　　Humble men, and innocent,
Serving evil lords so long,　　Upright men, and diligent,
Come and hail this Infant Birth!　　Come before Him, come and sing.
Come, and make a joyful sound;　　Let Him not in vain entreat,
God with Men henceforth is found,　　Come and kneel before His feet,
He is come to dwell on earth.　　Giving glory to your King.
As a Little Boy He's here;　　Ye shall have your hearts' desire,
Long-desired, we hold Him dear;　　Tasting, with the heavenly choir,
Very precious shall He be.　　Feasts of Love eternally.

Jacopone da Todi, *Lauda* LXIV

FRANCIS went back once more to the valley of Rieti, that he might spend Christmas there. This more southerly valley is gentler than Assisi's valley of Spoleto, and its people are happy and kindly. Francis had always loved it and now it was to be the setting for a wonderful resurgence of happiness in him, almost a return to the happy days of the springtime of the Order. The Portiuncula was now the stronghold of Elias, but the little towns of Greccio, Rieti and Poggio Bustone, the villages that clung to the mountainsides, the hermitages of the brethren that hid themselves among the rocks and the woods, were full of his old friends who loved him. For a few months he went in and out among them as he had always done, doing what he could for them. It was almost like the old days, and yet not quite like them, for in spite of his love and ceaseless thought for them they were aware of some fragile quality about this exquisite return, some quality about Francis himself that made their hearts ache. The peace that enclosed him, though he shared it with them, gave them a feeling of loneliness. More than ever they treasured up every word and action in their memories that they might not forget.

Francis had a plan for this Christmas, a plan for himself and for them. He had a good friend who lived at Greccio, Giovanni da

Vellita, a member of the Third Order. He had been, and still was, a well-to-do man, but he used his money and land now for God and His poor. He had wanted to do something for Francis and his brothers, and had made them a hermitage, and because he understood their tastes he had been very careful not to make it too luxurious. Greccio is built within a hollow in the mountains, and opposite the little town, on land he owned, were some caves in the rocky hillside, with woods above and below them. He built a rough hermitage about these caves. It was an ideal Franciscan hermitage for although it was not particularly comfortable it gave shelter from cold winds and had a distant view of the lovely valley of Rieti and the snowcapped mountains beyond. Views, like flowers, were not luxuries to Francis but revelations of the glory of God. He decided that he would spend this Christmas at the Greccio hermitage, and he asked Giovanni to help him make it memorable.

His mind was back in Bethlehem and he remembered the night when he had knelt in the Cave of the Nativity. The Child in the manger had been as near to him then as though he had held Him in his arms. It had been one of those experiences that cannot be entirely shared but he wanted to share it as far as possible. What could he do that these good people of the Rieti valley should be able to say, "Unto us a Child is born, unto us a Son is given," not just with their lips but as a cry of conviction from adoring hearts? They were a simple and childlike people, even as he was himself, and to behold with their bodily eyes the stable and the manger, and the gentle beasts, would help them to see the Babe. He opened his heart to Giovanni, and Giovanni understood what he wanted and did what Francis told him. He built a stable in the woods near the hermitage and he put a real manger in the stable and filled it with hay, and beside the manger he built a simple altar. He arranged that there should be a real ox and ass there on Christmas eve, and he kept it all the deep secret that children love. Francis, meanwhile, sent messages to the brethren who lived in the valley of Rieti, and to the people of Greccio and of the villages, and asked them all to come to mass at the hermitage on Christmas eve.

They counted the days to the holy night and then they came.
Down in the darkness of the valley of Rieti lights began to
twinkle, as men and women and children carrying lanterns made
their way along the narrow paths towards the mountain. Across
the upland valley the lights of Greccio had been shining out of the
little windows for some while. Now the citizens came winding
down the hillside, some of them with lanterns and some with
candles. All the myriad twinkling lights were like stars and there
were stars in the sky. The people came singing the ancient *laude*
of Umbria that had been handed down from generation to
generation, *laude* in honour of the Christ-child so soon to be born,
and as the converging bands of pilgrims met together the sound
of their singing floated up strongly and beautifully to those who
were waiting for them high up in the darkness of the woods.
They could not sing as they climbed, for the rocky paths were
steep, but in the soft thick darkness under the trees, where the air
was warm and sweet-scented with the resinous pines and larches,
the candle flames burned brightly. Up above them it was the
brothers who were chanting now, and light streamed down from
some place within the woods. The youngest got there first,
scrambling up the last steep bit of the way to the more level
ground, and then running towards the light. Their elders, toiling
behind them, heard their high excited cries of awe and joy, like
the calling of birds, and a few came flying back saying, "Padre!
Madonna! There is a stable there. There is a manger for the
bambino, and an ox and an ass, a real ox and ass! And Father
Francis is there. Come quickly! Quickly!"

The wood became a church and the stable the chancel of the
church. They knelt with bowed heads on the carpet of moss and
pine needles. The lanterns were set on the ground or hung on the
branches of trees and the pools of light about them showed ferns
growing in the earth, lichens and bright toadstools about the roots
of trees. Some of those who had brought candles still held them
between their hands and the flames, symbols of their prayer,
showed the young faces sunburnt and rosy, the older ones lined
and weather-beaten. Those who were nearest to the stable could
see a manger and the gentle beasts, the vested priest before the

R

altar and Francis the deacon, but those who were too far away to see much were not aware of any loss for the great peace and joy of this holy night enclosed them all.

Francis was more in heaven than on earth, all his being centred on the manger, and seemed hardly conscious of the people, yet when after the reading of the Gospel he came forward to preach to them he was the same great preacher who had shaken the crowd in the piazza at Bologna. Celano says, "his voice, his strong voice, and glad voice, clear voice and ringing voice, invited all to seek the highest good." Yet still he seemed not to see them. He saw the Child of Bethlehem, and greeted Him Who was coming, and when he spoke the word "Jesus" his hearers were awed with the sense of a Presence already amongst them. He saw the shepherds leaning on their crooks, looking up to the stars, and the Italian folk sitting in the wood were with him on the hillside above Bethlehem. Their lanterns lit the sheepfold and they heard the sheep bleating. Across the dark valley the lights of Greccio shone from white-walled Bethlehem. It was towards midnight. Francis blessed them and turned from them and there was a rustling in the wood as they once more knelt and put their brown hands palm to palm in prayer. It was midnight and the Host was lifted. "While all things were in quiet silence, and that night was in the midst of her swift course, Thine Almighty Word leaped down from heaven out of Thy royal throne." Giovanni da Vellita said afterwards that when he looked towards the crib he saw a bambino in the hay.

Francis stayed on at Greccio until the late spring, coming back from each visit to the people in the valley to spend days and nights in prayer, in the hermitage or in the woods that were now ringing with birdsong. Down below in the valley the vines were green and the orchards were pink and white with blossom. He was at the hermitage for Easter and preached to the brothers a very memorable sermon.

This was the manner of it. The brothers had thought to make their Easter dinner something special this year, for Father Francis was with them. They borrowed a white tablecloth and some fine dishes, and they arranged the table with pride and care. While they were busy in the kitchen Francis came into the refectory and it seemed to his startled eyes that the table was laid as though this was a nobleman's house. The brothers who were with him in the hermitage were his good and loyal sons but it seemed that even they had been unconsciously affected by the love of comfort that was creeping so insiduously into the Order. What could he do? He could not be angry with them on Easter day. He thought what he would do. A poor man had come to the hermitage that day and had had a pilgrim's staff and scrip with him. Francis borrowed them and went quietly away into the woods.

When the brothers came to dinner Francis was not there, but he was sometimes late for meals when prayer absorbed him and he had told them when that happened not to wait for him, and so they sat down and began to eat. Then came a knock at the door and one of the brothers went to open it. On the threshold stood Francis, the scrip slung over his shoulder and the staff in his hand. He walked to the open door of the refectory and cried out, "For the love of the Lord God give an alms to this poor and infirm pilgrim." Knowing and loving Francis's fine child-like dramatic instinct the Minister entered into the spirit of his performance and replied, "Brother, we also be poor, and since we be many, the alms we have be necessary to us. But for the love of that Lord whom thou hast named, enter the house, and we'll give you of the alms which the Lord hath given to us." And he gave Francis a platter with food upon it and Francis carried it to the fire and sat down on the earth floor with the plate on his knees, as they had done at the Portiuncula in the old days. And then he sighed and said, "When I saw the table worshipfully and sumptuously laid out, I thought within myself it was not the table of poor religious who daily go from door to door for alms. For it becomes us, dearest, more than other religious to follow the example of the humility and poverty of Christ, because we are professed and called to this before God and men." And then some of the friars began to weep because they were so ashamed.

Francis went as usual to the Whitsun Chapter at the Portiuncula, for that was his duty, but there was no fighting sermon, no protest of any sort, for that was all over. Yet that chapter of 1224 was a memorable one for it was then that Agnellus and his brothers were commissioned for England. English people can hold as one of their particular treasures the knowledge that Francis blessed these friars as one of his last actions before he went away into the wilderness to meet his God. They carried his "The Lord give thee peace" with them as a gift to England. On the September day when they landed in England Francis was kneeling in prayer upon Monte Alvernia.

Chapter Four

ALVERNIA

Gazing on Thee, Thou Bright and morning Star,
I am led far, I know not where I be;
My heart is melted like a waxen bar,
That moulded in Christ's likeness it may be;
O Christ, Thy barters keen and wondrous are!
I am stript naked, to be dust in Thee:
My heart transformed in me,
  My mind lies dumb,
  To see Thee come,
In sweetness and in Love.

Now on no creature can I turn my sight,
But on my Maker all my mind is set;
Earth, sea, and sky are emptied of delight,
For Christ's dear love all else I clean forget:
All else seems vile, day seems as dark as night:
Cherubim, seraphim, in whom are met
Wisdom and Love, must yet
  Give place, give place,
  To that One Face
To my dear Lord of Love.

Jacopone da Todi?
From *Lauda* xc "Amor de Caritate", which has been ascribed to Saint Francis

THE thought of Alvernia must always have been at the back of Francis's mind, that mountain that had been a gift to him and would lift him up to receive a gift from God of which perhaps he had some foreknowledge in the mingled fear and longing that came to him whenever he thought of Alvernia. Now, in the burning days of harvest, his thoughts turned to the holy angels. In common with the men of his time he had a great devotion to the angels, especially to the archangel Michael. He told his sons that the angels are companions to be revered and guardians to be called upon, that their presence must not be outraged and that we

ought not to presume to do before them what we should not do
before men. In those days a Lent was kept in their honour, and
the honour of Mary Queen of Heaven, a fast which lasted from
the Feast of the Assumption on August the 15th until the Feast of
Saint Michael on September the 29th. Francis knew that this year
God had called him to keep the angels' Lent on Monte Alvernia.

He chose the sons who were nearest and dearest to him to be his
companions; Leo, Angelo, Masseo, Ruffino, Sylvester, Illuminato
who had been with him on the crusades and probably Bonizzo
who had been with him through the suffering days on Monte
Rainerio. Of his close friends only Bernard and Giles seem to
have been absent. And so with these seven he set out on the long
journey northward, up the valley of the Tiber where the grape
harvest was in full swing, through the villages and the woods,
through the valley of the Arno to the foot of the mountain. He
was too weak for the steep climb up Alvernia but the brothers
borrowed a donkey for him to ride upon from a peasant. "Tell
me, art thou Brother Francis of Assisi?" asked the peasant, and
when Francis answered, "Yes," he said, "Take heed, then, that
thou be in truth as good as all men account thee; for many have
great faith in thee, and therefore I admonish thee to be no other
than what the people take thee for." This was the kind of remark
that appealed irresistibly both to Francis's humility and to his sense
of humour. He was so delighted with it that though he had just
got on the donkey he got off it again that he might kneel on the
ground and kiss the peasant's feet.

When they had climbed some way and had come through the
woods of the lower slopes, where in their season the wild cyclamen carpet the ground, and emerged on to the rocks above, they
stopped to rest, and Francis sat under a tree with the great view
spread out before him. Far down below were the villages built on
the little hills among their vines and olives, the Arno twinkling
through the plain, the great mountains in the distance blue and
cloud-like in the heat. Within their ravines and valleys were
so many places that he had loved throughout his life, paths along
which he had walked, castled villages where he had preached and
healed. He sat lost in memory, considering the great view. The

silence, the quietness of the heights, was profound. Then, says *The Little Flowers of Saint Francis*, "while he was thus considering, behold there came a great multitude of birds from divers regions, which, by singing and clapping their wings, testified great joy and gladness, and surrounded Saint Francis in such wise, that some perched upon his shoulders, some on his arms, some on his bosom, and others at his feet, which when his companions and the peasant saw, they marvelled greatly; but Saint Francis, being joyful at heart, said to them: 'I believe, dearest brethren, that our Lord Jesus Christ is pleased that we should dwell on this solitary mount, inasmuch as our little brothers and sisters, the birds, show such joy at our coming.' And having said these words, he arose and proceeded to the place which had been fixed upon by his companions; and so did Saint Francis come to the holy mount of Alvernia."

Far up above the rocks, where there were trees again, pines and great beeches, the Lord Orlando had built huts of clay and interwoven branches for the brothers, and a chapel which was called after Santa Maria degli Angeli. When he heard that Francis had come to Alvernia he was filled with joy, and the next day he and his servants came carrying food for the brethren, and he told them to send to him at his castle if there was anything they wanted. When he had gone Francis was distressed about this, for he feared that to have such care taken of them was not holy poverty. But the brothers must have felt it a weight off their minds.

Then the eight men entered into the quietness of that threshold of heaven that is always there for us, like an old church porch in a street where the traffic thunders by, if only we can manage to forget ourselves and our busyness for long enough to become conscious of it, to get out of the traffic and go in. These men had learnt how to do that, and according to their capacity they went in, some deeper than others, Francis deepest of all. He chose a hut a little apart from the others, under a beech tree, and asked that only Leo should come to him, to minister to him as a priest and to bring him bread and water. He asked the rest to help him with their prayers, for he knew that God had some purpose for him in this place, some work to be wrought in him and through him, and he wanted to be lifted up into that state of readiness which is the work of prayer. For days and nights he prayed that he might be conformed to the will of God, the prayer of his whole life that he had prayed in San Damiano. "Be found of me, Lord, so that in all things I may act in accordance with Thy holy will." And then one day he went out of his cell, and stood under the beech tree, and he began to have some premonition of what that will might be. The air was the pure cold air of the heights, the stillness absolute, before him was that great view and at his feet the precipice of rocks fell sheer away, rent into great chasms. The beauty and splendour of nature always lifted him up to God. With the rock of Alvernia strong beneath his feet he thought of Christ the rock, his strength and stay, rent by the sin of man. The mountain was speaking to him of the passion of Christ. He was caught up into prayer and he became convinced that the fissures in the rock had been torn at the moment when Christ died. Alvernia had shared the passion of Christ.

From that moment he became more withdrawn into prayer, and Leo, coming to minister to him, was aware of the withdrawal, and felt a sorrow akin to the sorrow of death. He had given Francis the whole of a son's devoted love and his father was being lifted away from him to some place where he was not able to follow. He prayed that God would have mercy upon him and in spite of his unworthiness give him a share in Francis's grace.

The conviction that to meet what was coming he must get away from men, even from Leo, was driving Francis all the time into a deeper loneliness. In the hut under the beech tree they could hear him if he called. He felt he would be more entirely in the hands of God if he was beyond the help of man. One day, as the Feast of the Assumption drew near, he asked Leo to stand at the door of the chapel, while he himself went deeper into the wood. Every now and then he called, and Leo answered, and when he reached a spot where Leo and he could no longer hear each other he knew that somewhere here was where he must be. He chose a ledge of rock that was divided from the way he had come by a deep chasm. An experience was coming to him that would set him apart from other men, set a chasm between him and them, and his deep unconscious sense of drama and symbolism was even now at work. The brothers made a little cell of interwoven branches on the rock, and bridged the chasm with a branch of a tree, and listened trembling to their instructions. Francis was a sick man and they must have been afraid for him. "Return now to your place," he said, "and leave me here alone; for, by the help of God, I intend to pass this Lent here, without any disturbance or perturbation of mind; therefore let none of you come unto me, nor suffer any secular person to come near the cell. But thou only, Brother Leo, once a day shalt come to me with a little bread and water, and once a night at the hour of matins, and thou shalt come in silence; and when thou art upon the bridge, thou shalt say, *Domine labia mea aperies*; and if I answer thee, thou shalt come to the cell, and we will say matins together; and if I do not answer thee, thou shalt depart forthwith." On the Feast of the Assumption he gave them his blessing and went away from them across the little bridge.

Mystics are explorers and all that now happened beyond that bridge happened in a far country. Francis tried to speak of the country in a few broken words to Leo when he came to minister to him, and in more detail to the seven brothers when he had come back to them again, but the words that are the currency of our everyday life in the body do not serve for the vision of God in the life of the spirit, and it can seem to the saints almost a desecration to use them to describe what they have seen. Angela of Foligno, one of the daughters of Saint Francis in the Third Order, said, "All that I say of this seemeth unto me to be nothing, I even feel as though I offended in speaking of it; for so greatly doth that Good exceed all my words that my speech doth appear to blaspheme against it."

Francis in his oratory on the rock gave himself courageously to that purgatory which in any world must precede the soul's union with God. Feeling the approach of a love terrible in its power and purity he was racked with that deep and searching sense of sin that pierced Peter when he cried, "Depart from me; for I am a sinful man, O Lord," and through these days and nights his suffering reached a point that he could hardly bear. "If the friars knew," he whispered to Leo, "there is not one of them who would not be moved to compassion and pity." But he was not left without help. Every midnight, in the great darkness of the world and of his soul, he heard the voice of Leo crying out the opening words of matins, "*Domine labia mea aperies*," and then his son would cross the bridge and they would kneel in prayer together and he would be comforted. One day, exhausted and wretched, he prayed that God would grant him some foretaste of the joy of heaven to help him bear the load of sin. Then it seemed to him that an angel was close to him, strengthening him. The great spirit had a viol in his left hand and a bow in his right, and just once he lifted the bow and drew it across the strings. Francis told his sons afterwards that had the music continued his soul would have left his body, for the joy of it could not be borne.

A falcon made herself his close companion. She had a nest close to his cell. In the daytime she would keep close to him to comfort him, and at night she made herself his clock, crying and flapping her wings when the hour for matins drew near. If she saw him more than usually sick and weary she would let him rest a little longer, but always she had him alert and ready for Leo. Francis took great delight in his falcon. The man, the angel and the bird brought him strength from God.

II

The days drew on to the Feast of the Holy Cross, September the 14th, kept holy by all Christians in remembrance of the day when the true cross had been won back from the Persian conqueror who had taken it away from Jerusalem. It was a day especially sacred for Francis because of what the cross meant to him, and because it was the patronal festival of the crusaders. The day had for him now a personal sadness. He had with longing offered himself to die a martyr's death upon the crusade, that he might have some share in the suffering and death of his Lord, and at that time his offering had not been accepted.

One night during these days Leo came to the bridge and called aloud, "*Domine labia mea aperies*," but for the first time there was no answer. He had been forbidden to cross the bridge if Francis did not answer him, but he was so afraid that his father might be now seriously ill that he disobeyed him and crossed the bridge. The cell was empty, but he went farther on into the wood beyond, for the moon was bright and he could see the way. Then he heard Francis speaking, and coming nearer he saw him kneeling in prayer and heard the words that he said. "Who art Thou, my dearest Lord? And who am I, a most vile worm and thy most unprofitable servant?" That was all his prayer, and he spoke the same words over and over again. Then it seemed to Leo that a light came from heaven and rested upon Francis, and though he himself could hear no words he believed that they were spoken, and three times over he saw Francis take his hands from his breast and stretch them up to the light. Then the splendour was withdrawn, and in joy, knowing that all was well with Francis, Leo turned, hoping to creep away unseen. But the fallen beech leaves rustled under his feet and Francis looked round and saw him and commanded him to stay where he was. Leo stood still and he trembled, for he had disobeyed and he was afraid Francis would be angry with him.

Francis came towards Leo but his eyes were now so dim that though the wood was bright with moonlight he did not know who it was who stood there, and he said, "Who art thou?" Leo said, "Father, I am Brother Leo," and kneeling at Francis's feet he asked for forgiveness. Francis knew the anxious love that had prompted the disobedience and he was not angry, but gentle and tender, and when he knew that Leo had heard his words, and seen the light and the lifting of his hands, he tried to tell him of what he had experienced in prayer. He said he had been kneeling in contemplation and he had beheld, as he was able to endure it, the goodness of God, and then he had seen the fearful abyss of his own vileness and out of the deep he had cried out, "Who art Thou, my dearest Lord? And who am I?" And then the Voice that had spoken to him so often spoke again from out of the light that rested upon him, asking him for three gifts, and he was distressed because he had nothing to give. He possessed nothing except his cord and tunic, and even they had been given him by

God. Then the Voice said, "Search in thy bosom," and putting his hands to his breast he found a golden ball there, and a second and a third, and he lifted them up to God, thanking Him that of His mercy he had given His servant something that he might offer. At first he did not understand what he was offering, and then he realized that the three golden balls were poverty, chastity and obedience. And he knew too that though God had come very close to him He would come nearer still, and that it would be soon.

After they had talked together Francis and Leo went to the little oratory and Francis knelt before the altar and prayed that he might know something of the will of God concerning him, so that he might be able to conform himself the more perfectly to that blessed will. Then he signed himself with the sign of the cross, and turning to Leo he asked him to open the book of the Gospels and read to him the first passage upon which his eyes fell. Leo took the book and opened it, bending in the dim candlelight to see the page, and Francis kneeling before the altar heard him read of the crucifixion of his Lord. Twice more Leo opened the book and twice more it opened at the story of the passion. Then Francis knew that his offering had been accepted. He was to share the suffering of Christ.

On the morning of the Feast of the Holy Cross, just before dawn, he was kneeling at the entrance to his cell, his face towards the east where soon now the light would break. Near to him was a rock which must many times have reminded him of the rock of the agony beside which he had prayed in the Garden of Gethsemane. He was praying now and the words of his prayer were these: "O Lord Jesus Christ, two graces do I ask of Thee before I die; the first, that in my lifetime I may feel, as far as possible, both in my soul and body, that pain which Thou, sweet Lord, didst endure in the hour of Thy most bitter Passion; the second, that I may feel in my heart as much as possible of that excess of love by which Thou, O Son of God, was inflamed to suffer so cruel a Passion for us sinners." He continued for a long time in this prayer and passed from it to deep contemplation, wherein the eyes of his soul beheld the Passion of Christ and His infinite love. Perhaps the eyes of his body, closed in prayer, were yet aware of the glory of the dawn, and his ears of the singing of the birds in the woods below him, as the light grew. He looked up and saw the sky filled with fiery and resplendent wings and in the midst of the glory a Figure. Two wings were spread above the head, two were outstretched in flight and two covered the body. It seemed to Francis that the Seraph was coming from heaven to earth, drawing near with rapid flight, and he was much afraid. Then the fear changed to joy and grief and wonder for he saw that the Seraph came to him as One crucified, with arms outstretched and feet conjoined. This was his Lord, looking upon him with gracious aspect and immortal love, so near to him now that he could see the infinite beauty of the suffering face, so near at last that the pierced feet rested upon the rock. Then it seemed to him that the Seraph smote him in body and soul, so that he was in great agony and yet in great joy, and afterwards was so close to him that they spoke together. This moment of union seemed to Francis to lift him out of time into eternity.

Then he was alone, yet not alone, for the burning love in his heart was the same love that had come from the height of heaven down to the depth of man's need, his joy was Christ's joy in redemption and his pain Christ's pain. Every prayer of his life had been answered. He had fulfilled the will of God as perfectly as a man may, his offering of himself had been accepted and he was wholly Christ's. In token thereof the seal of the cross that had been set upon his immortal soul years ago was now upon his mortal body also. He bore in hands and feet and side the wounds of Christ.

III

The return was to this world, beautiful in the sunrise with the golden light gilding the woods and the mountains, and the birds singing, but still this world. Yet Francis afterwards did not say that he had felt grief that his soul had not been allowed to escape from his body, sorrow at the realization that Alvernia had been his Mount Carmel but not his Calvary, and that he must live on in this world a little longer. For he had never drawn back from anything God asked of him and he was not changed at all, only more deeply in love with the will of God than he had ever been, more full of zeal to serve Him. He left his cell and went back to the brothers. His own wish was to keep what had happened a secret between himself and his Lord, and then he wondered if God was sending him back into human life to share his joy with his sons that they might be strengthened and purged by it. As always, he did not trust his own judgement, and calling the brothers together asked them if they thought the favours of God should be revealed or hidden. Illuminato, looking at his transfigured face, at his hands hidden in the sleeves of his habit and the folds of the habit covering his feet, knew he had been near to heaven, and replied, "Brother, thou knowest that not for thyself alone are the heavenly secrets revealed to thee, but for others also." Then Francis set aside his own wish and told them of the vision, and he told them that his Lord had told him certain things that he might never make known as long as he lived. He told them of the stigmata but only to Leo did he show his wounds, and only to him because he wanted his help, for they gave him pain and he needed Leo to bandage them for him. Only after he died did any beyond the faithful few have full knowledge of what had happened to him.

For Francis, not in spite of the pain but because of it, these days brought a renewal of his youth. It was like the rebirth of the first days of his conversion, only more glorious. That had been the start of the stony uphill journey and he had set forth singing, so glorious had it been to set his feet in the footsteps of Christ. But now he had attained to the summit and the Master he had followed had turned and, even in this world, looked upon him. He lived now in the light of that regard and because the pain he suffered was God's own redemptive pain it was a part of the light and could not dim his joy. Other saints who have come through the darkness to this light of union have felt that in spite of the difficulty they must try to tell us of it in their books and verse because they know what hope it gives to sinners to have their pledge that the place of union is not something that exists only in our aching longing, but is in truth the end of our journey, even if it is an end that for most of us will be reached only at some point still far beyond the point of physical death. Francis, though he was a singer, was not a writer and he was not able to write about what had happened to him, nor did he need to because it was written upon his body. That was fitting for he had always made "a tongue of his whole body". But yet he felt that he must try and express in some way the praise and adoration that filled his whole being. That fount of joy that had been sealed in by sorrow was free again now as when after long drought the wells have broken. He asked Leo for pen and parchment and wrote the psalm that has been called "The praise of the Crucified".

> "Thou art the Holy Lord God; Thou art God of gods, Who alone workest marvels.
> Thou art strong, Thou art great, Thou art most high; Thou art almighty,
> > Thou holy Father, King of heaven and earth.
> Thou art threefold and one; Lord God of gods.
> Thou art good, every good, the highest good; the Lord God, living and true.
> Thou art love, charity; Thou art wisdom; Thou art humility.
> Thou art patience; Thou, fortitude and prudence.
> Thou art security, Thou art rest; Thou art joy and gladness.
> Thou art justice and temperance; Thou art all our wealth and plenty.
> Thou art beauty, Thou art gentleness; Thou art the protector; Thou art the keeper and the defender.
> Thou art our refuge and strength; Thou art our faith, hope and charity.
> Thou art our great sweetness; Thou art our eternal life.
> Infinite Goodness, great and wonderful Lord God Almighty; loving and merciful Saviour."

If the words do not pour forth quite in the headlong fashion of the days of his youth, when he wrote the first Rule, they hold the same joy, only flowing more quietly because more deeply.

Those who have attained union with God come back to the world again not bemused visionaries but men and women of action. Set free from self they are able to serve those about them with all their practical as well as spiritual powers lifted to the highest point of usefulness. Francis, though so ill and crippled and already a dying man, was yet able for a short while to begin life all over again, travelling, healing, preaching and comforting with tireless love. So now during these last days on Alvernia he did not go back to his lonely prayer but stayed with his sons that he might serve and comfort them.

Leo had special need of his help for he was still going through a time of lonely misery and darkness, feeling more than ever that Francis had moved away from him to a place where he could not follow and that he had lost him. He realized too, as he looked at Francis, what it really means to be a lover of God, what the cost is, and comparing himself with Francis he despaired of himself. He was a very humble person who felt himself unworthy of love. He felt shut out alike from the love of God and of Francis, like a child in the dark on the wrong side of the door. There was a certain blessing in the Old Testament that he loved very much and he thought that if Francis were to write this out for him, and he were to have it with him always, it would keep him from despair. But he could not bring himself to ask Francis to do this. He could not presume to intrude himself and his wretchedness upon the notice of this great saint in his bliss.

While Francis was writing out his praises Leo was sitting humbly near him, watching him with dog-like devotion but silent in his misery. Francis, after he had written the words, "Loving and merciful Saviour", turned the parchment over and wrote something else on the other side, and drew a small picture, and then handed it to Leo saying, "Take this sheet and carefully keep it by thee till the day of thy death." Leo took the sheet and to his amazement read the very blessing that he had longed for.

"The Lord bless thee and keep thee.
The Lord show His face to thee and have mercy upon thee.
The Lord turn His countenance to thee and give thee peace."

After this Francis had written, "Brother Leo, may our Lord bless thee," and below he had drawn the outline of a head and resting upon it in blessing the sign Tau, with which Francis always signed his letters. In utter joy Leo took the parchment, and the darkness was lifted from his mind and soul, never to return. From that day until the day when he died he kept it folded over his heart. It can be seen today in the sacristy of the Sacro Convento at Assisi, the creases where he folded it clearly visible. He annotated it three times in his exquisite handwriting. The first note reads, "Blessed Francis wrote with his own hand this blessing for me, Brother Leo." And the second is, "In like manner he made this sign Tau together with the head with his own hand." The third is longer. "Blessed Francis two years before his death kept a Lent in the place of Monte Alvernia in honour of the Blessed Virgin Mary, the Mother of the Lord, and of the Blessed Michael the archangel, from the feast of the Assumption of the Holy Virgin until the September feast of Saint Michael. And the Hand of the Lord was laid upon him; after the vision and speech of the Seraph and the impression of the Stigmata of Christ in his body he made and wrote with his own hand the Praises written on the other side of the sheet, giving thanks to the Lord for the benefits conferred on him."

Francis gave Leo a task to perform for him. He asked him to consecrate the stone upon which the feet of the Seraph had rested, as Jacob had consecrated the stone of his vision that it might be holy for ever. Leo washed it and then anointed it with wine, oil and balsam. To the other brothers we can believe that Francis had words to say to each man alone that he would never forget. We know that he talked long with Ruffino. And so the quiet days passed and the autumn morning came when Francis, with Leo to take care of him, was to start his journey back to the Portiuncula.

The Lord Orlando came to take leave of him, bringing a donkey for him to ride upon, and the six brethren who were to stay longer praying upon the mountain were weeping because they must say good-bye. God had visited them upon the mountain, drawing them into closer union with each other as well as with Himself, and the ending of such holy days was hard to bear. And they must have known that Francis would not see Alvernia again. Masseo wrote a description of his farewell to the brothers and to the mountain which is kept still in the convent at Alvernia.

S

"Our dearest father had decided to bid farewell to the holy mountain on September the 30th, 1224 ... My Lord Orlando, the Count of Chiusi, had sent up the beast for him to ride on, since on account of the wounds in his feet he could not walk. Early that morning he heard mass as usual in the little chapel of Our Lady of the Angels. Then he summoned the brethren and commanded them under obedience: they were to remain lovingly together, to give themselves to prayer, and to recite their office by day and by night. Then he commended to their care the holy mountain: never were the brethren, now or in the future, to use this mountain for any secular purposes: on the contrary, they were always to look upon it as a holy place, and he would bless quite specially those who lived here or looked after the holy place reverently. To me he then said: ' Brother Masseo, I want you to know that it is my desire that only good religious should live here—the best of my Order. O, Brother Masseo, what more can I say?' Then he began to take his leave: 'Farewell, Brother Masseo,' he said, 'farewell. Farewell, Brother Angelo.' And he said the same to Brother Sylvester and Brother Illuminato. Then he said: 'Live in peace, my dearest sons, and God bless you. I am going away, but my heart stays with you. I am going with Brother Leo, the lamb of God. I am going to Santa Maria degli Angeli, and I shall never come back. Now I must go, farewell, and love one another! Farewell, holy mountain. Farewell mountain of Alvernia. Farewell, dear Sister Falcon, and thank you for your kindness to me. Farewell, mighty rock of Sasso Spicco. I shall never see you again. Farewell, little chapel of Our Lady: to you, O Mother of the Word, I commend these sons of mine.' And so he left, weeping, and he took our hearts with him. I, Brother Masseo, have written this through my tears. God bless us all."

Through the centuries the brothers have obeyed the command of Francis and kept the mountain holy. A convent and church have been built there and the Chapel of the Stigmata encloses the rock that Leo consecrated. After matins and lauds have been said the brothers walk in procession through the cloisters from the church to the chapel, a large wooden cross carried before them. There they kneel and pray, and keep silence beside the rock, then return the way they came. The cloister has only been built in comparatively recent years, but through the years when there was no shelter for them the brothers came and went through the winter storms as well as the summer nights of stars. Only twice was the tempest so great that they could not go. It is said that one of those occasions was a night of deep snow. In the morning, when the sky had cleared, the brothers saw the smooth expanse of white snow patterned with the footprints of hundreds of birds and small creatures who had gone to the chapel in their stead.

IV

Francis, Leo, and the peasant whose donkey Francis was riding, descended the mountain together. As they climbed down the steep path towards Borgo San Sepolcro Francis was withdrawn into prayer. When they came to the little town and made their way through the steep streets, the people crowding joyously around Francis, he was unaware of the turmoil, and when they were out in the country again he asked Leo when they were coming to Borgo San Sepolcro? That evening they reached the convent of Monte Casale and rested there for a few days in the peace and beauty. Sitting at supper with the brothers on the first evening Francis was told of one of their number who was cruelly ill with epilepsy. Full of pity he took a piece of bread from his plate, made the sign of the cross upon it and sent it to the sick man, who when he had eaten it was cured. This man was the first of many sick people who were cured by Francis after he had received the stigmata, for now he was more than ever a channel of the peace and love of God to those who suffered.

When he was a little rested Francis and Leo set forth upon the next stage of their journey home. From the height of Monte Casale, before he rode down from the hills, Francis had his last view of Alvernia and he lifted his hand and blessed it. "Farewell, Mount of God, holy mount, farewell Monte Alvernia; God the Father, God the Son, God the Holy Spirit bless thee. Abide in peace since we shall see each other never more."

At Cita di Castello in the plain Francis stayed for some while at the earnest prayer of the people, and he ministered to them and healed their sick. When he left them the snow was already falling in the mountains and it was no weather for a sick man to be travelling. The peasant who was with them considered that it was no weather for any man to be travelling and when their first evening found them snowbound in the hills, unable to get to the village where they had hoped to find shelter and forced to spend the night sheltering under a rock, his lamentations were bitter. Francis gently laid his hand upon him. His hand when strong and supple had always had power but now that it was weak and wounded and full of pain, and very little use to Francis himself, its power to help others was redoubled. The shivering peasant felt a glow of warmth all through him. He was comforted, and like a child in its cot he curled up under the rock and slept all night as happily and peacefully as though it were midsummer. Francis, Leo and the donkey spent the night the best they could, the donkey with his back turned stoically to the weather and Francis and Leo contented because they were together.

The next day they came to the Portiuncula. There was no sorrow in this homecoming. In the soul of a man who has come as close to God as had Francis fear and anxiety have no place. Even Elias had no more power to hurt him now. He now knew Him in Whom he had believed and could say with Julian of Norwich, "All shall be well, and all manner of thing shall be well."

Chapter Five

THE LAST JOURNEY

They are truly peace makers who amidst all they suffer in this
world maintain peace in soul and body for the love of our Lord
Jesus Christ.

Writings of Saint Francis

I

ELIAS on his side received Francis with reverence, awe and joy, for
though Francis was not aware of it the news of some miraculous
happening at Alvernia had preceded him home. In the history of
the Church three hundred men and women are known to have
received the stigmata, one of whom, a son of Francis, still lives in
southern Italy, but Francis was the first of whom we have knowledge. For years past the children had been crying, "*Il Santo!
Il Santo!*" when he entered a village, but now he was a saint
indeed and in its possession of him the Order was privileged above
all others. His union with the suffering of Christ had integrated
and saved his sons. They would have their troubles and dissen-
sions after his death but what he had suffered and what he was
would always hold them. Elias, welcoming him home, forgot the
irritations of the past. From now until the end their relationship
has a touching beauty about it. Elias fussed over Francis with the
tenderness of a devoted mother, and Francis gave his dying body
into Elias's keeping with peaceful obedience, gratitude and
humour.

But after his return to the Portiuncula he still had a few more
months of active work before him. As soon as possible after his
return home he set off on his last missionary tour, to the dismay of
the brothers, for his body was so broken with illness and pain that
they did not know how he would live through it. But the great
power of love that filled him gave his body a miraculous strength.
"Let us now *begin* to serve God," he said to the brothers. All that

he had done up till now seemed to him nothing. He had seen all the suffering of the world in the face of the crucified Seraph and he must spend himself for the suffering poor for as long as he could go on. He kept going right on into the summer. Celano says, "He filled all the earth with Christ's Gospel, so that often in one day he would make the circuit of four or five villages or even towns, preaching to everyone the gospel of the Kingdom of God. ... And though he could no longer walk he went round the country riding on an ass." Through these months he had an especial loving care of the sick, and in particular the lepers. This new rebirth had brought back to him the days of his conversion and as well as he could he tried to tend the lepers as he had done as a young man. They above all other men stood to him for the suffering Christ.

During this time not only his health but his eyesight got much worse and when he returned to the Portiuncula Elias took action with guile. Cardinal Ugolino was now at Rieti with the Pope and his court and unknown to Francis Elias wrote to him and told him of Francis's condition. The Cardinal replied that Francis must come at once to Rieti and be examined by the Pope's own physician.

Francis would rather have stayed quietly where he was, in the peace of his beloved Portiuncula, taking such pain as came to him as God's will for him, but he was glad to do what Elias wanted. In the past he had not been able to give his conscience into the keeping of the Minister General, and so he was all the more happy to be able to give his body. Accompanied by the faithful four who hardly ever left him now, Leo, Ruffino, Masseo and Angelo, he started out on his last memorable journey. In one sense it was a pitiful journey, a way of sorrows, for he was dragged from doctor to doctor and from place to place when there was nothing that anyone could do for him. Yet each resting-place, each station of the cross, was the scene of some heavenly occurrence, each like a light lit in a dark place, so that the journey in the end had been a gift to the whole world that has never been forgotten.

The first stage of the journey was a very short one. Francis, when he left the Portiuncula with the brothers, decided that he would like to stop at San Damiano on his way and pay a short visit to Clare and say good-bye to her. His scrupulosity about visiting her had vanished now with his other mental miseries and their love was what it had always been, only deeper. In the phrase of little Agnes he came very often now "to comfort her in Christ". And she comforted him, for she understood his suffering and his joy as perhaps not even Leo was able to do, for she in her different way had come to Mount Carmel also. Francis had meant to spend only one night at San Damiano, and to continue his journey the next day, but that first night he was suddenly taken very ill, and by the morning they all realized that he would not be able to go on for the present. All their plans were frustrated, but as so often happens, out of the frustration of man's plan God's plan came to fruition. Out of that long wait at San Damiano God brought slowly to birth a song which is one of the treasures of the world.

Under Clare's direction the brothers built a wattle cell for Francis in the convent garden, like the one he had at the Portiuncula. It was early summer and he could hear the birds singing and smell the flowers in the convent garden, and the love of the devoted four and of Clare and her sisters upheld him. Clare sat by him often, busy with her exquisite needlework. There is still to be seen, at Santa Chiara, the pair of sandals of soft leather that she made for him to ease his wounded feet. But his pains increased. To the wasting misery of his disease and the throbbing of the wounds was added torturing pain in his eyes and for a while he became totally blind. And then his cell became overrun with field mice. Had he been able to see sister mouse and her bright eyes he would not have minded so much, but in the total darkness which enclosed him it was an added misery to have the little creatures scampering everywhere. They allowed him no rest and tormented him so much that he could not even pray.

At last one night even he came to feel that his suffering had become more than he could bear. The hours before dawn, when vitality is at its lowest, can be hard to endure even for the sighted, but they can find comfort in watching for the sunrise. For the blind these hours are the worst of all because they know that even when the sun does rise it will make no difference. Francis, though

he had looked into God's face of love at Alvernia, actually began
to wonder if God was punishing him because he was such a great
sinner. He said, "My God, I am worthy of this, and even of
worse." And then, and all sufferers will know just how he felt,
the suffering itself began to feel like sin. It seemed like a dark
cloud that separated him from God and he prayed, "My Lord
Jesus Christ, Thou Good Shepherd . . . grant to me, Thy little
lamb, that no pain, however great, no infirmity or anguish shall
ever separate me from Thee." There could be no greater misery
than this, separation from God. When that thought came to him
the anguish had reached its peak and began to ebb. He could
realize again that God was with him, always had been with him
and always would be. He heard the interior Voice talking to him
and began to glow with a return of the joy of Alvernia. The
Voice asked him, if all the beautiful things of earth, the rivers, the
sun, the hills and the sea, were made of gold and balm and
precious stones, and if he could find a treasure more precious still
than all these, and he were offered it in place of his suffering,
would he not rejoice and be content? And Francis answered,
"Lord, I am unworthy of such a treasure." And the Voice said to
him, "Rejoice with all thy heart, Francis, for such a treasure is life
eternal which I have in keeping for thee, and even now promise to
thee; and this thine infirmity and affliction is a pledge of that
treasure."

Francis lay still in worship. He heard the first flutings of the
birds and knew that the sky was lightening. It was no longer a
grief to him that he could not see the sun, and would not again see
clearly the beauty of earth that he loved so well, for like his
suffering it had been given to him as a pledge of heaven. It was
passing from him now, for it had done its work, preparing him
by its reflections and shadows of blessedness for the heaven of
God's love that was to come, encompassing him about with songs
of deliverance. Yet in its passing he felt he loved it more dearly
than ever, adored God in it and for it as never before and was
infinitely grateful for all that God through the beauty of the world
had given him and taught him. He had loved his brothers and
sisters the birds and animals and flowers but now with heaven so

near his thoughts turned not so much to them as to those greater creatures of God, the sun and moon, the stars and winds and waters, and mother earth herself. Joy mounted in him, up and up with the song of the lark as she sprang towards the sun. When the warmth of the new day was on his face, and the life of the convent began to stir, he called the brothers that he might share his joy with them, for he never hoarded joy. When they had gathered round him Francis rose from his bed and began to sing.

Not now in the language of the troubadours, for the earth and sun were to him the earth and sun of Italy, the fire the one that burned under the pot in the homes of the poor. He sang in Italian, in rugged rhyme, as the peasants sang their laude, and the simple song that had grown out of the night of pain was so full of joy that it has become one of the deathless songs of all time.

"O most high, almighty, good Lord God, to Thee belong praise, glory, honour and all blessing!

Praised be my Lord God with all His creatures, and specially our brother the sun, who brings us the day and who brings us the light; fair is he and shines with a very great splendour: O Lord, he signifies to us Thee!

Praised be my Lord for our sister the moon, and for the stars, the which He has set clear and lovely in heaven.

Praised be my Lord for our brother the wind, and for air and clouds, calms and all weather by which Thou upholdest life in all creatures.

Praised be my Lord for our sister water, who is very serviceable unto us and humble and precious and clean.

Praised be my Lord for our brother fire, through whom Thou givest us light in the darkness; and he is bright and pleasant and very mighty and strong.

Praised be my Lord for our mother the earth, the which doth sustain us and keep us, and bringeth forth divers fruits and flowers of many colours, and grass.

Praise ye and bless the Lord, and give thanks unto Him and serve Him with great humility."

The three-fold rhythm was still the same, first the solitary darkness of prayer, then the illumination and afterwards the practical action. Francis was full of zeal now to conquer men's hearts for God with song. Having set his canticle to music he sent for Brother Pacifico, his poet laureate, and taught it to him, and to other brothers who had good voices. He planned to send his singers on tour through the world. When they came to towns and villages first a brother was to preach, and then they were all to sing the canticle, and then they were to say to the people, "We are God's jongleurs; and for that we have sung to you, we ask a reward: and our reward will be that you all abide in sincere penitence."

Francis was soon given proof of the power of his canticle. While he still lay ill at San Damiano he was told that the Bishop and the Mayor of Assisi had quarrelled. They were no longer on speaking terms and the Bishop had excommunicated the Mayor. Assisi appeared to be enjoying the quarrel for no one was doing anything at all to compose it. Francis was grieved and after some thought he made a plan. He added a new verse to his canticle, and then he sent one brother to the Bishop asking him to receive the Mayor, and another to the Mayor telling him to go with his magistrates to the Bishop's palace, and to his singers, he said, "Go and sing the Canticle of Brother Sun before the Bishop and the Podesta and the others who are with them, and I trust in the Lord that He will immediately humble their hearts, and they will return to their first love and friendship." For love of Francis everyone did what they were told, and when they were all gathered together in the open court of the Bishop's cloister one of the brothers stood up and told them how Francis had composed this canticle in his sickness, and then all the brothers sang it, adding the new verse which Francis had written.

"Praised be my Lord for all those who pardon one another for love's sake, and who endure weakness and tribulation;
Blessed are they who peaceably shall endure, for Thou, O most Highest, shalt give them a crown."

The voices that had rung very sweetly in the cloistered enclosure fell silent and to the everlasting glory of the laity it was the

Mayor who moved first. With tears running down his face, for he was devoted to Francis, he walked across to the Bishop and knelt at his feet and said, "Behold, I am ready to make satisfaction for everything as it shall please you, for the love of our Lord Jesus Christ, and of His servant blessed Francis." But Bishop Guido was only a few minutes behind the Mayor in the movement of charity. Taking his hands he raised him and said, "My office bids me be humble, yet because I am naturally prompt to wrath, it behoves that thou shouldst pardon me." Then they embraced each other and the quarrel was over.

II

After six weeks at San Damiano Francis was able to travel slowly on to Rieti. The rumour of the stigmata had preceded him and he was received with reverence and devotion by the Pope and his court, and by the whole city. It was almost as though he had been canonized in his lifetime, so great was the honour accorded him. He was lodged in the Bishop's palace, and here the sick were brought to him that he might pray for them and bless them, and many were healed. But although he was a channel of healing to others the doctors could give him no relief from his own suffering. He was content, knowing that only by bearing pain himself could he be used to set others free from it. It was said of his Lord, "He saved others; Himself He cannot save." That is the way of salvation. There is no other way. And so he bore it gladly, and found great comfort in meditating on the glory of God as revealed in creation. When we think how hard it is even for the best men and women to turn their thoughts outward when they are in dire pain, how absorbed they are by the struggle to maintain courage and patience, we realize what a spiritual achievement this was.

At Rieti he had a great longing to hear the viol played. After his God music had been the great delight of his life, and it was until the end. One of the brothers looking after him had been an expert violist before he joined the Order and Francis begged him to borrow a viol "and bring comfort to brother body who is full of pains". But the brother demurred. He now considered the viol a frivolous instrument and he did not know what people would think of him if he asked for such a thing. They were in the palace of the Bishop of Rieti. Not only was his own reputation as a holy brother at stake but also that of Francis as a saint. All the brothers were very anxious that Francis, the glory of the Order, should behave as a saint is expected to behave. They had their anxieties in these days for unexpectedness was a part of Francis. But he was a humble and good patient and he yielded at once. "Let it be," he said. "It is better to put aside good things than to give scandal."

But all that day he went on thinking of the beauty of music, until with the coming of night his thoughts were filled with the thought of the beauty of God. When night was in the midst of her course, and the little town lay still, Francis was alone and awake in the darkness. There was complete silence, very heavenly, and then gently and gradually entering into the silence, music. Someone was playing the viol under his window. The musician touched his instrument with an unearthly skill, and the music sounded now here, now there, as though the player were passing gently back and forth. Yet there was no sound of footsteps, only that heavenly music, such music as Francis had not heard since the angel had played to him on Alvernia. He forgot his pain for in the place to which the music lifted him there was no suffering.

But Francis was not happy in a town, lodged in a palace and the centre of reverence and adulation, and presently he was moved to the near-by hermitage of Fonte Colombo and here he spent the winter. None of the doctors who had attended him had been able to do anything for the disease of which he was dying, but one physician hoped to relieve the agony in one of his eyes by cauterizing his upper cheek. When Francis was asked if he would submit to the torture of this treatment he said peacefully that he had no will of his own about his body but was altogether in their hands. And so the ordeal by fire for which he had offered himself on the crusades was granted to him after all. Not one of the four brothers who looked after him, not even Leo, was brave enough to stay with him through this. They fled and left him alone. Elias, whom he had especially asked to be with him, did not appear, and so by himself he sat waiting and watching while the doctor heated the iron in the glowing heat of the fire. When it was red hot, and the doctor came to him with it, Francis stood up and looking steadily at the glowing beauty of the thing he signed it with the sign of the cross and said, "Be courteous to me, Brother Fire, for I have always loved thee." He met every challenge of his life supremely well but none more perfectly than this.

The treatment did him no good and they tried opening the vein above the ear, and piercing both ears with a red-hot iron, but the torture in the eye was not made any better by the added agony of the ears. The brothers who died in Morocco can scarcely have suffered more, but Francis remained at peace. One of the doctors told the brothers that he would hesitate to give such drastic treatment to the strongest man, yet this highly strung and dying monk was able to endure. Nothing could quench the joy of Alvernia.

One thing at least he was spared in his dying, for he was not given the modern drugs which can only dull the pain of the body by clouding the mind. His mind remained clear until the end. As his body weakened and failed his immense vitality seemed to burn all the more brightly in mind and spirit. During this winter of pain he wrote canticles and sent them to Clare, and he wrote letters, begging those to whom he wrote never to forget the reverence due to the Blessed Sacrament. This had always been a matter of great concern to him, for he knew how fatally easy it can be for Christians to get so accustomed to making their communions that they begin to take the humility and graciousness of God's coming almost for granted, and forget that nothing that can ever happen to them can be as wonderful as this. One of the letters ends with a typical flash of vision. He thinks of the Gospel carried to all people everywhere, and Christian bells ringing all over the world. He says to his sons, "And you shall so announce and preach His praise to all peoples that at every hour and when the bells are rung praise and thanks shall always be given to the Almighty God by all the people through the whole earth."

And so the winter passed and with the spring Cardinal Ugolino arranged for Francis to be taken to Siena, which was renowned both for its doctors and its health-giving air. The Cardinal, so hale and hearty himself, did all that his love could devise for Francis in his illness. They all did their utmost to keep him with them for a little longer and in the stories of these days one can sense the desolation of their helplessness in the face of death. The humble are generally humiliated, and Francis had been cruelly pushed aside by men who owed their existence as members of a great and beloved Order, in many cases their spiritual salvation, to him alone. Now, at only forty-two years old, he was leaving them, and they knew at last how great a man he was in his humility, how unique in the power of his love. They would never know anyone like him again and without him the world would be darker and colder and the future full of uncertainty and fear.

Neither the climate nor the doctors of Siena could do anything for Francis and while he was there he had a bad haemorrhage which brought him to the point of death. The brothers who were at Siena gathered round his bed weeping and lamenting, begging him to bless them, begging him to leave them some written message for the Order, asking him what was to become of them without him, terribly sorry for themselves and in a lesser degree sorry for him too in his pain.

Amazingly Francis managed to drag himself up out of his weakness and rally to their need. He bade them call Brother Benedict of Pirato, a priest who was ministering to him in the place of Leo. Why Leo was not with him at this time we do not know but we can be quite sure that only some illness of his own would have kept him away. Brother Benedict came and Francis at the point of death dictated to him words which read like a prose poem.

"Write how I bless my brethren who are in the Order, and who shall come, unto the end of the world. And since on account of my weakness and the pain of my infirmity I may not speak; in these three words I make plain my will and intention briefly to all my brethren, present and to come; namely, that in token of my memory and benediction and will, they should always love one another like as I have loved and do love them; that they should always love and observe our Lady Poverty, and always remain faithful subjects to the prelates and clergy and holy Mother Church."

Perhaps the great effort which Francis made to do what was required of him brought him back from death, for when Elias, who had been hastily sent for, arrived, he had rallied. Elias decided that he must be taken back to Assisi at once, for it was immensely important that he should die there. He was Assisi's own saint and if he were to die anywhere else they might never get his bones back. It is hard for us to realize, in our day, what it meant to a city of the Middle Ages to be in possession of a dead saint. They believed that not only did their patron saint defend their city, their lives and their interests upon earth, but he saved their souls too for in heaven his prayer procured their eternal salvation. And if he were a miracle-working saint pilgrims would come to his tomb, and that was good for trade. With the bones of a saint in their midst they had the best of both worlds, and they did not scruple to steal a saint if they had not got one of their own. Elias, and Assisi with him, were in a panic that Perugia would steal Francis. This was no idle fear. Years later, when the church of San Francesco was finished and Francis's coffin had been brought from the first temporary tomb in San Giorgio and secretly buried there, the knights of Perugia came after dark one night, forced their way into San Francesco and heaved up the paving stones with pick-axes in an unsuccessful effort to find the coffin. Not until centuries later was the secret burying place found, and the space round it opened out and turned into the chapel where today we may kneel and pray before the altar tomb with its candles and flowers. And so great care was needed in the planning of the journey home. The direct route from Siena to Assisi would bring them close to Perugia, and so Elias decided to turn aside at Cortona and take a longer way round the mountains. It would be far more exhausting for

Francis but that could not be helped. At whatever cost to the saint himself his birthplace must have his bones. For an added security Elias sent a message to Assisi asking that a company of armed knights should be sent to meet them in the mountains, so that if Perugia pounced Assisi could defend her holy property with the sword. There is no record of what Francis thought about all this but he was never too ill to be amused.

The first stage of their journey brought them to the hermitage at Cortona, where later Elias would build the beautiful Celle. Here Francis became ill with dropsy and they had to stay for a while at the hermitage. It was late spring and the thoughts of Francis and Elias must have been carried back to that other spring when they had been here together as young men and Francis had received Elias into the Order. They heard again the sound of the tumbling stream, and the birdsong ringing in the woods. Francis was suffering very greatly at this time yet the story that belongs to Cortona shows him compassionate and humorous as ever. A poor peasant came to the hermitage to pour out his woes to Francis, for his wife had just died and he had no food for his children. Francis had a new cloak which the brothers had just given him to replace one that he had given away to a beggar on the journey from Siena, and this he promptly gave to the man, warning him that he was on no account to give it up to anyone unless well paid for it first. At this point the brothers came hastily upon the scene, outraged and protesting. That they should have to procure yet a third cloak for Francis was too much. They held on to the cloak and so did the peasant. Nerved by the command of Francis he said he would not let go of the cloak except for payment down. In the old days of the Order there would have been no money in the hermitage with which to redeem the cloak, but now Elias was here and things were changed. With amusement Francis was aware of the brothers reluctantly parting with their few coins and the peasant going happily away. All was now concluded to his satisfaction. The poor man's children were fed, the brothers were once more united to holy poverty and he still had a cloak for the journey home.

From Cortona they went through the mountain passes to

Gubbio, another place of memories for Francis, and from thence to Nocera where the armed guard from Assisi met them. Francis journeyed now in a kingly manner, his litter carried in the midst of attendant and obsequious knights. He had dreamed in his boyhood of travelling just in this fashion, swords and shining helms about him, himself the centre of adulation and honour, and he had dreamed too of coming home from the wars a triumphant hero to his native city. The dreams were coming true now but in a manner of which he had not dreamed. He laughed and joked with his bodyguard. At Satriano the knights were hungry but when they tried to buy food from the villagers they asked so peremptorily that they were refused. "You have not found because you confided in your pence and not in God," said Francis. "But return now to the houses whither you went seeking to buy, and laying aside your shame ask alms there for the love of the Lord God." So the proud knights went begging like Brothers Minor and the villagers gave them what they had and they ate at the table of the Lord.

III

In the brilliant sunshine and great heat of midsummer Francis came back to Assisi. As soon as the citizens, watching from the walls, saw the cavalcade of knights slowly approaching they came streaming out of the city in pride and joy to welcome their saint in his last homecoming. They would not let him go to his beloved Portiuncula, where they knew perfectly well that he always wanted to be, for in that undefended spot Perugia might still get him, they brought him into the city and lodged him in the Bishop's palace and set an armed guard about it. Celano says, "The city rejoiced over the arrival of the blessed father, and the mouths of all the people praised God, for the whole multitude hoped that the holy man might soon die." If that statement shocks us it would not have shocked Francis. He knew human nature and its lively sense of favours to come.

Back in Assisi, no longer enduring the agonizing jolting of the litter and the weary useless pilgrimage from one place to another, allowed stillness and rest at last, Francis revived a little. He talked with those about him, speaking of the Order and his hopes and fears for it, and he dictated his last letter to his sons. He greets them all, the Minister General and all who shall follow him in that office, the ministers and priests and all the simple and obedient brothers, the first and the last. He exhorts them to discipline, obedience and courageous witness to the faith in word and deed, and he humbly confesses his own sin, but most of the long letter is concerned once more with the subject always so close to his heart, the reverence due to the Blessed Sacrament. In places the words pour out with something of his old impetuosity.

"Let the entire man be seized with fear; let the whole world tremble; let heaven exult when Christ, the Son of the living God, is on the altar in the hands of the priest. O admirable height and stupendous condescension! O humble sublimity! O sublime humility! that the Lord of the universe, God and the Son of God, so humbles Himself that for our salvation He hides Himself under a morsel of bread. Consider, brothers, the humility of God and pour out your hearts before Him, and be ye humbled that ye may be exalted by him. Do not therefore keep back anything for yourselves that He may receive you entirely who gives Himself up entirely to you."

The letter ends with the prayer of his whole life, the prayer that he and his sons may do the will of God as perfectly as they are able, and with his blessing, "May the Lord be with you forever. Amen."

His devotion to the will of God remained unshaken. Saint Bonaventure tells us that one of the brothers found it hard to bear the sight of his suffering, and said to him, "Brother, pray the Lord that He deal more gently with thee, for me seemeth that His hand is laid more heavily on thee than is right." But Francis had asked that he might share the redemptive suffering of Christ, and the answer to his prayer had been gathered within the will of God for him, and he would not rebel now against that adorable will. He "cast himself on the ground, jarring his frail bones in the hard fall. And, kissing the ground, he cried: 'I give Thee thanks, O Lord God, for all these my pains, and I beseech Thee, my Lord, that if it please Thee, Thou wilt add unto them an hundredfold;

for this will be most acceptable unto me if laying sorrow upon me Thou dost not spare, since the fulfilling of Thy holy will is unto me an overflowing solace.'"

There was another solace, that unity with his Lord that with the suffering had been granted to him at Alvernia. He spoke of it very simply, for it was beyond description, yet in a choice of words so perfect that they do convey some hint of the satisfied peace of his soul, that eternal satisfaction that can lie untroubled as deep water beneath the torment that belongs to this world only. One of the brothers asked him why he did not now do as he had always done and seek comfort in the Bible. Francis answered, "I need no more, my son. I know Christ, the poor man crucified."

He was sublime, yet through it all he remained endearingly human, much like all of us in illness, wanting comfort sometimes, afraid to be a nuisance, not really able to eat anything yet fancying that if something which did not happen to be there at the moment had been there he could have fancied that. Once during a feverish night he longed for the fresh wholesome taste of parsley, and asked the brother who was with him if he would get it for him. The brother was not wholly willing; how could he find parsley groping about in the garden in the pitch dark in the middle of the night? But Francis begged him to try and assured him that he would find it. So the brother went out into the garden, grabbed at some sort of fresh cool greenness, brought it in and looked at it. It was parsley.

However devoted and loving the immortal spirit may be the strain and labour of nursing can reduce the mortal part of a nurse to a state that falls very far behind the spirit's intention, and the heartbreaking part of it is that the more the patient is loved the greater can be the fall from grace. The nursing brothers were tired out and their patience was wearing a little thin. Francis knew he was being an unconscionable long time dying and his sensitive spirit was pitifully aware of their weariness. He was quite helpless and suffering intensely, and now there was this added pain of knowing himself to be a burden upon those who looked after him. Yet there was no self-pity in him and no hurt pride. He was concerned only for the brothers, and in a way that was typical of

him. He had never been overmuch concerned about the safety
and comfort of the bodies of those he loved, it was their precious
immortal souls that were of such concern to him, and so now
The Mirror of Perfection tells us that "he began to fear lest from
their too great labour on his account the friars should incur even
the least offence before God on account of some impatience.
Whence on a time he said with piety and compassion to his
companions: 'Dearest brethren, and my little sons, let it not
weary you to labour for my infirmity; since the Lord will return
to you all the fruit of your works for His humble servant in this
world and in the future.'"

Yet in spite of his lack of concern for the body he did wonder in
these last days if he had done wrong to be so hard upon his own.
He was well aware that he was dying now because brother ass
had been so broken by austerity that he had not been able to stand
up against the onslaught of disease. He had tried to maintain all
possible discipline throughout his illness, and whenever he had
allowed his suffering body the minimum of comfort his conscience had rebuked him, but now he wondered if perhaps poor
brother ass deserved a little kindness at the end. He discussed it
half humorously with one of the brothers, asking his advice about
it. The brother said, "Tell me, father, if thou deignest to do so,
with what diligence thy body, while it could, obeyed thy
behests?" Francis replied, "It has shirked no toil, has refused no
discomfort, if only it might do as it was bid. Herein have I and it
been in perfect agreement, that we should serve Christ the Lord
without any reluctance," The brother said, "Is it a worthy
rewarding of faithful friends to accept a kindness gladly, and then
in the time of his need not to requite a giver's merit? ... Be it far
from thee, father, stay and staff of the afflicted: be this sin against
the Lord far from thee." Francis said, "Rejoice, brother body,
and forgive me, for behold now I gladly fulfil thy desires, and
gladly hasten to attend to thy complaints."

Like all courageous men when they are dying he wanted to
know how long he had to live, and when one of his doctors,
Buongiovanni of Arezzo, a friend of his, came to see him, he said
to him, "What thinkest thou of this my infirmity of dropsy?"

Buongiovanni answered with the temporizing wariness of all doctors, "Brother, it shall be well with thee, by the grace of God." But Francis was not to be put off with such nonsense, and using a popular saying of the country people he said, "I am not a cuckoo to be afraid of death. By the grace of the Holy Spirit I am so intimately united to God that I am equally content to live or die." Then Buongiovanni told him straight out that he did not think he would live longer than the end of September or the beginning of October. It was good news. There was not much longer to wait now. Francis "spread his hands out to the Lord with very great devotion and reverence, and said with great joy of mind and body: 'Welcome, Sister Death.'"

After the doctor had left him he passed through a period of such great pain that he could hardly maintain his cheerfulness. One of the brothers stayed with him through it, talking to him of heaven where he would see face to face the God whom he had loved so well in life, and he was comforted, and when the pain had a little lessened as utterly happy as he had been after the night of pain at San Damiano. He sent for Angelo and Leo and asked them to sing his *Canticle of the Sun* to him, and when they had sung it he added one more verse, the last.

"Praised be my Lord for our sister, the death of the body, from
    which no man escapeth. Woe to him who dies in mortal sin!
Blessed are they who are found walking by Thy most holy will,
    for the second death shall have no power to do them harm."

From that day until the end music took possession of his soul. He had all eternity in which to worship God but time was slipping from him, and the minutes and hours as they came and went must be offered up to his Lord in praise and thanksgiving. The brothers sang to him often and as he was able he sang with them. They sang the *Canticle* and they sang psalms and *laude*. The sentries who kept guard, and paced backwards and forwards beneath the high window of the room where Francis lay, listened to the singing. They heard it by day, when the burning sun of late summer increased the fever and pain of those who suffered, and by night under the stars. They looked up in wonder and awe at the window from which it came. No groans or sighs of weariness came from that window, only singing.

Elias doubted if this was as it should be. He did not think Francis was dying with sufficient solemnity, and he feared for his reputation. He wondered what people were thinking. He was afraid they were saying, "Why does this man show such light-heartedness, who is near death? He ought to be thinking of death." And so he went to Francis and as tactfully as he could asked that the singing should stop. Throughout his illness Francis had been so humbly obedient to the Minister General that no doubt Elias thought he would be instantly obeyed. But in this thing only he was not obeyed. "Suffer me, brother, to rejoice in the Lord, both in His praises and in my infirmity," said Francis, "since by the grace of the Holy Spirit helping me, I am so united to my Lord, that by His mercy may I well rejoice in the Most High."

He had said the same thing to his doctor. "By the grace of the Holy Spirit I am so united to God." The union of Alvernia was growing deeper still and he was marvelling at it. The coasts of the country must have been clear to him now, as clear as the shore to the Apostles when they came home in the dawn from the night of fishing on the lake of Galilee, and saw the gracious figure of Christ building a little fire on the beach to welcome them in.

Yet his pain was very great and he did not pretend it was not so. One day a pitying brother asked him which he would rather have, the cruel death of a martyr or this long drawn-out agony. He said, "Son, that to me has been and is dearest and most acceptable, which it pleases my God to let happen to me; yet in regard to the distress of my suffering, this sickness, were it but to last three days, is more grievous than any martyrdom."

One day it seemed that he could not live longer and the brothers gathered round him begging that he would bless them. Bernard was kneeling on his right and Elias on his left. Then followed an incident typical of the love and understanding of Francis. He was blind and near to death, yet his knowledge of the need of others was as strong as ever, and as he stretched out his wounded hands to bless his sons he was intuitively aware that

Elias was kneeling on his left. Elias had hurt him almost unbearably yet Elias was now heart-broken. He crossed his arms so that his right hand rested on the head of the Minister General. To be quite certain he asked if this was so and when they said yes he murmured, "That is as I wish." Then raising his voice he blessed Elias. "My son I bless thee in all things, and through all things, and as the Most High has multiplied my brothers and sons in thy hands, so upon thee and in thee do I bless them all. May God the King of all, bless them in heaven and on earth. I bless thee as far as I can and more than I can; and what I cannot do, may He do in thee, He Who can do all things."

The crossed arms are now the symbol of the Franciscan Order and the words, "As far as I can and more than I can," its inspiration.

How could Elias refuse him anything after this? He could not, and when Francis begged that he might go home to the Portiuncula he acquiesced. It was just what they had hoped to avoid, for Perugia could so easily snatch their saint away from the unprotected little Portiuncula, but to his everlasting credit Elias took the risk. Francis loved the Portiuncula more than any spot on earth and if he wanted to die there Elias was determined that he should, and he obtained the consent of the city for his removal.

And so on a day late in September, in the year 1226, Francis was carried on his bed out of the Bishop's palace into the fresh air. It was a long time since he had had the blue sky over him and the warmth of the sun directly on his body. He was not fond of palaces and it must have felt to him like coming out of prison. The brothers carried him gently down through the narrow streets to the city gate called the Portaccia, and out into the country beyond, along the way that led from Assisi past San Damiano to the Portiuncula and on to Perugia. He had travelled this way so often that he must have known by heart every uneven paving stone in the street, every curve on the road. With the heightening of awareness that blindness had brought to his remaining senses the tramp of the feet about him, each voice speaking to him or of him with devoted love, would have had a great power and significance, as though the whole Order from the beginning to the end of its earthly time were carrying him on his way to eternity. Each birdcall, each rustle of wind in the trees, the scent of the rosemary bushes and the growing things along the way, had a loveliness sharper and more intense than in his sighted days. He could take leave of the earth with a new sort of poignancy because he was blind.

They went on and a different sort of scent came to him, the stench of the leper hospital of the Crucigeri. Instantly to his inward sight they must have been all about him, the leper in whom he had seen the suffering Christ, the leper to whom his embrace had brought healing, the recalcitrant leper whose body he had washed in the hospital, all the multitude of sick men whom he had served with such devotion, and he took his leave of them with love. They had given him his bearings and in a moment or two he knew that they had reached the place where there was a clear view of Assisi. He asked his bearers to stop and turn around that he might face Assisi. They did so and he raised himself upon his bed as though gazing at the strong old walls that he had helped to rebuild when he was a boy, the terraces over whose ramparts he had leaned as a child, the houses climbing up one behind the other on the mountain slope. Then he raised his hand and blessed the city and its people. "Blessed be thou of the Lord, holy city faithful to God, for through thee shall many souls be saved and in thee shall dwell many servants of the Most High, and from thee shall many be chosen for the eternal kingdom."

They went down to the Portiuncula and through the gate in the quick-set hedge to the enclosure, and Francis was put to bed in a cell close to Santa Maria degli Angeli. The last journey had ended.

Chapter Six

THE LARKS

Love, Thou didst enter very softly in
  To hold this heart of mine.
  No sound, no stir, no sign!
How couldst Thou cross my threshold all unseen?

O sweet and gentle Love, Thou art the key
  Of heaven's city and fort:
  Steer Thou my ship to port,
And from the tempest's fury shelter me.
           Jacopone da Todi, *Lauda*, LXXXI

FRANCIS was only a few days at the Portiuncula before his death, and reading the accounts of these days it would seem that for most of the time he had passed beyond pain into a peace of body as well as mind and spirit, what Shakespeare calls the "lightning before death". They passed with a measured orderly beauty, as one by one he set his affairs in order before turning to the symbolic acts of his dying. He had always liked order, for love with its refusal to encroach or grab, its awareness of the utmost that is due, is always orderly. First, in this lucidity of mind between pain and death, he dictated his will. He had nothing to leave except his memories. They are written down with simplicity and beauty, interwoven with his deep pleading that these things may be remembered and the Order held to its first obedience and its first holiness. This will is his confession of faith, affirming that he stands where he always did, determined to keep the rule of Gospel poverty purely and simply until the end. There are some stern commands and warnings yet he writes with a humility and gentleness that make this testament a very moving revelation of himself. It ends with a fatherly blessing and the words, "I, Brother Francis, your little one and servant, in so far as I can, confirm unto you within and without this most holy blessing. Amen."

Once more it was the season of Saint Michael and the holy angels. Two years had passed since he had kept their Lent upon Alvernia, two years of intense agony and intense joy, the agony and joy of the Redeemer that he had prayed that he might share. In the chapel he could hear the brothers chanting the praises of the angels, and he could hear the ringing of the bell. It was that moment of the autumn when the birds start singing again and the sun is so warm that it is like another spring. The dying often seem to feel themselves back again at their starting point, reliving the days of their youth and remembering the things that they thought they had forgotten. They are no longer the old man or woman only but the whole person, all that they have been and done gathered into a unity to face the end that is also the beginning.

The boy who had been Francis was back again now, and he had loved gay garments and bright lights upon a festival. The dying saint who was this boy thought that for this festival of death he would like to be well clothed upon his bier, and have lighted candles about him. He had put comfort from him long ago but his body being dead would not feel the pleasure of a clean new shroud, or of a soft cushion for his head in place of a stone, so there could be no sin in it. Was there anyone who would understand and sympathize? He remembered the Lady Giacoma di Settesoli, and as well as a desire for candles and a cushion there awoke in him a great longing for dear Brother Giacoma herself, with her humour and understanding and her restful competence. He called one of the brothers and told him to send a messenger quickly to Rome, to the Lady Giacoma, asking her to come to him and to bring with her certain things that he wanted. With his usual definiteness he knew exactly what these were; a gown of grey cloth, a napkin to cover his face, a cushion for his head, wax candles, and some of the almond sweet cake that she made. The brothers must have been dumbfounded, especially Elias, but they chose their messenger and would have sent him off had there not come to their ears the sound of horses' hoofs and jingling harness. The cavalcade of some great personage was approaching through the woods. Then the porter who watched at the gate in the quick-set hedge came running to say that the Lady Giacoma herself was riding towards them with her two sons, now Roman senators, and a retinue of servants. Now what was to be done? No woman was allowed inside the quick-set hedge. An anxious brother went to inquire of Francis, who replied serenely, "Blessed be God, who has sent our Brother Giacoma to us. Open the gates and lead her inside, for the rule concerning women is not for Brother Giacoma."

So she got off her horse and came quickly to Francis's cell and knelt down beside his bed, laughing and crying together because she was so happy to be in time, yet so desolate because with one look at him she knew she was only just in time. She had brought with her everything he wanted, the new grey gown, the cushion, the napkin, the candles and the almond sweet cake. The cushion was a very fine one embroidered with lions and eagles in gold thread upon red silk, just the sort of cushion to rejoice the heart of Francis the boy, and the gown she had woven herself from the wool of the lamb he had given her. She told the brothers later that at home in Rome she had been praying and the interior Voice had told her that she must go quickly to Assisi if she wished to see Francis again, and that she must take with her the things she had brought. Francis was so happy at her coming that some strength returned to him. He was pleased that Brother Giacoma had brought the almond sweet cake and he sent for Brother Bernard his firstborn son to share it with him. A gust of desperate joy blew through the Portiuncula, and they almost began to hope that he was not going to die after all. But Francis himself knew better. He asked Brother Giacoma to stay until the next Sunday because he would die on the Saturday.

Though he rejoiced in the comforting and comfortable presence of Brother Giacoma Francis had not forgotten Sister Clare. Even had she been allowed to break enclosure she would not have been able to come to him for she also was very ill. All this while his thoughts were with her and when a brother told him that she was weeping bitterly because she could not see him again he was deeply grieved for her. He dictated a letter to her and her nuns that like his testament was an affirmation of his faith and loyalty and an appeal to them to stand fast. He knew that they would. He could trust Clare to keep her integrity intact in exactly the same manner as he had kept his. There were few of his sons who were so utterly at one with him as she was. He said to her, "I, little Brother Francis, wish to follow the life and poverty of Jesus Christ our Most High Lord, and of His Most Holy Mother, and to persevere therein until the end. And I beseech you, my ladies, and counsel you, to live always in this most holy life and poverty. And watch yourselves well that you in no wise depart from it through the teaching or advice of anyone."

When the writing was finished he said to the brother who was to take it to her, "Go and bid Sister Clare put aside all sorrow and sadness on account of not being able to see me. But let her know in truth that before her death, she and her sisters shall see me, and shall be much consoled concerning me." He was quite right. Clare had her consolation and it came to her in this way. The night after Francis died he lay upon his bier clothed in the habit that Giacoma had woven for him, his head upon her cushion and candles burning about him, and the citizens of Assisi passed by all night long to look their last upon his face that had become young and beautiful in death, and to gaze in awe upon the wounds in his hands and feet. Early the next morning they carried him with songs of praise, with candles and trumpets and palm branches, from the Portiuncula to his grave in San Giorgio, the church where he had learnt his lessons as a child and as a man preached his first sermon, but on their way they stopped at San Damiano. The brothers carried the bier into the chapel and brought it to the grille behind which Clare and her sisters were waiting. They moved the iron grating and held the body up in their arms and Clare looked upon the satisfied peace in the face of Francis and was happy. Nor did she ever again feel herself parted from him.

Now that Giacoma was here and Clare was comforted Francis's thoughts returned to his Lady Poverty. The Portiuncula was especially her home. She had always lived here with him. He pleaded with the brothers that they should never leave the Portiuncula. "If you are thrust out on one side, enter it again on the other," he said to them, "for surely this place is holy and the dwelling of God." His God was the poor man crucified. The last days and the last hours were passing and what could he do to bind his sons once again in their first loyalty to Him? He could no longer plead much with them in words but he could make of his whole body a tongue to preach the Gospel. He asked them to remove his tunic and lay him naked on the ground. When they had done that, and he lay with his left hand covering the wound in his side, he said, "I have done what it was mine to do; may Christ teach you what is yours."

Then the Father Guardian of the Portiuncula showed an understanding born of his love. He brought Francis his tunic and breeches, and the sackcloth cap he wore to cover the scars left by the treatment for his eyes, and said, "This tunic and breeches and cap are lent thee by me in holy obedience; and that thou mightest know that thou hast no right of property in them, I deprive thee of all power of giving them to anyone else." Francis's face lit up with joy for there was very much in those few words; an acknowledgement that Francis had been loyal until the end to the Lady Poverty, almost a promise that the Order would be too, and then that tender half-humorous remembrance of old days, when to the despair of the brothers Francis had given away or cut in pieces one after another of the garments given to him.

When they put him back on his bed he was very content but that night he was in pain and could not sleep. In the morning he was better and asked that the brothers should come to him. They stood by his bed, Elias, Bernard, Leo, Ruffino, Angelo, Masseo, and all the sons whom he loved the best, and Bernard begged him that he would forgive them their sins and bless them, and Francis answered, "See, my son, I am called by God: I forgive my brethren, whether present or absent, all their offences and faults and, as far as I can, I absolve them: do thou proclaim this to them and bless them all for me." To Bernard himself he gave a special blessing because he was his firstborn. Then he asked that a loaf should be brought and broken in pieces for him, because he was too weak to break it himself, and he gave a piece to each of the brothers and they all of them had their last meal together. The brothers realized that his thoughts were now centred on his Lord and that he was thinking of Maundy Thursday, because he asked them, "Is it Thursday?" It was actually Friday, but they read him the gospel for Maundy Thursday.

All that day and the next he was sinking. The brothers sang his *Canticle of Brother Sun* to him, and at the end he said, "Welcome, Sister Death." Then turning to his doctor he said, "She is to me the gate of life." He asked the brothers when the end came to lay him again on the bare ground as they had done three days ago, to sprinkle ashes over him and read to him the account of the Passion of his Lord in Saint John's Gospel. On the evening of Saturday, October the 4th, when they saw that he had not long to live, they did all that he had asked of them. They had just finished reading to him, and were waiting in awe and expectancy, when they realized that with the last flicker of life left in him he was singing the 142nd psalm.

> "I cried to the Lord with my voice: with my voice I made supplication to the Lord.
> In his sight I pour out my prayer, and before Him I declare my trouble:
> When my spirit failed me, then Thou knewest my paths.
> In this way wherein I walked they have hidden a snare for me.
> I looked on my right hand, and behold: and there was no one that would know me.
> Flight hath failed me: and there is no one that hath regard to my soul.
> I cried to Thee, O Lord; I said: Thou art my hope, my portion in the land of the living.
> Attend to my supplication: for I am brought very low.
> Deliver me from my persecutors; for they are stronger than I.
> Bring my soul out of prison, that I may praise Thy name."

Francis of Assisi went singing into eternity, but when his voice had failed there was still music, for in the golden afterglow the larks were singing.

"Certain birds which love the light, and have a great horror of darkness, at the hour of the holy man's transit from earth, which was the time at which twilight is wont to set in, came in great multitudes over the roof of the house, and flew round and round it joyfully for a long time together, giving clear and joyous testimony to the glory of the saint who had been wont to invite them to sing the praises of God."

LIST OF BOOKS

The Legend of Saint Francis by the Three Companions (The Temple Classics).

The Mirror of Perfection (The Temple Classics).

The Life of Saint Francis of Assisi, Saint Bonaventure.

Two Lives of Saint Francis, Thomas of Celano.

The Writings of Saint Francis of Assisi, translated by Father Paschal Robinson.

Selections from *The Little Flowers of Saint Francis*, edited by Hugh Martin.

Saint Francis of Assisi, Father Cuthbert, O.S.F.C.

Life of Saint Francis, Paul Sabatier

Saint Francis of Assisi, G. K. Chesterton.

Saint Francis of Assisi, R. H. Moorman.

Saint Francis of Assisi, T. S. R. Boase.

Saint Francis of Assisi, Essays in Commemoration.

Franciscan Italy, Harold Elsdale Goad.

In the Steps of Saint Francis, Ernest Raymond.

Little Plays of Saint Francis, Laurence Housman.

Jacopone da Todi, Evelyn Underhill.